# HOW VOTERS DECIDE

A model of vote choice based on a special longitudinal
study extending over fifteen years and the British election
surveys of 1970–1983

HILDE T. HIMMELWEIT
PATRICK HUMPHREYS
MARIANNE JAEGER

Open University Press
Milton Keynes · Philadelphia

Open University Press
Celtic Court
22 Ballmoor
Buckingham MK18 1XT
*and*
1900 Frost Road, Suite 101
Bristol, PA 19007, USA

First published 1981
First published in this edition 1985
Reprinted 1988, 1990, 1992, 1993
Copyright © Hilde T. Himmelweit, Patrick
Humphreys and Marianne Jaeger

**British Library Cataloguing in Publication Data**
Himmelweit, Hilde T.
   How voters decide. — 2nd rev. ed.
   1. Voting — Great Britain — Simulation methods
   2. Voting — Great Britain — History —
   20th century
   I. Title     II. Humphreys, Patrick
   III. Jaeger, Marianne
   324.941'085'0724     JN956

ISBN 0-335-10591-2


**Library of Congress Cataloging in Publication Data**
Himmelweit, Hilde T.
   How voters decide.
   Rev. ed. of: How voters decide/Hilde T.
Himmelweit [*et al.*]. 1981.
   Bibliography: p.
   Includes indexes.
   1. Voting — Great Britain — Longitudinal studies.
   2. Great Britain — Politics and government — 1945 —
   I. Humphreys, Patrick.     II. Jaeger, Marianne.
   III. Title.
   JN956.H68 1984     324.941     84-19030


Printed in Great Britain by
St Edmundsbury Press Ltd, Bury St Edmunds, Suffolk.

# Preface

The emphasis of this book is on the individual voter—the factors that influence the decision whether to vote, and if so, for which party. It complements studies which concentrate on the macroanalysis of elections although, of course, its findings have relevance for predictions of the outcome of elections.

For a social psychologist vote decisions are of special interest; everyone has to make the decision on the same day, the options are the same for everyone with the decision having to be made repeatedly so that each person builds up a repertoire of past decisions. Although each election is unique in terms of the political and economic climate in which it is fought, it is also part of a sequence, making it possible to develop a *model of electoral choice* that identifies the influences that bear on the decision and the factors which affect their relative role.

To develop and test such a model, a special longitudinal study was designed, unusual in its length in that it extended over fifteen years and in the wealth of information obtained about each individual through repeated questioning. This made it possible to trace the development and change over time of people's political attitudes and vote choice. We studied the same group of men from the time they cast their first vote in 1959 at age 21 through to their sixth vote in October 1974. Longitudinal studies are laborious to undertake and have many problems associated with them, not least because they refer to events now past. Their unique value, however, lies in the opportunity they provide for the testing of models of behaviour.

Political scientists and psychologists have stressed the need for longitudinal data to be collected at the time when the event occurred instead of using data based on recall of that event, with the distortion that reliance on memory produces. This is why Butler and Stokes carried out their panel study of voters' responses from 1963 to 1970 and Särlvik and Crewe theirs of voters in the 1974 and 1979 elections. Since these studies covered several of the same elections as our study, we not only drew on their published findings but also, where appropriate, re-analysed their data. In this way, we were able to check and extend the validity of the conclusions gained from a detailed study of a small number of voters using large panel samples. Some of the analyses in this book involve looking at decision making in successive elections, one at a time. For these we used the four large-scale representative British election surveys covering the 1970, 1974, 1979 and 1983 elections, as well as our own study.

We have used what we call a *societal psychological approach*, a systems approach which takes more account of the interdependence of the individual and society than is usual in traditional social psychology, examining both the social reality and the individual's experience of that reality. That is why it was so important to obtain information about the same individuals over a long enough period — in this case from their early twenties to their middle thirties — to be able to examine the influence of both societal changes as well as changes in their own lives on outlook and vote choice.

For reasons which will become apparent in the book, the core of the cognitive model we developed is a *consumer model of voting*. The model, which has been tested in Britain during the changing political and economic climate in this country (from the period of optimism and apparent economic abundance in the 1960s to one of despondency, economic recession and high unemployment in the early 1980s), offers a means of analysis of future British elections and also a useful perspective for understanding the behaviour of voters in other Western countries. At any rate, we hope that social scientists in these countries will be encouraged to examine its applicability.

This edition differs considerably from the first edition. It contains three new sources of data taking the analysis beyond the period of the initial study, which ended in 1974, to include the 1979 and 1983 elections. The 1979 election is of special interest in that for the first time since World War II a sizeable number of working class Labour voters did not just defect from the Labour party but went right over to the Conservatives. The 1983 election was the first election in which the Alliance formed between the Liberals and the newly created Social Democratic Party took part, attracting a 25% share of the vote.

The three additional data sources are the Särlvik and Crewe 1974–1979 panel study based on the February 1974 representative British election survey, the 1979 British election study, and the 1983 survey of over 4,000 voters carried out by Crewe on behalf of the BBC at the time of the 1983 election.

The book has been substantially revised. Some chapters have been extensively rewritten and new ones added. Discussions with political scientists in this country and in the United States made us aware that the way the model had been presented did not make sufficiently explicit its general applicability nor how it related to alternate models of voting behaviour. Consequently Chapter 1, A Cognitive Model of Vote Choice, has been extensively rewritten to set it in its historical context and to bring out more clearly the different facets of the model and their interrelation, showing how their role varies depending on the problems of the day, the state of parties as well as the voters' beliefs and value systems.

Because the longitudinal study on which we developed the model was small and unrepresentative, we have gone to unusual lengths to validate its usefulness for modelling the vote choices of the electorate as a whole by testing it on more than 15,000 men and women voters in four elections using the panel and representative British election studies spanning in all a period of 20 years. Chapter 2: the Data Base sets out the studies we have analysed.

Chapter 6 is new. It deals with social determinants and their role in vote choice relative to that played by the voters' attitudes and beliefs.

Chapter 11: The Middle Ground, originally a case study of the Liberal voters, now includes the Alliance voters, examining how far they differ from the Liberal voters of earlier elections.

A new chapter (Chapter 13) on the implications of the work for political scientists has been added to complement the chapter on its relevance for social psychologists. The final chapter on political implications has been considerably expanded in the light of the results of the 1979 and 1983 elections taking account of the arrival of the Alliance on the political stage.

All in all, about a third of the book is new with every chapter containing additional analyses.

The book addresses itself to several audiences: to the political scientist interested in elections and political socialization; to the social psychologist interested in the process of decision making, in the relation of cognitions and attitudes to behaviour and in the individual's representation of the social world, and to the sociologist interested in the changing role of social class membership and social mobility. The study adds to the politician's understanding of the voters' goals and values, of their appraisal of political issues and leaders, their reactions to the Conservative, Labour, Liberal and now the Alliance parties, and of the conduct of election campaigns. To the pollsters, the study offers a different, and we believe more promising, approach to the sampling of public opinion and vote intention. To address such a diverse audience poses special problems which we have attempted to lessen by using the specialized vocabulary of each discipline as little as possible, by placing only those tables in the body of the book which are essential to the argument and by providing separate chapters on the implications of the study for these different audiences.

The final chapter on political implications includes discussion of the factors relevant to the future support for the Conservative, Labour and Alliance parties and, using the 1983 election as a case study, discusses the parties' election campaigns and the role played by the press and by broadcasting.

*October, 1984*                                                    H.T.H.; P.H.; M.J.

# Acknowledgements

Financial support for the initial study came from two separate grants from the British Social Science Research Council (now Economic and Social Research Council). The analysis of the surveys of the last two elections contained in the revised edition was made possible by grants from the London School of Economics and the Markle Foundation. The opportunity to carry out these analyses and to begin the revision of the book was afforded to the first author by a Fellowship at the Center for the Advanced Study of the Behavioral Sciences in 1983 financed by the John D. and Catherine T. MacArthur Foundation. We are very grateful to these organizations for their financial support and, in the case of the Center, for providing such excellent conditions for gaining new insights and for the interchange of ideas with political scientists.

The book owes everything to the men who, first as adolescents and later as adults, were ready to talk to us about themselves, their families, school, work, their values and aspirations. When the research changed to a study of political attitudes and voting, they were equally willing on numerous occasions to answer questions about their voting, and their views on social and political issues. We are very grateful for the co-operation they so willingly gave.

A longitudinal study makes many demands on the researchers. A study revived periodically at each election requires not only rekindling of interest but also great skill on the part of those researchers who join the study. We were very fortunate in the help given by David Phillips, Richard Johnston and Rod Bond, not only for their mastery of a complex data set and their skills at analysis, but for the ideas and insights they contributed.

We should like to thank Richard O'Reilly and Yogesh Despande of the Computer Unit at the London School of Economics for their help with the many computing problems associated with the analysis of longitudinal data, and the technical staff of the Social Psychology Department, particularly Steve Bennett, for their work in the preparation of the many diagrams. We owe much to Morag Rennie, Pat Christopher and Jean Goodall for their ready and patient typing of the drafts of the book.

First David Butler and subsequently Ivor Crewe were extremely helpful in making their data base available early on. Ivor Crewe has greatly facilitated the revision of the book by providing us with his papers on the 1983 elections.

The year at the Center proved helpful in enriching our understanding of the thinking of political scientists through discussions with M. Fiorina, S. Barnes and J. Dennis, to whom we owe a great deal. Richard Brody, Paul Sniderman, Merrill Shanks and Henry Brady gave us the benefit of their experience as did, earlier on, Bob Lane, Bill McGuire and Bob Abelson. On the methodological side we gained much from discussions with Lee Cronbach and Clyde Coombs, and more recently with Lincoln Moses, Chris Achen and David Kenny. David Kenny in addition carried out a LISREL on our data to tease out the relative role of party identification and attitudes. We are extremely grateful to these colleagues and to Paul Jackson, Lynn Gale and Dina Berkeley who displayed great ability and patience in carrying out the new analyses required for the revision of the book.

We have left to the last our thanks to Angus Campbell from whom we had encouragement, friendship, ideas and invaluable advice and who also made possible the visits to the Survey Research Centre, University of Michigan. Angus Campbell's untimely death has left a great gap in the academic community, not only because of his exceptional stature as a social scientist but also as a human being. We dedicate this book to his memory, linking his name with that of Kurt Lewin who has been such a profound influence on us all.

H.T.H., P.H., M.J.

# Contents

# 1

# A cognitive model of vote choice

Clarifying the nature and extent of popular influence in government will require a knowledge of more than what is in the voter's mind. But all theories of democracy must contain propositions about the public's response to the actions of government and the proposed actions of those who contend for electoral support. (Stokes, "Voting" in the *International Encyclopaedia of the Social Sciences*, p. 394, 1968)

The process whereby the voter decides whether and how to vote — the microanalysis of elections — is of obvious interest to political scientists and politicians. It also has relevance for social psychology in that it relates to issues central to the field: the distinction between transitory reactions and stable, more enduring attitudes; the role of attitudes and beliefs in affecting behaviour and the way individuals' "cognitive maps" (or internal representations) about their social world develop and adapt to changes in their own lives or to changes in the economic, social and political climate of society.

As a decision, voting has certain characteristics which provide a particularly good opportunity to learn more about decision making in general. Firstly, the decision is recurrent. This made it possible, in our study, to relate the voter's decision in a particular election to his record of voting on as many as five earlier occasions. Secondly, the options are the same for everyone, permitting easy comparison, and thirdly, the decision is made by the electorate on the same day, in the same economic and political climate. Finally, given the pervasive role of the mass media, and of broadcasting in particular, it can be argued that the electorate has access to much the same information, or is at least exposed to a common pool of information about otherwise remote issues when making the decision. This is indeed rare in decision making. We can therefore see more clearly than in decisions where options differ across individuals, the role played in the choice by the voter's history and background and the extent to which "ideological thinking" varies with education. Although the parties from which a choice has to be made remain much the same across elections, their platforms change, as does the social and economic climate in which the elections are fought. Each election is, therefore, unique and also part of a sequence, permitting examination of the relative contribution to the voter's decision of his or her previous vote decisions and current attitudes.

In most non-trivial decisions, the individual is much involved; the consequences are as real as his or her role in bringing these consequences about. This is not so in the case of voting. Despite the importance of the aggregate decision, the majority of the electorate do not feel very involved. They believe that their individual decision, being one of millions, makes little difference to the outcome, and the public as a collection of individuals does not see itself as having much influence on political events or even on the conduct of the party of their choice. This is not surprising. After all, it is only at election time that the public's views are seriously canvassed and any interest taken in their lives, their fears, their babies. More recently, with the increase in the number of voters over sixty, kissing babies has given way to sincere handshakes with frail but vocal old age pensioners.

To be taken off the shelf, dusted down and asked to perform once every four or five years does not generate much enthusiasm for the act of voting, or convince the public that it is worth their while to invest in the study of political issues. It is also not easy to know where to turn for guidance. Politicians do not help. At election time each party sets out a tempting *table d'hôte* of policies, implying that if only their party were to come to power all their proposals would be implemented. No one mentions that the cost of implementing one policy might well jeopardize the implementation of a second equally desirable one or even threaten the continuation of long-established services that the voters had come to take for granted. Electioneering is about persuasion, not education.

Our focus is on the individual voter not as a person in isolation but as a member of many groups and responsive to the social and political context. The approach we have adopted, like Campbell *et al.* (1960) before us, is a systems approach as advocated by Kurt Lewin (1951). He sought, as we do, the means for understanding people's behaviour in the study of the changing environment and the individual's interpretation of that environment, and looked for indications of institutions' changing roles in the public's perception of these institutions and changes in that perception. In the case of voting, there is not only the interdependence of the political and economic climate and the parties' and the voters' responses but also the dependence of the present on the past. Changes in the individual's circumstances, changes in the life history of issues and in the parties' records and promises, as well as the individual's past voting record, interact to affect the relative strength of the influences that bear on the decision.

To understand vote choice it is therefore less important to estimate statistically the exact magnitude of hypothetical parameters, since these apply to a particular election only (and can only be estimated *after* it is over), than to develop a model of voting that indicates the sources of influence and their direction, and the conditions under which each is likely to be more or less important. The model of vote choice needs therefore to be sufficiently general but also sufficiently clearly structured to be readily applied in different political climates. In this book we develop and test such a model of voting, which is essentially a cognitive model.

## Other models of voting

Explanations of how voters decide have varied over the years. Here we provide a brief and inevitably selected account of some of the models and their evaluation so as to place the model we propose in some historical context.

Schumpeter (1950) pointed out that for the effective working of a democracy the ideal citizen should be interested and well informed, ready to seek additional information where needed, able to make correct inferences and relate particular policy proposals to his or her well articulated value system about desirable goals and permissible means. Then, and only then, will such a citizen decide how to vote doing so uninfluenced by pressure groups or propaganda.

When Berelson and Lazarsfeld (Berelson *et al.*, 1954, Lazarsfeld *et al.*, 1944) carried out the first surveys questioning the voters themselves during presidential election campaigns in the 1940s, they found that the voters were a far cry from Schumpeter's ideal citizen. In general they were disinterested and ill informed. Also the policies under consideration were inadequately presented by the parties. In making their decision, voters relied primarily on interpersonal influences, on trusted people around them.

> The usual analogy between the voting "decision" and the more or less carefully calculated decisions of consumers . . . may be quite incorrect. For many voters political preferences may better be considered analogous to cultural tastes . . . both have their origin in ethnic, sectional, class and family traditions . . . both seem to be matters of sentiment and disposition rather than "reasoned preferences" . . . they are relatively invulnerable to direct argumentation and vulnerable to direct social influences. (Berelson *et al.*, 1954)

At the same time, Berelson also reported that *during the 1940 campaign* there had been significant gains by voters in knowledge about issues and parties' stands.

Campbell, Converse, Miller and Stokes, (1960), social psychologists at the Institute of Social Research, Michigan, conducted comprehensive surveys of voters covering the United States presidential elections of 1952 and 1956, this time on a national scale. Similar surveys have been carried out for every subsequent presidential election right up to the present day, including from time to time short-range panel studies covering two or at most three elections.[1] The surveys varied somewhat in content, but typically, in addition to demographic data, included questions asking for the voters' evaluation of issues, candidates and parties (their performance and view on policies) as well as people's evaluations of the present and future state of the economy and of their own financial situation. Individuals were asked whether and how they had voted and also "generally speaking do you see yourself as a Democrat or a Republican, or do you not see yourself in this way?", followed by a question asking for the strength of that identification (from very strong to not strong). The answer to these two questions gave a measure of the individual's *party identification*.

[1]These studies are carried out by the Center for Political Studies which is one section of the Institute of Social Research, Michigan.

These surveys have had a profound influence on the progress of the study of electoral behaviour in both the United States and Europe for a quarter of a century, not least because most researchers have re-analysed the surveys rather than collected new data about these or other elections on particular issues or theoretical viewpoints.

These surveys have played a central role, partly because of their calibre and expense, but also because the first two surveys were used by Campbell *et al.* (1960) to develop a model of vote choice which continues to influence the thinking of political scientists in the United States and Europe. For convenience sake, we shall refer to this model as the *Michigan model*. In Britain Butler and Stokes carried out election surveys based on what Crewe (1974) has described as Michigan Model Mark II.

## THE MICHIGAN MODEL—
## A SOCIAL PSYCHOLOGICAL VIEW OF VOTE CHOICE

Campbell, Converse, Miller and Stokes who designed and analysed the 1952 and 1956 surveys were as dismayed as Berelson had been at the lack of involvement and ignorance that the surveys revealed among the voters, and at their readiness to vote for a particular party even though they might disagree with its policies.

Finding that party identification correlated with vote choice and, unlike people's position on issues, was remarkably stable across time, the authors saw in attachment to party the key to accounting for people's decision. This attachment, they suggested, had its roots back in the individual's childhood and generally reflected parental vote preferences with current group memberships and affiliations having some additional influence. We discuss this issue in Chapter 4 on political socialization.

Party attachment and vote choice were seen to be functions of social group processes, thus continuing the theme of group influences stressed by Berelson and Lazarsfeld.

> We propose to consider the parties as social groups . . . Parties provide a psychological anchoring and have causal priority over short term political attitudes . . . Identification with a party raises a perceptual screen through which the individual tends to see what is favourable to his partisan orientation. The stronger the party bond, the more exaggerated the process of selection and perceptual distortion will be. (Campbell *et al.*, p. 133)

Party identification was considered to develop in adolescence through modelling parental preferences. Like manners, it was bred in the home and acted upon when the individual had to cast his vote. Having once voted for a party, the individual began to label himself as belonging to that party, and was then more likely than not to vote for it on subsequent occasions.

The Michigan model of vote choice postulated that a predisposition or habit was established (mediated by the individual's background or class) which, once developed, was not easy to dislodge. Lapses of observance, i.e. abstentions or even flirtations with another party, were judged to be of little consequence, no more than short-term fluctuations within a basically consistent pattern of party preferences. The model allowed that subsequent reference groups would exert some influence, notably those associated with achieved status due to inter-generational and intra-generational mobility. But, like the voter's parents, the new reference groups were seen as exerting a *direct* influence on the voting decision rather than an indirect influence on attitudes and beliefs which, in turn, influence party choice.

> The party that wins favour appears to depend predominantly upon social transmission from the family or early reference groups. The critical initial decision appears to be taken most frequently under strong social influence early in life, when involvement in politics is at a low ebb, and presumably political information is most scanty as well . . . the self-reinforcing aspects of psychological identification progressively reduce the probability of change in party allegiance. (Campbell *et al.*, p. 212, 1960)

This theory saw the voter as believer (ardent or lukewarm) in a party, like a believer (ardent or lukewarm) in the church of his parents, faith or identification reducing the need to match the candidate's or the party's stand with the individual's own views. Party identification, according to Campbell *et al.*, had the double function of facilitating choice and acting as political litmus paper for determining which policies to favour.

The voters' views, including their beliefs about the parties' past performance and future policies, were influenced not only by party identification but also by societal and individual experiences. However, such attitudes and beliefs were judged to play only a very secondary role in the decision. For although Campbell *et al.* (1960) acknowledged that intense feelings about an issue might change an individual's partisan commitment, they concluded that in the 1950s,

> the period of our studies, the influence of party identification on attitudes has been far more important than the influence of these attitudes on party identification itself. We are convinced that the relationships in our data reflect primarily the role of enduring partisan commitments in shaping attitudes towards political objects. (p. 135)

In his book *Voters' Choice* Pomper (1975) provides a vivid description of the prototype of the voter in the Michigan model. He calls him the *dependent* voter.

> The dependent voter does not make an autonomous choice on the basis of the issues and candidates. He relies instead on indirect and uncertain relationships; . . . political discourse is limited, sparse and desultory . . . . Family background, cultural milieu, all of the inchoate pressures of "socio-economic status" seem subtly to work on the voter in a process which is neither rational nor accompanied by high interest . . . Party is a type of social group, a group that happens to be political. Attachment to this group is, therefore, psychological in character, and is not essentially a political phenomenon . . . . In place of individual judgement, group influences determine the dependent voter's choice. A person thinks politically as he is socially, for his vote is formed in the midst of a group decision. (p. 16)

Once a theory or model gains influence it does more than offer an explanation for the observations made. It indicates to future researchers what is figure and what is ground, i.e. what needs explanation and what might be taken for granted or ignored. The popularity of the Michigan model meant that throughout the 1960s researchers showed little interest in the differences, if any, between the beliefs of those who remained loyal to a particular party and of those who strayed. Instead, research concentrated on voters able to identify with one of the two main parties rather than on the independents and those refusing to give themselves a political label.

## THE "RATIONAL VOTER" MODEL — AN ECONOMIC VIEW OF VOTE CHOICE

The social psychological model with its emphasis on a voter's group membership rather than current concerns fitted the calm period of the 1950s where few issues divided the electorate. Not so in the 1960s when the electorate and the parties took different positions on the Vietnam War, the Civil Rights Movement and many other issues of the day. Voters were able both to express their own views and to identify accurately the position of each party or candidate.

As discussion of people's views on issues came to the fore, a second model was increasingly considered, that of the voter as a rational decision maker that had been put forward earlier by Downs in his influential book, *An Economic Theory of Democracy* (1957), and subsequently developed by Key in *The Responsible Electorate* (1966). Downs' theory used concepts from economics like opportunity costs and pay-offs, and started by considering why people bother to vote at all.[2] He distinguished between the immediate pay-off which would result from the chance of affecting the outcome of the election by casting one's vote which is, of course, very small and a second pay-off that comes from the *act of voting itself* — as expression of one's duty as a citizen.[3] Moscovici elegantly described this as "the last religious act in a secular age",[4] where people with little faith or interest still turn out in large numbers for the civic or ritual act of voting.

Downs considered voters behave rationally since they can differentiate between alternatives, place them in some kind of order and then make a decision so as to maximize utilities or to minimize regret. Unlike the social psychological model, Downs stressed the role played in this decision by the parties' current policy platforms:

> Parties formulate policies in order to win elections, rather than win elections in order to formulate policies. Parties' purpose is to win votes, they will spell out the aims and costs of proposals only in so far as this is necessary for this purpose given the actions of the opposition parties. (1957)

[2] A not unimportant question particularly for the United States where the turnout for a Presidential election is hardly above 50% and that for Congressional elections between 35 and 45%. Turnout in British general elections tends to be in the high 70's but plummets to around 40% in many local elections.

[3] Downs saw the individual's voting as a capital sum he pays out at each election for the benefit of living in a democracy.

[4] Personal communication, 1980.

Thus Downs saw the result of an election as an equilibrium between voters' decisions and parties' policy formulations, borrowing the market analogy of the equilibrium achieved between maximizing the utility behaviour of the individual consumer (voter) and the profit maximizing behaviour of the firms providing the goods for purchase (in this case the parties who desire to maximize votes). Downs' rational voter therefore faces a choice, provided and restricted by the platforms of the opposing parties.

The voter's final decision is based on evaluation of those proposals offered which matter to him or her together with some general evaluation or image of the parties. The analogy here with consumerism is that, in choosing between goods, the individual will take the firms' general reputation for quality of product into account.

Downs suggested that voters can adopt an "information shortcut", using their image of the party ideology or outlook as a guide where information about a specific issue is lacking or difficult to come by. But they will do this only so long as their party's ideological position continues to conform to their expectations. Also where the voters' views have changed over time while the party platform has not, party identification will cease to affect vote choice to any marked degree. Note that here as much emphasis is put on the party's history as on that of the voter, two aspects which are underplayed in the Michigan model.

Key (1966), developing Downs' model further, emphasized that how far voters behave rationally and responsibly depends also on the clarity of the alternatives presented and the amount of information made available. Comparing in seven different elections vote switchers to those who remained with the party, Key found significant differences in their attitudes, with the vote switchers' attitudes no longer fitting those of the majority voting for the party. We provide supporting evidence in Chapters 3 and 7.

Key assigned an important role to voters' concern with issues that tallies with the findings of the Michigan surveys of the 1960s and early 1970s and was described by Nie *et al.* (1975) as "the rise of issue voting". These later surveys showed an increasing awareness on the part of the electorate about the parties' stands on issues with the voters' seeking a match between their own views and those of the party for which they will vote. At the same time, volatility of voting increased (i.e. the tendency of a voter to switch votes between one election and another) accompanied by a steady decrease in the proportion of voters who expressed any party identification and among those who did so a decrease in the strength of that identification.

Pomper (1975) drew another portrait of the voter of the 1960s and 1970s whom he called the *responsive voter*.

> The character of this voter, and the influence upon his choices, are not permanent, but change with the circumstances of the times and with political events. Issues are often important to the responsive voter. In the proper environment, public questions and the candidates' issue positions become critical to the electoral decision. Variety in electoral behaviour is most evident, not determinism. (Pomper, 1975, p. 8)

For Downs party identification enters into the voter's decision but it is a moving average, reflecting the voter's evaluation of party performance over a series of elections, and not a relatively fixed attachment once developed.

A variant of the voter's rational model of vote choice was suggested by Popkin *et al.*'s (1976) article entitled, "What have you done for me lately?", and developed further by J. A. Smith (1980) in his *Analysis of Presidential Elections*. It was called an *investment model*. While the rational model takes into account the parties' strategies to maximize votes and the implications of these for the clarity and honesty with which proposals are offered to the voters, the investment model stresses additionally the *role of the candidate or leader* of the party. The analogy with the manager of one's investments is clear; the voter takes into account the track record of the candidates, the trust that can be put in their promises, their ability to deliver, their standing with significant institutions, their capacity to arouse loyalty and their general likeability.

Key (1966) and subsequently Fiorina (1981) provided evidence to show that voters base their evaluation of the incumbent party and leader on their performance in office, i.e. it is a *retrospective evaluation* rather than an assessment of the party's proposals for the future.[5] Campbell made the same point in 1960, showing that when things go well, people do not associate this with the activities of government but do so when things go badly. Lipset's (1984) recent analysis of elections in democratic countries between 1979 and 1983 shows that neither the right nor the left are spared. He computed for each country a misery index based on inflation and unemployment rates. In the 17 countries where the index was high, the government lost the election, half the governments had been to the left, the other half to the right of centre. On the other hand, among the four countries that had a low misery index all four governments were re-elected, two were left-wing and two right-wing.

## A cognitive model of vote choice — a societal psychological approach

Although models centred on the "economic rationality" of the voter take into account party and candidate performance, they tend to concentrate on the final decision process only, and ignore the influences that lead to particular evaluations of issues. In the Michigan model the past does enter: party identification is thought to have its roots in early socialization and in attachment to subsequent reference groups, with time and the habit of voting increasing that attachment. But in both models too little account is taken of the social context in which the elections are fought, the cultural values of the society of the day and the *life history of issues*, i.e. the way political ideas develop, crystallize, are put into practice and, in the

[5]Lemieux (1974) suggested that in the British context this should operate even more strongly since the party in office is more directly responsible for policy than the President because of the checks inherent in the American constitution.

process, transformed. Nor is the role of the individual's value system considered, how assessment of specific proposals is coloured by their broader perspective on society. We show in Chapter 4 that this matters a good deal.

Explanations of events have a powerful role to play in shaping our attitudes towards, and our subsequent dealings with, those events. Nor is attitude change a once-and-for-all affair; rather people's perceptions, attitudes and their adaptation to circumstances are in a continuous state of flux, largely imperceptible, only rarely dramatic (Kelman, 1974). This is why it takes time for beliefs to erode, for new ideas to take root and for minority views to become the social representation of a society and its new ground rules (Moscovici et al., 1984).[6]

Concern with the life history of the issues themselves and with the social context in which the issues arose played a prominent part in the pioneering studies of voting conducted by Berelson and Lazarsfeld in the 1940s. Subsequently, in the race for the best prediction using the most sophisticated statistical techniques, the life history of issues and of voters took second place. We seek to redress the balance through our analyses of surveys of British voters spanning two decades.

Our study began in the early 1960s, at the height of the popularity of the Michigan model. However, we saw no reason to follow that model in treating the voting decision as differing from any other decision by postulating one dominant, permanent source of influence with cognitions relegated to a subsidiary position. On the contrary, we saw the decision as influenced by a variety of factors whose importance would vary with the individual's circumstances, the problems of the country and the distinctiveness of the parties' platforms.

Our model assumes a voter who is — following Pomper's description — responsive rather than dependent, active rather than passive. Pride of place in the model is given to the individual's cognitions. The individual, with his personal set of attitudes and beliefs, looks for the best match or the least mismatch between these and his or her perception of the platforms and the record of the parties. The voter's information gathering about the parties' stand might be searching or superficial, accurate or misleading, and his own views transient or stable. What matters is that the act of voting, like the purchase of goods, is seen as simply one instance of decision making, no different in kind from the process whereby other decisions are reached.

In developing the model we paid careful attention to how a person perceives the consequences of his particular vote, how far he anticipates the future in making the decision and how accurately he assesses the parties' stands.

The model incorporates elements of both the Michigan and the rational and investment models. In line with the Michigan model it emphasizes the role of

---

[6]It is worth reflecting that the Victorians considered poverty the responsibility of the poor. Today few societies do so and consequently governments of whatever political persuasion, however miserly or reluctant, have to be seen to be taking measures to help the poor. The view that poverty also has to do with the institutions of society has, in Western society of the twentieth century, become such a social representation or ground rule.

early political socialization and that of cross pressures. It sees the habit of voting as exerting a direct effect on vote choice and, as in the Michigan model, interacting with party identification. The biggest change lies in the role we assign to party identification. We see it, not as the invariant dominant factor eclipsing all others, but as variable in its strength and interacting with other cognitions and preferences. Here we follow Downs' model. Party identification will have a weak effect where the individual's views are clear and reflected in one or other party's stand. Its influence will be stronger and may well tip the scale when individuals lack clear-cut preferences among the available policy proposals, when the parties and candidates fail to demonstrate distinctive policies or styles, or when information is hard to come by. Like the rational model it assumes that people have views about political issues, recognize the parties' stands and, in rank ordering the utilities of the parties, consider also their evaluation of the parties' and leaders' performance.

The model is more inclusive in a psychological sense than the rational model in that it takes into account individuals' past habit of voting for one rather than another party, their value system, influences in the environment, and access and responsiveness to sources of information as well as the social context in which the election is fought and in which the parties display their wares.

At the core of the cognitive model is what we have called *a consumer model of vote choice*, to emphasize that the same principles hold as those which guide the individual in purchasing goods for consumption. The name may fit the title of McGinness's (1969) book, *The Selling of the President*, but it would be wrong to assume that this indicates that the voter thinks of the two parties as two brands of detergents, distinguished only by their packaging. In the model due weight is given to the importance of election campaigns. A voter whose preferences for two parties, e.g. the Conservatives and the Liberals, are fairly even, may at the last minute be influenced by a particular posture of a politician,[7] by the media or the polls.

An obvious requirement for any model, if it is to have analytic and predictive value, is that it should work in different historical contexts. Our model, being more inclusive and more flexible than the other models, does just this. It permits the importance of different parameters to vary by elections. Thus, in the United States in the 1950s, where few issues divided the voters, the decision may well have been more influenced by vote habit and party identification compared with the late 1960s and 1970s where the country was divided on such issues as the Vietnam war, minority rights, law and order and the extension of state and federal aid.

Butler and Stokes (1974) point out that, for issues to affect vote, three conditions

---

[7] In Chapter 9 we show that very small differences between the preferences for the parties are still good indicators of party choice. Such preferences represent the utilities for each party. A change in the salience of an issue or in the voter's position on it may be sufficient to make the difference.

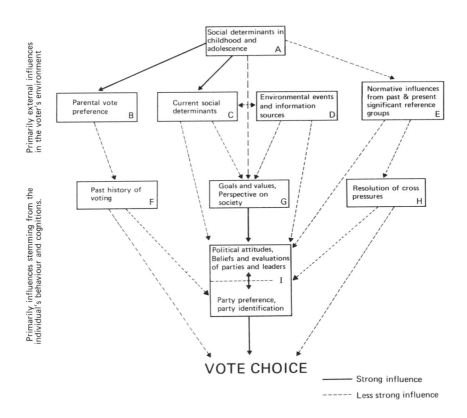

Fig. 1.1. A cognitive model of voting.

A  School and home influences; social, educational background of parents; individual's age, sex.
B  Parental Vote Preference during individual's adolescence.
C  Level of educational attainment, current social status, nature of employment.
D  Political and economic events, societal changes, information sources including the mass media. Linkages are two ways as the individual's social determinants and goals and values lead to selective exposure to information sources.
E  Influence of neighbourhood, friends, marriage partner, place of work, trade union membership and membership of other organisations.
F  Individual's voting history.
G  Includes measures of authoritarianism, political efficacy and interest; value orientation; goals.
H  Resolution of cross pressures relates to past as well as present.
I  Includes the individual's political orientation, attitudes to issues, beliefs and evaluations of parties and politicians, and party identification.

need to be met: first, voters have to care about the issue; secondly, there should be a diversity of views about this issue among the electorate; and thirdly, the parties or candidates should be seen to take different stands. In the American presidential election of 1972 the three criteria were met: Nixon and McGovern offered markedly different solutions to the Vietnam war, which voters correctly associated with the respective parties.[8]

These three conditions applied in the British elections between 1970 and 1983. Examples of such issues are the power trade unions should have, industrial relations generally, nationalization, immigration and comprehensive education. For example, in 1970 Enoch Powell's views defining the conservative perspective on immigration, despite Mr Heath's and the party's repeated repudiation of them, created a clear differentiation between the parties on this issue.

Finally, our model requires neither stability of attitudes nor consistency along some ideological dimension in order to form an accurate prediction of vote choice. Although in practice both consistency and "ideological thinking" influence the decision, each election is like a new shopping expedition in a situation where new as well as familiar goods are on offer. Not only can the role of issues vary from election to election, but the relative importance of past habit or party identification can vary with the party preferred. We shall show how the past plays a stronger part in the case of the Conservative vote, i.e. the party of tradition, while issues play a more significant role in the Labour vote. By comparison with the Conservative party, Labour is a party of change. As shown in Chapter 11, the Liberal voters, mostly different people in every election, are the comparative shoppers *par excellence*, making their decision almost entirely in response to the current situation and the tenor of the election campaign.

Figure 1.1 presents the consumer model in schematic form.

## Testing the model

To understand the role that an individual's cognitions play in the voting decision, reactions to a sufficiently wide range of political issues need to be assessed. Some issues reflect the major concerns of the society (e.g. the need to keep inflation and unemployment down) and are important for everyone, while others may have significance for some voters and not others. Each election sets its own particular agenda, but past issues, particularly where these are unresolved, may continue to matter. Therefore views on issues being emphasized by the parties at a particular election need to be sampled, as well as issues that were important at earlier elections.

But this is not all. In their study of the civic culture of political attitudes and

---

[8]This contrasts with the 1968 election where Humphrey and Nixon expressed similar sentiments and were at pains *not* to offer clear options (see Pomper, 1975).

democracy in five nations,[9] Almond and Verba (1963) showed that individuals' attitudes to political issues and their readiness to engage in political activities were rooted in their general orientation towards self and society, two aspects of which were of special relevance: the individuals' readiness to trust and their authoritarianism. Strumpel (1976) also pointed to the need to account for attitudes towards the political system and its parties by reference to individuals' goals which are rooted in the conditions of the society, the individual's place in it, and in his or her perception of equity in the allocation of resources. The effect of shared successes and hardships is quite different from that of unevenly distributed rewards and sacrifices. It follows that the individual's social class and other experiences related to the structure of the society are likely to influence his or her general perspective on society. We return to this issue in Chapter 4.

All this makes good sense. The rhetoric of politics even more than its reality is, after all, about all kinds of choices, from the type of society to aim for and preferences for particular goals (e.g. "to each according to his needs" versus "to each according to his output") to preferences for particular means in the pursuit of shared goals (e.g. bringing down inflation by means of an incomes policy or by free collective bargaining).

THE STUDIES USED

A study on which we had already embarked, on the influence of home, school and later of work on an individual's aspirations, outlook and goals, provided an appropriate starting point. It was very suitable for a variety of reasons. Being a follow-up study of middle and working class adolescents first studied in 1951 and re-interviewed as 25-year-old men, a considerable amount of factual and attitudinal data had already been collected, more than is generally obtained in election studies based on door-to-door interviewing of representative samples. Also, as 1951 was election year and we had asked the adolescents how they would have voted had they been old enough, we were able to chart the process of political socialization over a period of 23 years, beginning when parental influence was at its height and tracing its erosion as new attachments and the changing social and political environment made their mark. And finally, since we already knew the sample well, we felt we could ask them more questions and do so more frequently than would have been possible with a sample of strangers. As the 1962 interview already included several political questions, we decided to superimpose the voting study on this broader study. After each of the 1964, 1966, 1970 and October 1974 elections the men answered questions about their vote choices and, in 1970 and 1974, additional questions about their own situation, their feelings about themselves, their authoritarianism as well as their reactions to 20–30 individual political issues.

[9]This study is based on surveys conducted with 5000 people in Britain, Germany, Italy, Mexico and the United States.

For the initial development and testing of an explanatory model, richness of information is more important than the representativeness of the sample. Indeed, the fact that the men in the survey who provided the data for the initial test were all of the same age yet varied in background, education and social status proved a decided advantage. It meant not only that their political socialization first at home and later as adults occurred at the same period in the country's history, but also that we could study the development of vote choice from its inception and so trace the relative role of party attachment and attitudes more neatly than could be done with a representative sample containing people of all ages.

To examine the generality of an initial model, we repeated the analyses on the representative British election surveys of the 1970, 1974, 1979 and 1983 elections and on two panel studies, one conducted by Butler and Stokes (1963–1970), and the most recent one by Särlvik and Crewe (February 1974–1979). Thus the generality of the model originally developed on a sample of 178 men followed over a period of 15 years was tested in the ways we describe in the following chapters on six separate British election surveys covering a period of 13 years and involving more than 15,000 men and women.

THE POLITICAL CONTEXT

When studying the reactions of people in the real world, as distinct from its representation in the aseptic ambience of a psychological laboratory, the particular socio-economic and historical context in which the enquiry takes place is always important and changes in this context provide valuable tests for the robustness of any explanatory model. This is particularly so in the case of voting. The 15 years or six elections covered by the initial study saw three changes of government and numerous political, economic and social changes. The men we studied cast their first two votes (1959, 1964) in a period of relative economic optimism and full employment and their last vote (1974) at a time of economic despondency, high unemployment and great concern about inflation.[10] These two decades cover the period of Britain's entry into Europe and Labour's changing stand on this issue. They saw the steady erosion of British prestige and influence abroad and a loss of confidence at home. During this period, different strategies were tried to contain, weaken or build on the power of the unions. Two of these were the Industrial Relations Bill in 1970 and the Social Contract in 1974. There was an increase over the years in the number, severity and duration of official and unofficial strikes. The importance of immigration as an election issue varied from election to election, but there was a continuous tightening of restrictions on the entry of immigrants imposed by the respective governments of the day. This period

[10]"What would you say is the most urgent problem facing the country at the present time?" In December 1970, 35% of the electorate mentioned prices and cost of living; by November 1974 64% did so (Gallup Poll Bulletins, 1974).

also saw changes in the secondary state school system, a liberalization of laws on capital punishment, homosexuality and abortion, the growth of the Women's Movement, the enactment of the Race Relations Act and the reduction of the voting age from 21 to 18. There was a growth of the protest movement against the Vietnam war, the conclusion of that war, an escalation of the conflict in Northern Ireland, the oil crisis, the exploitation of North Sea oil, as well as the growth in the political muscle of the regions, notably Scotland. The chronicle of change is endless: some, like inflation, unemployment and strikes, touched directly on the lives of our respondents, while others, like entry into Europe, at first seemed more remote.

The data base provided by the initial longitudinal study, supported by the large-scale national surveys of the general elections, spanned more than two decades of change in Britain's fortunes and way of life, allowing us to test the general validity of the model by seeing how far the relationships predicted apply to elections fought in different economic and political climates. It also enabled us to examine the stability of beliefs and preferences over time and their role in the decision, as well as the effects of the victory or defeat of a preferred party on subsequent voting. The period covered three changes of government — from Conservative to Labour in 1964 from Labour to Conservative in 1970, and back to Labour in 1974.

We added to our data base national election surveys covering two further elections, not just to bring our analyses up to date, but also because each raised new and interesting questions. The 1979 election brought the Conservatives back to power with a large majority. The election took place after the "winter of discontent", where the number and vehemence of the strikes, especially those by ambulance drivers and grave diggers, shocked the electorate and demonstrated to them that Labour's special relationship with the unions was insufficient to act as an effective brake. What made the election unusual was the considerable number of defections by former Labour supporters among the skilled working class who now voted Conservative. This represented a fundamental change in the electoral vote pattern that had persisted over twenty years in which conversions from left to right and right to left were rare; instead voters had expressed discontent with a major party for which they had previously voted by abstaining or voting Liberal.

The period between 1979 and 1983 saw a deepening of the recession, a reduction in the rate of inflation and also a massive rise in unemployment to an unprecedented 3½ million, with certain areas of the country and heavy industries being the most hard hit. And then came the Falklands war in 1982 which at a stroke changed the public's assessment of Mrs Thatcher. Just before the war began she had the lowest rating of any Prime Minister since polls began, but as soon as the war started the public's assessment of her rose to an all time high and remained so until the election a year later.

The 1983 election, which brought in the Conservatives with an overall majority of 144 seats in the House of Commons, made history as the first election in which the newly created Liberal–Social Democratic Party Alliance took part. "The Gang of Four'' Labour veterans, three of whom had held ministerial posts in former Labour governments, decided to leave the Labour party and in March 1981 formed the Social Democratic Party. Later in November 1982 they linked with the Liberals to fight the election jointly as the Alliance with the aim of ''breaking the mould of British politics''. In the last part of this book we shall pay particular attention to the shape of this mould: the structure of political attitudes and the nature of voting ideology (Chapter 10) and provide an assessment of the problems facing a party which aims to break or transform British politics through seeking the middle ground (Chapters 11 and 14).

STEPS TAKEN TO TEST THE VALIDITY OF THE MODEL

In the chapters that follow we consider the various aspects of the model. Chapter 3 examines the extent and nature of vote volatility and the principles that underlie them. In Chapter 4 we explore the influence of political socialization and of the individual's circumstances, especially social mobility, on their vote preference and on their perspective of society, showing that this in turn affects the individual response to specific policy proposals. Special consideration is given to the role of cross pressures. We end Chapter 4 by presenting, with the help of path analysis, a global picture of the influences across time of those factors outlined in the model. It is here that the length of time we have studied our sample and the range of information we have obtained come into their own.

In Chapter 5 we show that, on the basis of knowing a person's attitudes and values, we can accurately predict his voting behaviour. Most voting studies carry out predictions with hindsight, that is, knowing the *results* of the election, they divide the sample on the basis of the votes they have cast and, using optimizing statistical techniques, determine how well they can discriminate between them on the basis of the voters' attitudes. We have carried out and report on such discriminant analyses, but in 1974 we also made *genuine predictions*, that is, we predicted how our sample and the BES 1974 and 1979 representative samples would vote *before* the results were known. We based the predictions on the voters' evaluation of particular policies and on their perception of the likelihood of each of the parties implementing them once in power. By combining these two sets of data, the individual's utilities or preferences for each party were obtained and he was assumed to have voted for the party which for him had the higher utility. Even without the benefit of statistical optimization that occurs in discriminant analysis prediction was very accurate (Chapter 9).

Chapter 6 demonstrates that attitudes relevant to vote do not merely reflect the individual's social group membership nor that vote choice is closely linked to social determinants.

On their own predictions, however accurate, are not sufficient to prove the validity of the model. We also need to show that voters who change their attitudes across elections are more likely to change their vote than those whose attitudes remain unchanged and that the direction of vote change parallels the direction of attitude change. Where a particular individual's set of beliefs and attitudes conflicts with those of the majority of the party for whom he has voted, the voter should be more likely to change his vote at the subsequent election, compared with someone whose attitudes fit well with the party of his choice (Chapter 7). One necessary element in the decision chain requires that the voter's perception of differences between the parties' policies is not merely a reflection of the voter's own party preferences (Chapter 8). Finally, we need to show that past habit and present attitudes each make an independent contribution to the decision and that vote is better predicted where attitudes and values, as well as past behaviour, favour the same party than where they conflict (Chapter 9).

Through testing the various propositions of the model, we obtained a picture of the voter as someone who, though little interested in politics, is still accurately informed about many of the parties' platforms and holds definite views on a range of political issues, but not on every policy contained in the parties' manifestos. Since we were particularly interested in the cognitive maps of voters and had on three occasions obtained their reactions to more than 20 issues, we were able to explore Converse's contention that the political views of the general public are too disparate and unstable to amount to any kind of "ideological" thinking. In Chapter 10, by analysing the longitudinal and the BES 1974, 1979 samples, we show that the views of the British voters at all levels of education were in fact organized along certain "ideological" dimensions which relate meaningfully to the individual's party choice.

The cognitive map or organization of these views, though remarkably stable over time, was affected by events and the parties' response to these events, as were attitudes to individual issues. Changing attitudes to the Common Market during this period are a case in point. Changes in attitudes over time are not necessarily evidence of indifference or lack of political sophistication. There is clearly a need to look at the *life history of issues*. It makes good sense that politically concerned individuals, in favour or against a proposed policy, may have second thoughts on the effects of that policy once it is implemented. There is, after all, a great difference between theory and practice, as indicated by the changing views of Members of Parliament of all parties and the positions taken by respective Governments and by the Opposition on Britain's membership of the EEC.

In Chapter 11 we report on the characteristics of the voters for the middle ground: the Liberal voters and now the Alliance voters who made their first appearance in the 1983 election.

The model throws fresh light on the voters' thinking, their reactions to the three parties, the parties' responsiveness to voters' concerns and on the conduct and impact of election campaigns. These we consider in the final chapter on political implications (Chapter 14). The implications of this type of study and its model for social psychology and for political science are drawn in Chapters 12 and 13.

# 2

# The data base

Although there is considerable overlap in the interests of political scientists and social psychologists studying political behaviour, there are important differences which affect the priorities they attach to different aspects of research. Social psychologists are primarily interested in the *process* which results in a particular decision or behaviour rather than in the prevalence of that behaviour in the population. They are concerned to obtain data in the format and breadth best suited to model the behaviour in question and tend, therefore, to design special studies even where this means using small and often unrepresentative samples.

Political scientists, on the other hand, equally interested in the reactions of voters, wish primarily to use them to draw inferences about the nature and outcome of elections, about party stability or about the changing nature of the party system or the electorate's outlook. For them, the prevalence of a given behaviour or opinion is of prime importance. They want to draw direct inferences from the replies of the sample to the electorate as a whole or to demographically significant subgroups. In their case, if there has to be a choice, breadth of information must be sacrificed in favour of size and representativeness of the sample. Consequently political scientists tend to develop or test new theoretical insights by re-analysing existing national election studies rather than by designing new studies.

Both strategies have a cost; the former that of generalizability, the latter that of flexibility and breadth.

Fortunately, we do not have to make a choice between these two costs, because we adopted an approach incorporating both strategies. For the development and initial validation of the model we designed a special study and later carried out extensive secondary analyses of existing British election cross-sectional and panel surveys to determine how well the model mirrored the decision process of the electorate as a whole.

A special study was necessary given the nature of the model in which a crucial role is assigned to individuals' views about their society and its institutions, to their preferences for given policies and styles of government as well as to their awareness of the parties' stands. In the model, the voting history of an individual affects the decision making. We therefore needed to trace the voting histories of the same people from their inception over a sufficient number of elections to examine the relative stability and influence of previous vote choices. Since elections are relatively rare events occurring normally only every four or five years, the follow-up study had to be very long. Ours extended over 15 years. We also wanted to chart changes in people's views about the same issues over time as well as their views on new issues raised in a given election campaign. This meant that the number of questions we needed to ask of our long-suffering respondents grew with each election.

Our first priority then was to find a sample willing to go along with these stringent requirements. We decided to use one with whom we had already established good contact, having first studied them as adolescent boys in 1951 and re-interviewed them 11 years later as young men aged 24 to 25. While the sample provided unusually good conditions for the development and initial validation of the model, the results could not, without additional checks, be used for drawing inferences about the vote choices of the general population.

As noted in Chapter 1, we carried out the same analyses on the representative British election surveys covering the period of our study from 1964 to 1974 made available by the Survey Data Archive at the University of Essex. We did the same with the two British election panel studies of that period: the extensive seven-year panel study by Butler and Stokes, which like ours began midway between the 1959 and 1964 elections[1] (their sample was recontacted three times: in 1964, 1966 and 1970), and the Butler and Crewe 1970–February 1974 panel study. Both panel studies built on representative samples, but, like ours, suffered attritions.

We extended the scope of our enquiry by analysing survey data from the 1979 and 1983 elections to see how far the model applied in a different political and economic climate from the one in which it had been developed.

Of particular interest in these later surveys is the Särlvik and Crewe 1974–1979 panel study which was built on the February 1974 representative sample. These respondents were re-contacted three times: in October 1974; at the time of the 1975 Referendum concerning Britain's membership of the EEC; and at the time of the 1979 election. For the 1983 election we used the representative survey conducted for the BBC by Crewe on the day of the 1983 election, Worcester's compilation of poll results, *British Public Opinion* (1983), and a panel survey covering the 1983 election campaign which Worcester conducted for *The Sunday Times* (1983).

The second phase of our research consists then of extensive testing of the general applicability of the model. Table 2.1 lists the studies covered in our analyses giving for each their sample size and the name(s) of the principal investigators. In the case of the panel studies, sample size represents the number of panel survivors, i.e. the sample which had answered questions at *each* occasion

---

[1]Our first set of interviews was conducted in 1962, theirs in 1963.

TABLE 2.1

Surveys included in the analysis

A. REPRESENTATIVE SURVEYS

| Source | Election year | Size of sample | Names of principal investigators |
|---|---|---|---|
| British election study | 1970 | 1843 | Butler and Stokes |
| British election study | 1974 (Feb.) | 2462 | Särlvik and Crewe |
| British election study | 1974 (Oct.) | 2365 | Särlvik and Crewe |
| British election study | 1979 | 1893 | Särlvik and Crewe |
| BBC Study | 1983 | 4146 | Crewe |

B. PANEL STUDIES

| Source | Duration of study (elections covered) | Final sample size | Response rate | No. of elections | Names of principal investigators |
|---|---|---|---|---|---|
| 1. Longitudinal study of men aged 25 | 1962–October 1974 (1964, 1966, 1970, Feb., Oct., 1974) | 178 | 40% | 5 | Himmelweit, Humphreys and Jaeger |
| 2. British election study 1963 representative sample | 1963–1970 (1964, 1966, 1970) | 718 | 36% | 3 | Butler and Stokes |
| 3. British election study 1970 | 1970–Feb. 1974 (1970–Feb. 1974) | 1096 | 59% | 2 | Crewe |
| 4. British election study Feb. 1974 | Feb. 1974–May 1979 | 765 | 40% | 3 | Särlvik and Crewe |
| 5. MORI/*Sunday Times* Panel Survey | 29 April to 3 June 1983 (before announcement of election to shortly before Election date 9 June) | 942 | 77% | 4 recalls | Worcester |

when a contact was sought.[2] The response rate refers to the percentage of the original representative sample that the survivors represent.

We would like to stress here the importance we attach to the validation of the general applicability of the model. Inevitably more space in the book is allotted to the longitudinal study. This is partly because it needs more description than the well known election surveys and partly because it contains more information than is usual in such studies. But it would be wrong for the reader to dwell on the fact that the model was developed on an unrepresentative sample. The re-analyses of the large samples clearly demonstrate that the model accounts well for the vote decisions of the electorate as a whole, not only for the five (1964–1974) elections covered in our study but also for the two subsequent elections of 1979 and 1983.

In the section that follows we outline the longitudinal study, discuss the characteristics of the sample and provide a thumbnail sketch of the men whom we got to know so well.


## The longitudinal study

By building on a study of adolescent boys we benefited not only because of the contact we had previously established which made returning to the same sample that much easier, but also because it proved particularly suitable in another respect. In the original cross-sectional study of adolescent boys aged 13–14 we had tried to chart the cognitive maps that young people build up about their society. Since the study took place in the election year of 1951 we had asked the boys how they would have voted had they been old enough, providing us with the unusual opportunity to trace political socialization from a very early age and to follow its progress across a *23-year period*.

The original study was conducted not as a study of political attitudes but to assess the relative influence of home (its social and educational background and the quality of family relations) and that of the divided secondary state school system on the adolescents' attainments, aspirations and attitudes to self and to society. The purpose of the study required oversampling of grammar schools relative to their number in the divided secondary school system.[3] In all over 600 pupils took part: all the third forms of four grammar and five secondary modern schools in the Greater London area drawn from socially different neighbourhoods. Close contact with the schools and the boys was established at that time. We saw the boys on three occasions, each time for several hours.

---

[2]In computing the sample size of the 1974–1979 panel survivors we took all those who had been successfully contacted in February and October 1974 as well as 1979, irrespective of whether or not they had taken part in the survey at the time of the Referendum.
[3]More than half the sample came from grammar schools; the correct proportion for the country as a whole at that time was around one out of five. Details of that study and its results can be found in Himmelweit and Swift (1969, 1971), Himmelweit and Bond (1974).

Initially, we had no intention of doing a follow-up study and therefore had made no attempt to keep in touch.[4] Yet when we decided to do so 11 years later (in 1962), all those successfully contacted agreed to be interviewed and many remembered the earlier study. Then, as in adolescence, they were very ready to talk about themselves and to express their views. The interviews generally lasted two to three hours. In addition, the men filled out questionnaires which they posted back.[5]

The follow-up study allowed us to: (1) examine the relation of adolescent performance and outlook to achievement and outlook in adult life; (2) examine the relation of societal and personal experiences to the development of goals, values and social attitudes; (3) relate social and political attitudes to voting behaviour. Despite the interval of 11 years and the fact that in early adulthood there is generally a good deal of geographical mobility, we were able to re-interview 450 or 73% of the original sample now aged 24–25. The result of this part of the survey proved sufficiently promising for us to embark on a continuing voting study, *restricting the sample at each successive wave to those who had replied at all previous stages.*[6]

In 1964, 1966, 1970 and October 1974, on the day after the general election, the men received a postal questionnaire asking how they had voted, and if they had not, which party, however slightly, they preferred; the reasons for their choice (from "best of a bad bunch" to "the party appealed to me"); when they had decided whether and how to vote (ranging from before the date of the election was announced to the day of the election itself); and what their reactions were to the outcome of the election. In 1970, eight years after the detailed interviews conducted in 1962, the men completed a more extensive questionnaire containing questions about their job, their goals and values, their well being, how they managed on their earnings, and two scales: one measuring authoritarianism, the other a sense of powerlessness versus competence. These questions and scales had already been presented in 1962 as had many of the questions concerning social issues. New questions were added in 1970 to reflect the concerns of the day.

One of the problems facing all longitudinal studies is how to deal with the fluctuating importance of particular issues over time. We decided on a compromise. We repeated questions about those issues which analysis had shown to be relevant

[4]To set out coldly to do a longitudinal study extending over more than twenty years would require more determination and more tolerance for boredom than the researchers possessed. Indeed after the first three elections we had decided to stop. But then the lure of a better test of the model or its refinement for which we needed new data gained the upper hand once the 1974 election was announced.

[5]Eighty per cent did so. One interviewee was so concerned about the time he had taken in answering questions that he insisted on paying the interviewer's taxi back; another wrote that he would be happy to see us, and had all the time in the world. Unfortunately by the time the necessary permission had been obtained he was no longer available, having left the prison in which he was serving a sentence.

[6]This meant that in 1964 we contacted only those who had replied in 1962 and, after the general election of 1966, only those who had replied *both* in 1964 and 1962. The same procedure was followed for the elections of 1970 and October 1974.

to the decision making, and added questions about matters that had gained importance since the last election. These included such issues as student unrest, demonstrations and a fuller range of questions about strikes, immigration and the trade unions; others were added in 1974. A brief account of the measures used at various stages of the study is given in Appendix 1.

The results of the study up to and including 1970 based on 246 subjects lent strong support to the "consumer" model of voting, except that one important element was missing (Himmelweit and Bond, 1974). While we knew which policy issues people favoured, we did not know whether they could correctly identify the parties' respective stands on these issues. We therefore decided, despite dwindling numbers at the time of the October 1974 election, to embark on one final round of questioning, once again repeating the voting questions and many of the questions and measures used in 1962 and 1970, adding new ones representative of the main concerns of the day (e.g. "stop unemployment from rising", "control inflation") and of issues included in the various manifestos (e.g. "sell council houses to tenants", "introduce statutory control of wage increases", "abolish grammar schools", "subsidize the cost of essential foods").

As before, the respondent was asked to evaluate each of the policies using a five-point scale ranging from very good to very bad. This time they were also asked to answer the following question, "How likely would each of the three parties have been to introduce the policies had they won?" and to indicate the likelihood of implementation of the policy by each of the three main parties in turn using a five-point scale ranging from very likely to very unlikely.

RESPONSE RATES

In 1962 we had interviewed 450 men. For the first two rounds — separated by an interval of two years in each case — the response rates were as high as 82% (371 of 450 in 1964) and 88% (325 of 371 in 1966), and for the last two rounds — each separated by four years — 76% (246 of 325 in 1970) and 72% (178 of 246 in 1974) respectively.

One hundred and seventy-eight men stayed with the study throughout the 13 years, providing full information at each round of questioning.

Our response rate was substantially higher than that of the two major panel studies of British elections during this period, each of which began with a representative sample. The four-year panel study of Butler and Crewe (1970–1974) yielded a response rate of 59% compared with our 72% over the same period. The Butler and Stokes panel study, extending over seven years (1963–1970), had a response rate of 42% compared with our response rate of 55% over the same period (1962–1970). The response rate of the Särlvik and Crewe panel study of Feb. 1974 to 1979 was 41%.

COMPARISON OF PANEL SURVIVORS
WITH THOSE WHO DROPPED OUT EARLY

In Appendix 2 we provide details of the effects of attrition. Apart from a somewhat greater loss of working class men in the earlier rounds only, exhaustive comparison between those who stayed with the study and those who did not showed no differences in inter-generational mobility, in the relation of class to voting, in interest in politics, party preferences or attitudes to social and political issues. Butler and Stokes (1974) similarly report no significant differences on relevant characteristics between drop-outs and those who stayed the course. Särlvik and Crewe (1983) found "no more than a trivial bias" in the comparisons they made on their 1974–1979 panel except with regard to reported voting turnout.

COMPARISON OF LONGITUDINAL PANELLISTS
WITH THOSE OF THE NATIONAL SAMPLE

We made four comparisons of our longitudinal sample with the national election studies. These are reported in detail in Appendix 2.

The first comparison concerned inter- and intra-generational mobility which was greater among our respondents than in national samples, partly due to the oversampling of grammar schools in our study, partly due to the period under study. Our sample grew up at a time of considerable expansion of higher education and at a time of full employment. The recent Nuffield enquiry into social mobility shows that due to changes in the occupational structure of Britain there has been a marked increase in upward inter- and also intra-generational mobility compared with the 1950s (Goldthorpe, 1980).

Our second comparison was on voting turnout which we found to be higher than in the national sample. The voting turnout reported by our sample in October 1974 was 85%, that of Särlvik and Crewe's panel 82% compared with a national turnout of 73% (Appendix 2, Table 4).

The third comparison concerned voting patterns. In 1964 the voting of our sample was very similar to that of the national sample, but from then onwards even though the proportion of Conservatives in the electorate remained constant, our sample showed a steady drift away from Labour to the Conservatives which was related to the high degree of upward social mobility among the men (Chapter 4).[7]

Finally our fourth comparison examined reactions to social issues. In our study four types of social issues related to voting: issues which reflect a generally liberal attitude (abolition of capital punishment; the easing of the law on homosexuality; treatment of immigrants); economic issues (welfare provisions, control of big business, nationalization); industrial relations issues (management–employee

[7]In 1964 35% of our sample voted Conservative; by October 1974 40% of our sample did so compared with 31% of the general electorate. In the same election 21% voted Labour compared with 37% of the electorate.

relations, power of trade unions and seriousness of strikes); and issues to do with selective secondary schooling. Here we compared the respondents' answers to identical questions given in two large-scale surveys we had conducted in 1971 and 1975 (Himmelweit *et al.*, 1981). Apart from the fact that our sample (which was better educated compared with the general public) tended to be somewhat more liberal in their attitudes to immigrants, and less in favour of the restoration of capital punishment or the increase in police power, their perception of trade union power, their views on control of immigration, or on comprehensive schooling were remarkably similar to the views expressed on these topics by the larger, more heterogeneous sample.

In any case, what really matters for the testing of the model is not the distribution of answers to individual questions but the extent to which these views relate to the decision whether and how to vote. This is where comparison with the relationships found in the larger samples becomes important. For the same reason, the fact that our sample, though no more Conservative in their party preferences than those whom we could not follow up, contains at every election a greater proportion of Conservative voters compared with the general electorate is not crucial for the validation of our model.

## A thumbnail sketch of the attainments, feelings and outlook of the men in the longitudinal study

We present below a brief picture of the attainments, background and outlook of the men we studied for so long.

Half of the 246 men who stayed in the study at least until 1970 had attended grammar school, half had come from a working class background, and by the age of 25 (in 1962) 27% were in a professional or in a managerial job; 43% in middle level or routine clerical posts; and a further 29% were doing manual work. Eight years later, in 1970, the proportion in upper middle class jobs had almost doubled (46%) whilst those in working class jobs had been reduced from 29% to 20%. The pattern is repeated when we consider the job level of those who remained in the sample until 1974.[8] How far is this reflected in their feelings about themselves, their careers and their jobs?

To see whether the individuals' feelings would undergo a change as they became older, or as a result of career changes, or a combination of both factors, we asked the same three questions of our sample when the men were 25, 33 and 38 years of age. These were: "How do you feel you have done in your career so far?"; "How much do you like your job?"; and "If you look at your life today, taking everything together, your work, your leisure life, how do you feel about yourself?". In 1962, at age 25, the replies reflected optimism and contentment. More than a quarter felt that they had done better and 56% as well in their careers as they

[8]See Appendix 2, Table 3.

had hoped. Ninety per cent liked their job and 48% liked it very much. Indifference or dislike were rare. They seemed pleased with life in general (71% describing themselves as happy and a further 24% as fairly happy).

Even allowing for the tendency of people to reply positively when asked how they are, replies to other questions which may not have this particular bias indicated that the men were indeed relatively confident. Two out of three saw the world as full of possibilities open to everyone, and three quarters rejected the statement ''Ordinary people like myself are quite powerless''.

As part of the original study we had asked a series of questions about the role that work played in the individual's life. The replies were interesting. While four out of five disagreed with the statement ''Work has no interest for me apart from the money'', they were almost equally divided between those who agreed and those who disagreed that ''Even though I enjoy my spare time, my real sense of achieving something comes from my work''. More disagreed than agreed that ''Even if I did not need the money, I would need to go to work to keep my self-respect''. Work, it would appear, mattered to this group of confident young men. They liked it, but it did not dominate their lives, as it might well have done a generation earlier.[9]

People's interest in politics was low; this does not, of course, prevent them from having views about political matters. What it does mean, however, is that if we are to understand people's motivations or to account for their holding different views on particular issues, we need to consider how these relate to their basic goals and values and to their general orientation towards people and institutions (their authoritarianism, for instance).[10] We therefore asked the respondents in 1962 and again in 1970 to rate the importance of sixteen goals using a seven-point scale ranging from extremely important to not at all important. A factor analysis of the ratings yielded four main factors representing different sets of goals (Table 2.2). Table 2.2 indicates the percentage of the sample who in 1962 rated the goal as very important (categories 1 or 2) and as not at all important (categories 6 or 7).

The table shows that interest in, even more than the rewards of, work were of overriding importance, and an easy, leisured life was not. Few people wished to change society, or were concerned about improving society. Their concerns were with their immediate environment, with personal growth. *To be*

[9]One needs to be careful not to read too much into the replies of people who felt safe in their jobs and able to change jobs. Their replies might well have been different if the questions had been asked today when unemployment and redundancy loom large. Maria Jahoda (1979) shows how prolonged unemployment erodes an individual's self confidence.
[10]Criteria for what is more or less basic are, of course, difficult to establish. One criterion, but only one, would be the relative stability of the replies by the same sample across time. Yet so much depends, when comparing the stability of values with those of attitudes to specific issues, on whether these issues have remained in the limelight. Where they have, the stability might be greater than when the issue has ceased to be discussed.

TABLE 2.2                                                          *Longit. study*

Percentage frequency of goals considered very important and not at all important by the men at age 25

|  | Very important (%) | Not important (%) |
|---|---|---|
| 1. *Conventional success goals:* | | |
| To have an interesting job | 89 | 1 |
| To have enough money for health and comfort | 75 | 3 |
| To have a house of one's own | 66 | 7 |
| To get ahead in life | 61 | 6 |
| 2. *Goals expressing concern with society and self-realization:* | | |
| To feel free to express myself | 68 | 2 |
| To be with people I can trust | 62 | 6 |
| To make the world a better place | 38 | 13 |
| To feel needed | 37 | 15 |
| To change society | 19 | 54 |
| 3. *Goals expressing a hedonistic outlook:* | | |
| To have a good time | 22 | 12 |
| To have lots of leisure | 19 | 19 |
| To enjoy myself and have few worries and responsibilities | 19 | 41 |
| 4. *Goals seeking a quiet, conforming life:* | | |
| To lead a quiet life | 14 | 35 |
| To be like the others and not to stand out from the rest | 10 | 42 |

*with people I can trust, to feel free to express myself* and *to feel needed* were important goals.[11]

We also examined the extent to which the passing of time (a person's increasing age) and the individual's job status and job mobility affected his feelings about himself and the importance he attached to particular goals.[12] Time had an effect: there was less exuberance; whilst still liking their jobs as much as before, in 1974 the men were less sanguine about their career prospects and significantly fewer decribed themselves without qualification as *happy* (47% in 1974 compared with 71% in 1962); instead the percentage who saw themselves as *fairly* happy increased.

[11]The priorities our sample attached to goals and values compared with those of a large-scale survey we conducted in 1971 were very similar — indeed, the importance of an interesting job, the need to express oneself, to feel needed and the little importance attached to having lots of leisure, a quiet life, few responsibilities or to be like the others were the same for both sexes and all ages. They reflect general, well internalized values in our society.
[12]We did this through a repeated measures analysis of variance with one main effect being the time period (1962–1974) and the other individual's job status, defined through classification into one of five groups: three stable groups, upper middle, lower middle and working class; and two *upwardly mobile* groups, those who had held lower middle class jobs in 1962 and had moved into upper middle class jobs by 1974, and those who had moved from working to middle class jobs. All results reported in the text were based on main effects or interactions significant or better than the $p0\cdot02$ level.

There were significant status differences at both points in time (Fig. 2.1). The pecking order was always the same. Those in upper middle class jobs liked their jobs the most, thought their prospects the best, and also assessed their lives in the most positive terms; those in stable working class jobs did so least. The groups, in descending order of satisfaction with their lives, were: the stable upper middle class; those who had moved from middle to upper middle class jobs; the stable lower middle class; those who had moved from working to middle class jobs; and finally the stable working class.

Interestingly, the two mobile groups expressed feelings in 1962 halfway between those expressed by the group from which they came and the group to which they had moved.[13] By 1974, their ratings were more similar to those of the group to which they had moved.

Time or age and the individual's social status and social mobility affected the priorities the men attached to the different goals (Fig. 2.2). In 1962, conventional success goals were least important to the upper middle class and most important to the working class; by 1974 the picture had been reversed, the stable working class group, seeing advancement blocked, had become far less interested in getting ahead, while for the upper middle class group, still on the ladder of advancement, success had become more important in their thirties than it had been in their twenties. Campbell and Converse (1980) as well as Strumpel (1976) show how adaptation to the reality of career prospects leads to a re-evaluation of goals.

By contrast the wish to create a better world, to feel needed and to express oneself had by 1974 become significantly more important for all groups. But once again the upper middle class and the working class reacted differently; for the upper middle class it became more important, for the working class less important. What is interesting, though, is that the differences between the groups had become smaller when the men were in their thirties than 12 years earlier. Certain needs concerning interpersonal relations seemed to be very generally felt. In 1962 the sample attached little value to being like the others and not standing out from the rest, and few wanted a quiet life. In their thirties they repudiated these goals even more.

The sample was neither diehard nor progressive; it was essentially a middle-of-the-road group which, like the electorate as a whole, was not particularly interested in politics, in making the world a better place or in changing society. Their concern was with seeking satisfaction within their everyday environment at work and at home. Yet, as we shall see, despite their relatively low interest in politics, the political views of this group were neither haphazard nor random.

---

[13]Their more optimistic outlook might well have contributed to their advancement. There were not sufficient numbers of downwardly mobile people in our sample to consider them as a separate group.

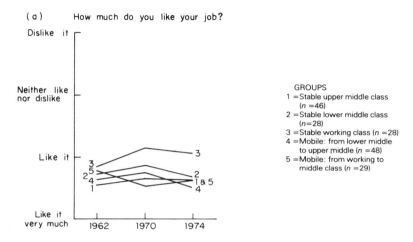

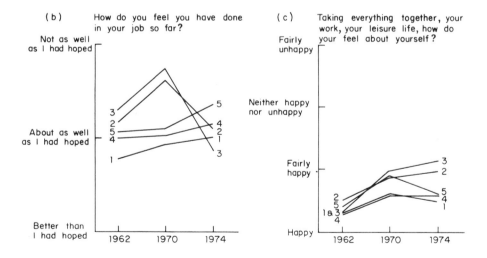

Fig. 2.1. Changes over time of feelings about self of five groups of men grouped in terms of their social mobility (1962–1974).

*Significance of results:*
(a) Groups: $p = 0.01$; Time: N/S; Interaction: N/S.
(b) Groups: $p = 0.001$; Time: $p = 0.02$; Interaction: N/S.
(c) Groups: $p < 0.03$; Time: $p < 0.001$; Interaction: $p = 0.08$.

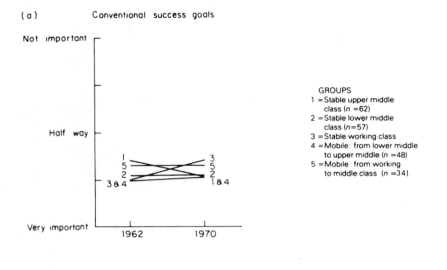

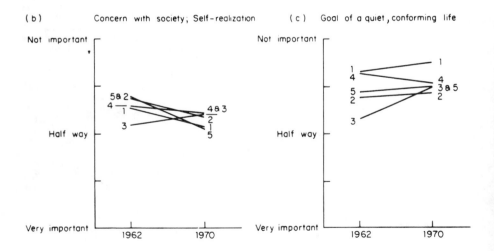

Fig. 2.2 Changes over time of the factor scores of selected goals and values of five groups of men grouped in terms of their social mobility (1962–1970).
*Significance of results:*
(a) Group: N/S; Time: N/S; Interaction: $p = 0 \cdot 002$.
(b) Group: N/S; Time: $p = 0 \cdot 000$; Interaction: $p = 0 \cdot 006$.
(c) Group: $p = 0 \cdot 001$; Time: $p = 0 \cdot 04$; Interaction: $p = 0 \cdot 01$.

SUMMARY

In this chapter we have outlined the two-phased approach we adopted. For the development of the model and its initial test we designed a longitudinal study using the sample of a previous enquiry of men who were all the same age, and therefore were politically socialized and voted in the same economic and political climate. We traced their voting history and political attitudes over a 15-year period from the time they were old enough to cast their first vote in 1959 until their sixth in October 1974. Since these men had previously been studied as adolescents aged 13–14 we were able to trace their political socialization across a 23-year period from adolescence to the time when the men were in their late thirties.

In the second phase, we validated the general applicability of the model by carrying out secondary data analyses of the representative British election surveys covering the 1970, February and October 1974, 1979 and 1983 elections and of two British election panel studies: 1963–1970 and Feb. 1974–1979.

The order of presentation of findings and tables is always the same. We begin with the results of the longitudinal study followed by the analyses of the relevant representative cross-sectional and panel studies. Each table number is followed by the designation of the sample to which the table refers. Our study is described as the longitudinal study (Longit. study), the cross-sectional British election surveys as BES followed by the election year of the study (e.g. BES 1970) and the panel studies as BES panel 1964–'70; 1970–Feb. 1974; and 1974–'79 respectively.

# 3

# The new norm:
# Variability, not loyalty

The period 1959–1974 under study was one of maximal electoral change. The Conservative party's fortunes went into a decline after the 1959 election, and in 1964 Labour crept into office with a minute majority. Two years later, in 1966, Labour was returned with the highest proportion of votes cast since Labour's landslide victory of 1945 and with the largest increase in majority ever won by a party in office prior to 1983. By 1970, Labour's popularity had waned and the Conservatives came to power, only to be ousted four years later (February and October, 1974). In the February 1974 election three million more voted and four million more voted Liberal compared with 1970. As a result, "the Conservatives polled their lowest share of the vote since 1929; Labour their lowest since 1931; the Liberals their highest since 1929; and 'other parties' their highest since the Coalition Election of 1918" (Clements, 1975).

The 1979 election once again brought about a change of government. The large Conservative majority in 1979 was a far cry from the tiny majority which had brought the Conservatives to power in 1970. In 1983 the Conservatives were re-elected with 144 seats, that is, with an increased overall majority in the House of Commons, and this despite the fact that their share of the vote was less than in 1979, and even less than in 1964, when they lost the election to Labour.

The reasons for the changing fortunes of an almost identical share of the votes have to do with the vagaries of the British electoral system. An election in Britain is won not on the basis of which party obtains the largest share of the votes but, because of the first-past-the-post system, by the relative distribution of votes within each constituency. Instead of one national election, there are *de facto* 650 elections, one fought in each constituency returning a member of parliament. Three factors favoured the Conservatives in 1983: the re-drawing of the boundaries of the constituencies which guaranteed them an additional 50 seats; the fighting of every seat by the SDP/Liberal Alliance which reduced the effectiveness of the opposition vote, and the poor showing, for the second time, of the Labour party.

Panel studies offer an unusual opportunity to examine the extent and type of vote change of individual voters across elections. This type of micro-level analysis is complementary to one which examines aggregate changes across the voting population. Although there is clearly a link between these two approaches, they do not always yield the same results. This is because many aggregate changes depend on the size and relative vote preferences of the first-time voters in that election and of those who have died. Also, aggregate stability across elections may either reflect genuine constancy among the electorate or hide its volatility where changes in vote cancel each other out.

The longitudinal and the two BES panel studies together covered a total of seven elections from 1959 to 1979. In the longitudinal study, we obtained data on six elections. The two BES panels each covered four elections. In all three studies the first vote was obtained not at the time of the relevant election like the other votes, but by asking the respondent on first interview to recall his or her vote of the previous election. We hesitated at first whether to include recalled vote, since we ourselves (Himmelweit *et al.*, 1978) and Särlvik and Crewe (1983) had each made a study of the accuracy of recall of the vote of the previous election. The results of the two studies were very similar and showed that around 25% made mistakes in recalling their previous vote, with more errors for those who had abstained (often recalled as having voted) and for those who had voted Liberal, probably because for many this choice was a one-off affair. Nor were the errors random, people tended to err so as to make the past choice consistent with present choice. Since the majority voted for one of the major parties, this inevitably gave an inflated impression of consistency of vote and of loyalty for these two parties. Despite these inaccuracies we decided to include recalled vote so as to cover a larger number of elections. Also errors serve to depress, rather than inflate, the volatility of the voters with which we were concerned.

In this chapter, the surveys we examined to assess the volatility of individual voters covered a 20-year period.

## Volatility

The voting histories of the three panels reflect the changeability of the electorate, so much so that *consistency proved to be the exception and variability the norm*. In the BES 1963–1970 panel study only 50% made the same decision in each of the four elections from 1959 to 1970, with as many as one in four, and never less than one in five, of the electorate moving between voting and not voting in two successive elections. Movement between the parties ranged from 8% to 13%, but most of it was accounted for by movement to and from the Liberals. Butler and Stokes concluded that:

> The most notable feature of the shifts in individual preference is their sheer volume. Our evidence indicates that the movements of party strength between successive elections may involve a turnover of something like a *third* of the electorate. Indeed,

in the five intervals of change that we have examined in the 1960s, there were never as much as two-thirds of the public positively supporting the same party at two successive points of time; the fraction remaining steadfast through several successive intervals of change was even smaller. Such figures indicate how widely the sources of change are dispersed through the electorate. *Electoral change is due not to a limited group of "floating" voters but to a very broad segment of British electors.* (Butler and Stokes, 1974, p. 268) (Our italics)

The proportion of steadfast voters in the 1970s was identical to that obtained by Butler and Stokes for the elections in the 1960s. Indeed, contrary to the widespread assumption that volatility is both high and on the increase, Särlvik and Crewe (1983) found no evidence of any increase through examining in detail six sets of two adjacent elections. *The "stability of change" was remarkable: about one in three voters changed allegiance between two elections; 40% changed at some point between three elections, and 50% between four. Individual election issues and circumstances seemed to make little difference, all the more surprising since, as we shall show later, those who switched once were more likely to switch again.*

Voters in the longitudinal sample were less steadfast over the six elections studied there. Only 30% came to the same decision throughout. In the large-scale panel studies, which unlike ours covered a wide age range, the four elections came at different periods in the individual voters' history, so that for some their own past voting habit might have acted as a brake on their willingness to change. Voters in the longitudinal study had no such habit to draw on. In 1959 they were first-time voters showing the inflated abstention rate characteristic of their age group.

Their age may also have led to greater volatility in that they were likely to experience more changes and have more contacts with new groups than occur later in an individual's life. Also the young are more open to change as can be seen from their readier response, for example, to the Liberal upsurge in February 1974, where as many as 27% voted Liberal.[1]

Most of our analyses are about the voting decision itself; we did not distinguish between abstainers. However, just to see how many in each election had no preference at all, we asked those who had abstained whether there was a party which, however slightly, they preferred to the others. We then computed a party preference distribution for each election, adding to those who had voted for a party the abstainers who had expressed a preference for that party. Appendix 3, Table 1 shows that the voting and party preference distribution for each of the six elections were very similar and that the percentage of "true" abstainers was always very small, generally no more than 3%, apart from the 1970 election. In 1970 as many as 6% of the abstainers, mostly drawn from previous Labour voters, were unable to name any party they preferred, however slightly. They were disillusioned with the lot.

[1]Alt *et al.* (1977) noted that the Liberal share of the vote was 19% but that there was a higher incidence among the young and among white-collar workers, the two groups overrepresented in our sample.

TABLE 3.1                                                              *Longit. study*

Percentage of voters who changed votes across two adjacent elections by vote cast at the first of the two elections

|              | 1959/64 (%) | '64/'66 (%) | '66/'70 (%) | '70/Feb.'74 (%) | Feb.'74/Oct.'74 (%) | '59/Oct.'74 (%) |
|--------------|-----------|-----------|-----------|---------------|-------------------|---------------|
| Conservative | 43        | 14        | 25        | 32            | 16                | 44            |
| Labour       | 23        | 15        | 42        | 26            | 14                | 41            |
| Liberal      | 55        | 68        | 59        | 26            | 30                | 63            |
| Abstained    | 69        | 73        | 57        | 72            | 22                | 76            |

Table 3.1 shows that the proportion of Labour and Conservative voters who changed *varied* across elections and that Liberals and abstainers always *changed more* than Conservative and Labour voters. The final column in Table 3.1 indicates the degree of change in votes between the first and the sixth election. Many of those who voted the same way on those two occasions had voted for a different party or abstained during one or more of the intermediate elections. Even so, change was considerable: over 40% among major party voters and over 60% among Liberals and abstainers.

Table 3.2 adds a different perspective, reporting on the proportion in each panel who voted consistently for each of the three parties or who consistently abstained.

TABLE 3.2.                                               *Longit. and BES panel studies*

Percentage who made the identical decision across all elections by type of vote

| Decision made | Longitudinal study (%) | BES Panel[a] 1963–'70 (%) | BES panel[a] Feb.1974–'79 (%) |
|---------------|----------------------|-------------------------|-----------------------------|
| Voted Conservative | 16              | 25                      | 23                          |
| Voted Labour       | 10              | 23                      | 24                          |
| Voted Liberal      | 2               | 1                       | 2                           |
| Voted Other        | —               | —                       | 1                           |
| Did not vote       | 2               | 1                       | 1                           |
| Proportion constant | 30             | 50                      | 51                          |
| Number of elections | 6              | 4                       | 4                           |
| n                  | (175)           | (786)                   | (718)                       |

[a] Source Särlvik and Crewe (1983)

## Voting histories

So far we have looked at the overall stability of vote choice across elections. Here we take a closer look at the voting histories of our own and of the Butler and Stokes' 1963–1970 panel sample covering the same elections. These can be considered in a variety of ways: quantitatively, indicating how many times an individual has made an identical decision; qualitatively, noting the various parties for whom an individual has voted on one or other occasion; and historically, relating types of changes to particular elections. In order to group individuals who shared the same voting profiles, taking these three aspects into account, we used Multiple Scalogram Analysis (MSA), a technique developed by Louis Guttman (Lingoes, 1973) which groups individuals who have identical data profiles. For the longitudinal sample these profiles consisted of the decisions made in each of the five elections between 1964 to October 1974. For the Butler and Stokes sample, the profiles were based on the three elections between 1964 and 1970 and the voter's recall of his or her decision in 1959.[2] We had complete voting data for 178 in our study and for 750 in the Butler and Stokes panel.

The analyses yielded an amazing number of profiles: 80 distinct patterns for our sample across five elections and 188 patterns for the Butler and Stokes sample over only four elections. Many patterns were unique to individuals. To make meaningful comparisons between different profiles, we obviously needed to reduce their number. By ignoring the chronological order in which these votes were cast we reduced the profiles of our sample to 45 and those of the Butler and Stokes sample to 42. Even so, as many profiles were shared by only a few individuals further simplification was needed. As, over a period of several elections, the majority of voters had voted for one party more than another, even if they had not supported it consistently, we classified the voters according to the party for which they had voted more frequently and the parties to which they deviated. We ignored one abstention, calling anyone a *consistent voter* if he or she had voted the same way on five occasions, or even on four occasions, abstaining only once.[3] A *floating* Conservative, Liberal or Labour voter was someone who, while voting for the party more frequently than for any other had abstained more than once or had, in the course of the voting history under study, voted for another party. Voters who had voted for two parties equally frequently or had abstained as often as they had voted were few in number and were considered separately (Appendix 3, Table 2A,B).

Because our sample was relatively small, we had to restrict the analysis to a comparison between the consistent and the floating voters for the Conservative and the Labour party, comparing, for example, the consistent Conservatives with Conservatives who deviated either to Liberal or Labour or chose not to vote. The larger Butler and Stokes sample also made it possible to distinguish between types of floating voters for each party. We explored the differences between consistent and floating voters, examining how far change was due to apathy, to differences

---

[2]We omitted the decision in the 1959 election from the profiles for the longitudinal sample, as we wanted our analysis to start after the men's initial inertia or failure to register as a first time voter had been overcome. The 1959 vote for the Butler and Stokes sample is problematic, because it was a recalled vote (the study started in 1963). We were forced to include it, however, as the profiles based on only three elections were too restricted for analysis.

[3]More than one abstention was counted as qualitative change.

in the perception of, and liking for, the parties or to differences in their attitudes to political issues in order to see whether change was a deliberate choice or a random response to the need to make a decision.

Despite the idiosyncratic character of the voting histories, certain similarities about the rates and types of defection across elections were found in all three studies.

1. The most frequent kind of switch between elections was from a vote to an abstention and vice versa, amounting to around two-thirds of all switching. What differed across elections was the proportion moving away from the various parties to abstentions, and the proportion moving from abstention to voting for one or other party. In 1970 and again in 1983 far more Labour than Conservative voters abstained; in other elections the relative proportion was more evenly balanced. In 1974, the move from abstention to voting for a party favoured the Liberal and Labour parties; in 1979 and 1983 it favoured the Conservative party.

2. The Liberal vote was a vote of departure rather than arrival. It was the refuge of the discontented of either major party, and generally a one-off affair. Of the recruits to the Liberals in the mid-1960s, only 33% voted for the Liberals in 1970. The percentage was similar for those who voted for the Liberals during the great upsurge of Liberal popularity in February 1974. Only 31% made the same choice in 1979 when the Liberals were in a much stronger position than in 1970, not because they retained more voters but because they were more successful in gaining new ones.

3. *There were as few consistent Liberal voters as there were consistent abstainers.* In election after election there was a great deal of movement *to* and *from* the Liberals. In the Butler and Stokes study, out of a sample of 750 voters followed over four elections, there were only 11 consistent Liberals and 35 consistent abstainers.[4] Even in the few months between the February and the October elections of 1974 as many as 31% of the Liberals changed their vote compared with only 15% of Conservatives and 12% of Labour voters.

4. The amount of vote change varied across elections. The smallest number of changes occurred between the elections that were closest in time (1964 and 1966, and February and October 1974), and the largest number of changes between 1959 and 1964 and between 1970 and the February 1974 elections.

5. The size of the defections and recruitment to Conservatives and Labour, varied with the election in question, but at every election, parties gained new recruits and lost voters who had supported them previously, i.e. there was a *movement both ways*. This was so even in 1983, when the popularity of the Labour party was at its lowest.[5] What matters for the overall share of the vote by different parties is the relative proportion of defections between the parties and the subsequent port of call of those who defect. In 1979, the Liberals lost most of

[4]In constructing this sample a "consistent" voter had to vote for the same party four times, or three times and abstain once; a "consistent" abstainer had to abstain four times or abstain three times, voting once.
[5]For example, 23% of the 1979 Conservative supporters went elsewhere — a quite sizeable proportion but significantly less than the 37% who forsook the Labour party.

their 1974 gains to the Conservatives, who also made a substantial number of new recruits from Labour and from abstentions. The same was true in 1983. However, in 1966 the picture was reversed: this time it was Labour that gained from the other parties and recruited more of the non-voters than did the Conservatives.

6. *Habit has an effect.* The elections of 1959 and 1964 were the first two in the voting career of our sample and the two 1974 elections the last two for which we had data. Table 3.3 shows that those who had voted for the same party at the first two elections were more likely to be still voting for that party some ten years later, compared with those who had abstained first time round. *But the effect of habit must not be overstated.* When we examined the proportion who continued to vote for a party we found that the initial two elections proved the decisive ones. After that, there was hardly any increase in stability.

TABLE 3.3                                                                                    *Longit. study*

Percentage of faithful[a] Conservative and Labour voters in the two 1974 elections by whether they had voted for the party in 1959 and 1964 or had abstained on the first occasion

| Voted for that party in | 1959 1964 | Percentage faithful | | | |
|---|---|---|---|---|---|
| | | Con Con | Abstained Con | Lab Lab | Abstained Lab |
| February 1974 | | 71 | 55 | 81 | 47 |
| October 1974 | | 67 | 65 | 68 | 42 |

[a] Faithful denotes those who voted the same way in the 1964 and either the February or the October 1974 elections.

7. *Volatility, like habit, is learnt.* Significantly more voters who had changed their allegiance between 1964 and 1966 changed again between 1966 and 1970 compared with those who had voted the same way in both elections. Similar results were obtained when making comparisons across other elections (Himmelweit and Bond, 1974).

Särlvik and Crewe (1983) also found that those who voted for the same party on two occasions were less likely to change than were those who had changed before. Only 24% of those who had voted for the same party in both 1974 elections changed allegiance in the 1979 election, compared with a switch by 59% of those who had voted only once for the same party in the 1974 elections. While the differences in the proportions of those who changed versus those who were steadfast varied by election, change was particularly marked in the February 1974 election.

8. *Homing*, as defined by Butler and Stokes, is the tendency to return to base after a brief flirtation with another party. We found no evidence of homing among Liberal voters or abstainers. In the case of the major party voters, it varied with the fortunes of the party. Butler and Stokes see homing as an important indicator of vote stability. But the concept is unclear. In a long voting career, what constitutes "home"? Is it the number of times — irrespective of gaps in between — that an individual has voted for a party? If so, the statement is tautological.

If by "home" is meant the party for whom someone has voted on at least two successive occasions, how do we select which two elections, given the uniqueness of each election and the fact that any two represent different stages in the voters' history?

9. *Conversions were rare.* Until 1979, conversions from Labour to Conservative or from Conservative to Labour were rare. Between 1959 and 1974 they did not exceed 5% in any pair of elections.

The 1983 election, and to a lesser extent the 1979 election, proved to be exceptions to this. In 1983, as many as 7% of Labour voters switched to the Conservatives, while movement in the opposite direction by Conservative voters was only 4%. Although the 1979 election already saw the beginnings of a left-to-right move larger than in previous elections, it is too early to tell whether such conversions will be temporary, will last or will even become more prevalent. Much depends on the future of the Alliance and on the polarization of the major parties' policies.

10. *The Liberal vote was not a halfway home.* Those who in one election had voted for the Liberals or had abstained, tended next time around to return to the party from which they had come, making the Liberals a turn-around station rather than a halfway house in the journey from right to left or from left to right.

## CONSISTENT AND FLOATING VOTERS

While everyone acknowledges the prevalence of floating voters and their importance in affecting the outcomes of the elections, political scientists have generally paid little attention to them and to their reasons for changing votes. This was in part because Campbell *et al.* (1960), as well as Butler and Stokes (1974), saw such changes as episodic, unpredictable deviations from a basic firm allegiance to a party. Political scientists have also tended to dismiss the floating voter because they saw him as politically apathetic, deviating through lack of involvement rather than out of disillusionment with one party or greater attraction to another (Blondel, 1969). More recently, this view has been challenged here and in the United States. Benewick *et al.* (1969) found a substantial proportion of floating voters "well-informed and interested in politics" and Pederson (1978), analysing the American SRC election surveys from 1952 to 1970, found no consistent relation between the degree of interest in politics and a change in vote. It varied, depending on the special features of the individual campaign:

> In races involving an incumbent, the apathetic voter groups change quite disproportionately and facilitate the incumbent's stay in office. In non-incumbent races, by contrast, in which shifts from the normal party vote require attention to, and comprehension of, events and issues, the interested voters groups are the more prominent agents of change. (p. 28)

Are floating voters less interested in politics and election campaigns than consistent voters? Do they have greater difficulty in deciding how to vote and so postpone their decision? Do they consciously toy with voting for another party?

And finally, is theirs more often a vote against their former party than a vote for the party to which they turn?

The answer to these questions was sought rather differently by each of the three studies, but the results were similar. Rather than report on each study, we shall do so selectively to illustrate different facets.

Our comparisons and those by Särlvik and Crewe suggest that the majority of voters changed for good reasons: either because they disliked some policy or the overall performance or style of the party for which they had previously voted (e.g. the stridency of the Heath campaign in February 1974), or because they found the policies of other parties more to their liking. Where none met their expectations, voters tended to abstain.

## APATHY AND INVOLVEMENT

The results of the two panel studies provided no support for the contention that the floating voter "floats" out of apathy. In 1962, 1970 and 1974, we questioned our sample about their interest in politics. Few were very interested, most only moderately so. There was no significant difference in the degree of interest reported by the floating voters and that reported by people who consistently voted either Labour or Conservative. Full details of these comparisons are given in Appendix 3, Table 3.

Butler and Stokes asked their sample about their interest in the election campaign rather than in politics in general, offering them a choice of replies ranging from *a good deal, some interest*, to *not much interest*. Their replies give a mixed picture: the floating Conservative voters were somewhat less interested than those who consistently voted for that party, but there was no difference between floating and consistent Labour voters. In fact in the 1970 election floating Labour voters were the more interested ones.

## PERCEPTION OF, AND ATTACHMENT TO, PARTIES

*Perception of differences between the parties.* It might be argued that, compared with the consistent voter, the floating voter deviates because he sees less of a divide between the major parties or between his preferred party and the Liberals. There were no differences between the responses of floating and consistent voters in the Butler and Stokes sample when asked about their perceptions of differences in 1964, 1966 and 1970. What all voters shared in common was the tendency to see fewer differences between parties the day after the election where the voter had backed the losing party and more where he had voted for the winning party. In 1966, the Conservatives, and in 1970, the Labour voters, saw fewer differences compared with those who had voted for the other major party.

*Party attachment.* It has been suggested that identification is more stable across time than votes cast. Converse (1966) reports for the United States "a remarkable individual stability in party identification even in this period of extravagant vote change". More recent evidence suggests that partisanship, in particular strong partisanship, is decreasing and is less predictive of one's actual vote (Pomper, 1975). In Britain, too, party identification is less variable than vote, although here it has decreased over the years (Crewe *et al.*, 1977).

The traditional view would lead us to expect little difference in partisanship between the floating and the consistent major party supporters. This was not so. Whereas 95% of our consistent Conservatives identified themselves as such in 1974, only 67% of the floating Conservatives did so. In the case of Labour voters the percentages were 81% and 69% respectively. We had asked for party identification in 1974 only but Butler and Stokes did so after each election, as well as in the mid-election years, 1963. Figure 3.1 shows the trend across the four periods measured. Once again, the results are quite clear-cut. The proportion of floating major party voters who identified with the party of their choice was always less than the proportion of loyalists.

*Liking for the parties.* Although the majority of floating major party voters liked the party they supported, their attitudes were less favourable than those of the consistent voter, and their dislike of the opposition less strong. Among both consistent and floating voters, liking a party, like party identification, varied with the parties' fortunes. Not unexpectedly, major party supporters liked their party more when it won than when it lost. By the same token, dislike for the opposition was greater when one's own party *won* than when it lost. In general, supporters of both parties were more favourable towards the Liberals than the opposition, with the floating voters being more positive than the loyalists (Fig. 3.2).

Thus by their behaviour, as well as by their identification with, or liking for, their party, the floating voters were less committed than the loyalists.[6]

A detailed study by Särlvik and Crewe of their panel yielded very similar results. Those who subsequently left the party were already less enamoured of it than those who stayed and, equally, in 1979, embraced their new party less than did those who had previously voted for it. They were also lukewarm in their perceptions of the leaders of the parties.

Another reason for vote change comes from an analysis of *the political opinions of those who switched*. In examining opinions on policy issues in 1979, Särlvik and Crewe found a greater correspondence between the views of the changers with their new party than with the views of the party from which they had come. For example, of the 1974 Labour voters, whose views on nationalization were closer to those of the Labour party than to the Conservative party, only 7% changed in 1979, compared with 34% of those whose views were closer to those of the

---

[6]The extent of the difference varied with the parties' successes in general elections. In 1964 and 1966, when Labour won the general election, there was an increase in the proportion of floating Labour voters who identified with Labour and a decrease in the proportion of floating Conservatives who called themselves Conservatives. The reverse was the case when the Conservative party came to power in 1970.

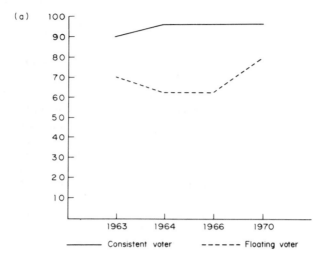

Fig. 3.1 (a) Proportion of consistent and floating *Conservative* voters with "correct" party self-identification. (BES panel 1963–'70)

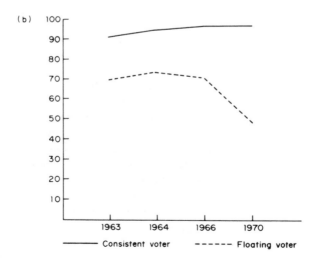

Fig. 3.1. (b) Proportion of consistent and floating *Labour* voters with "correct" party self-identification. (BES panel 1963–'70)

Conservative party. Other policy issues provide further examples, showing that change of vote is not random but relates meaningfully to the individual's initial or changed outlook. We examine this relationship in more detail in Chapter 7.

Discrepancies between the individuals' outlook and the policies of the party for which they voted, their lack of liking for party and leader complicate their decision. It is not surprising therefore that the majority of changers made up their minds later and were therefore potentially more affected by the vicissitudes of the election campaign than were the consistent voters. Also in comparison with consistent voters, a higher percentage of floating voters voted for negative reasons,

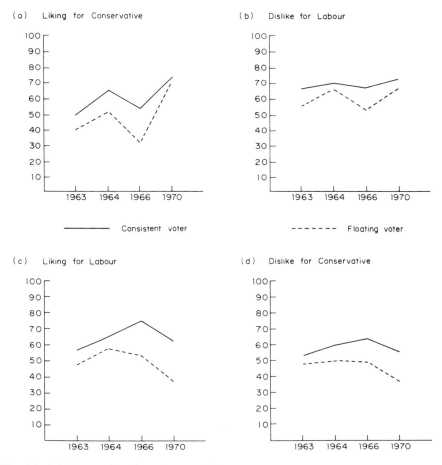

Fig. 3.2. (a,b) Proportion of consistent and floating *Conservative* voters who have a favourable attitude toward the Conservative party and an unfavourable attitude toward the Labour party. (c,d) Proportion of consistent and floating *Labour* voters who have a favourable attitude toward the Labour party and an unfavourable attitude towards the Conservative party. (BES panel 1963–'70)

disliking their own party rather than being attracted to another. We are talking here about the relative frequency of voting for negative rather than positive reasons as between consistent and floating voters. In the electorate as a whole, the tendency was to vote for positive reasons. Here too the 1983 election was exceptional. In all parties, more floating and consistent voters chose their party as "the best of a bad bunch" than for positive reasons. In this respect, Labour fared worse than the Conservatives, and on a par with the Alliance: only 33% selected either party for positive reasons (see Table 3.4).

TABLE 3.4                                                                *BBC/Crewe 1983*

Reasons given by the British electorate for vote choice in 1983 (comparative BES 1979 figures are given in brackets)

| | Percentage distribution | | |
|---|---|---|---|
| Vote cast | Negative (%) | Positive (%) | Both equally (%) |
| Conservative | 48 (44) | 40 (41) | 12 (15) |
| Labour | 54 (35) | 35 (50) | 11 (15) |
| Alliance | 57 | 33 | 10 |

While dislike of a party's policy or style may make an individual ready to change his vote, whether he will in fact do so depends also on the strength of the underlying party identification. Although 85% of people identify with one or other major party, the strength of that identification makes the difference; in 1970 about 20% of Labour and of Conservative voters identified strongly with their parties, by 1979 only 10% did so.

*Liking the decision made.* Butler and Stokes asked the voter after each election to assess the strength of his or her preference for the vote cast. Our sample was asked on each occasion whether they had voted for a party because it appealed to them or because it was the best of a bad bunch (Appendix 3, Table 4). Certainly compared with the loyalist voter the floating voter was consistently less enthusiastic about the party he had chosen, but there was little evidence that the majority of floating voters used their vote as a protest vote. Most voted for a party because it appealed to them, the strength of their preference varying considerably from election to election.

ATTITUDINAL FIT TO PARTY

We have shown that the consistent voter differed from the floating voter in ways which would appear to have a bearing on his choice. But it could still be argued, in line with *cognitive dissonance* theory, that the individual's lesser valuation of the party he leaves is the result of the need to justify his choice rather than a reason for it (Festinger, 1964).

Plausible though this explanation is, it is not the correct one. We have one measure of *relative estrangement from the parties* which is not open to such an interpretation. In Chapters 5 and 6 we report on a series of discriminant analyses where the replies to attitude statements were used to discriminate between voters for the different parties. Such analysis gives an overall measure of the accuracy of "prediction" of vote from attitudes and also, for each voter, three measures of relative attitude fit to the majority of Conservative, Labour and Liberal voters in the sample. For any given voter, the three measures, which are called posterior probabilities add up to 100%. Over 50% indicates a good attitudinal fit, one of less than 50% a poor fit. Using the posterior probabilities obtained for the Butler and Stokes 1970 sample, we found that attitudinal fit to the preferred party was closer for consistent voters than for floating voters. The fit was particularly poor among floating voters who had voted for the other major party or voted Liberal rather than abstained (Table 3.5).

In Chapter 7 we show that those with poor attitudinal fit to the party for which they had voted were more likely to defect next time round.

TABLE 3.5                                                      *BES panel 1963–'70*

Percentage of Conservative and Labour voters with good attitudinal fit to their preferred party grouped in terms of their voting pattern across four elections

|  | Percentage with good attitudinal fit[a] |
| --- | --- |
| Preferred party: Conservative | |
| Consistent voter | 50 |
| 2 Abstentions | 46 |
| Also voted Liberal | 47 |
| Also voted Labour | 29 |
| Preferred party: Labour | |
| Consistent voter | 56 |
| 2 Abstentions | 42 |
| Also voted Liberal | 24 |
| Also voted Conservative | 20 |

[a] The measure of good attitudinal fit is the posterior probabilities for the preferred party obtained from the discriminant analysis of the 1970 vote choice using nine measures of political attitudes. A good fit is one where the posterior probability for the preferred party exceeds 50%.

TIME AT WHICH DECISION IS MADE

All the surveys yield the same result; consistent voters tend to have made up their mind before the beginning of the campaign, while floating voters in sizeable numbers make up their mind during the campaign and indeed only in the last few days. This is one of the reasons why the polling organizations now claim that reliable forecasts can be made only from polls taken the day before the votes have to be cast. The timing of the vote decisions of our sample at the different elections are given in Appendix 3 Table 5.

## Portrait and implications

We have looked in some detail at the voting histories of the three studies. In our sample, we were looking at the beginning of the men's voting careers, while in the other two panels the elections sampled occurred at different stages on the voting history of the men and women concerned. Even allowing for one abstention, over only four, let alone six elections, voting for the same party throughout was the exception not the rule. The majority were floating voters who had a preferred party to which they returned or from which they deviated, but when and how varied across elections and across individuals. This variation proved so great that the attempt at fine grouping on the basis of the voting history of the respondents, taking account of quantitative, qualitative and chronological aspects, had to be abandoned as there were so many idiosyncratic pathways. Habit had some effect in that the voter was more likely to vote for a party for which he had voted before, but the consequence of such "rootedness" or habit was limited and must not be exaggerated. Age made no apparent difference; older people were as volatile as the younger voters and women just as volatile as men.[7]

What markedly distinguished the floating from the confirmed voter in both studies was not apathy, as has been suggested, but their weaker identification with, and liking for, their own party and their attitudes towards the other parties. Above all, volatility was related to the closeness of the floating voter's attitudinal fit to those of the majority of voters for his preferred party.

All the evidence, then, points in favour of a positive decision to *move away* from a party rather than to a deviation due to apathy leading to a random selection of an alternative party. It has been the practice of pollsters to take recall of vote as an accurate statement of vote cast in previous elections but our data show the size of the error to be considerable. Because errors are not random, but biased in favour of consistency, they lead to an overestimate of the faithful, especially of the faithful for the two major parties.

The fact that these days floating voters are so numerous, that the consistent voter can so easily become a floating voter, and that the potentially floating voter makes up his or her mind late, puts a particular burden on the election campaign. It may also account for the ever increasing swings in the polls when these are carried out at different stages of a campaign.[8] If fewer voters establish the habit

[7]Other forms of rootedness which did make a difference, namely the example of significant reference groups, are discussed in Chapter 4.
[8]The extent of the swings is well illustrated by Clements's (1975) report on two large cross-sectional surveys, one held five days before the February 1974 election, the other held only two weeks earlier. The intended vote for Conservatives dropped from 45% to 38·5%, that for Labour from 40% to 31%, while the intended vote for the Liberals rose from 12% to 28%. Clements draws the conclusion that electoral choice is so volatile that only polls carried out on election day itself will have sufficient predictive power. "Timing has — in the current situation — become the critical dimension in public opinion polling."

of voting for one party and volatility increases still further, it will place an increasing burden on the timing and conduct of the election campaign.

While many fear that such volatility is harmful for the effective working of the parliamentary system, others like Budge (1982), who analysed the electoral volatility of 23 post-war democracies, take a rather different view. Budge finds volatility to be widespread, but rather than viewing it as a potential de-stabilizing force, he suggests that it might be a way of adapting the democratic system to changing conditions, i.e. a much-needed flexibility in that it makes parties more responsive to the public's changing concerns and attitudes. On the other hand, it may have the effect of making the parties less committed, less ideological and less assured, responding to the floating voter with ''floating'' policies. Only time will tell whether not being able to take the loyalty of any major segment of the population for granted will make the parties more or less effective at governing.

# 4

# The process of political socialization

Studies of political socialization[1] examine the ways in which children develop an understanding of the political system and the influences that help shape their political interest, views and values. This is a field in which political scientists concerned wtih political participation and with the stability across generations of political values and party attachment have been active, as well as social and developmental psychologists.

Three main approaches have been used. The first, based largely on work with children like the pioneering studies of Easton and Dennis, (1969) and Hess and Torney (1967) in the United States and those of Jahoda (1964) in this country, link affective feelings about one's country and its leaders and growth in political understanding to stages reached in cognitive and social development. With increasing age, young people become more critical, learn to distinguish between occupant and role, enlarge their knowledge of their country's political system, and gradually replace "a raggle-taggle array of sentiments" (Adelson and O'Neill, 1966) with a more coherent system of political beliefs.

The second approach, owing more to Freudian than cognitive developmental theories, seeks a partial explanation for the individual's readiness to embrace certain political views, e.g. racial prejudice or political extremism, or to experience a sense of political efficacy or alienation, in particular types of childrearing (Block et al., 1969; Mussen and Haan, 1981; Kinder and Sears, 1985). This approach came into prominence in the aftermath of the Second World War with the seminal work by Adorno and his colleagues (1950) of the *Authoritarian Personality*, the subsequent work by Maccoby et al. (1954) and others, as well as Rokeach's (1960) work on dogmatism.

The third approach, and the one adopted here, while taking the other two on board, concentrates particularly on the relative influence of different socializing experiences through the individual's contact with, and membership of, significant groups: in childhood through family, school, neighbourhood and peers and as

[1]A term coined by Hyman (1959).

adult through further education, work, marriage and social and political groups. Contact with these different groups helps to shape the individual's view of self and society and to set expectations and norms, providing what Schank and Abelson (1977) call the individual's cognitive "scripts".[2] It is with the development of such politically relevant cognitions and more particularly with the individual's political behaviour that we are concerned here.

The term *political socialization* has generally been used with reference only to the young, yet the same process continues through life.[3] Each new group exerts an influence, whether the group is joined voluntarily or by force (as for example in the case of conscription and imprisonment). Dahrendorf (1979) describes the effects of such influence, consciously perceived or not, intended or unintended, in terms of roles and rules:

> Societies are fields of social roles. Man finds himself . . . confronted with a plurality of expectations which he may not have invented but which he cannot escape either. Roles, that is expectations crystallised around positions, are themselves a part of wider fields: families, communities, enterprises, associations, regions, countries. Thus, wherever we look, society is structure, rules and the guardian of rules, and people are agents of social structure even where they break rules. (Dahrendorf, 1979, p.47)

Political theories provide insights into the weight to be assigned to given group membership. Marxist theory points to the strength of influence of social class membership, while theories about marginality and relative deprivation draw attention to motivational factors or need states which might sensitize the individual to certain political values or movements.

Others have investigated the influence of education, especially higher education on the development of ideology, on party attachment and on political participation, both protest and conventional (Kinder and Sears, 1985).

One powerful source of influence has received relatively little attention in these studies, namely that of the *Zeitgeist*, including changes in the cultural, political or economic climate of a society as well as those generated by important national and international events: changes which might lead to changes in evaluation of existing institutions of a society as well as to altered expectations and social representations (Moscovici, 1984). This happened, for example, in the 1960s with people becoming less deferential to, and more critical of, established institutions, demanding greater accountability and participation. The change in outlook which has persisted since that time has important political consequences.

Our longitudinal study in which the men gave their views on a number of issues in 1962 and again in 1970 and 1974 covers a sufficiently long period to explore how far given changes in society are reflected in corresponding changes in the men's views. Jennings and Niemi's (1981) study carried out in the United States over much the same period (1965–1973) was specially designed to examine the

---

[2]These are coherent and stable interpretations of sequences of events.
[3]For a recent and comprehensive review of these approaches the reader is referred to the *Handbook of Political Socialization*, edited by Renshon (1977) and to Kinder and Sears (1985).

relative influence of societal changes and of changes in the individuals' circumstances.

This chapter is divided into three parts: the first deals with the influence of the home on the adolescent's party preferences and the subsequent erosion of that influence; the second part examines the influence on political attitudes and voting of the individual's social class position at two points in time 12 years apart, together with the effects of inter- and intra-generational mobility. Finally, using data from the longitudinal study on the development and change of political attitudes, goals and values along with information about the men's work and education, we were able to build up a rounded picture of the various direct and indirect influences on voting.

As in other chapters, we relate our results here to other larger studies, in particular to three: one British, and two American. These studies are valuable because they are more recent (the children and adolescents studied were brought up in the 1960s and 1970s when ours were already adult), and include measures of political views, knowledge and interest, as well as party preferences. We had to rely on recall by our respondents of their parents' party preference while in these three studies the parents themselves were questioned, making it possible not only to investigate the young person's accuracy of their perception of parental views, but also to examine parent–child agreement uncontaminated by bias introduced by recall.

The British study (Dowse and Hughes, 1971) examined the relative influence of home and school. Data were obtained within one city from over 600 11- to 17-year-old grammar and secondary modern school pupils. Of the parents, half returned the questionnaires they had been sent.

The second study, and the most extensive conducted anywhere, is that by Jennings and Niemi (*Generations and Politics*, 1981). A random national sample of high school seniors in the United States aged 16–18 years and their parents were questioned in 1965 and both again after an eight-year interval in 1973. In 1973 a further sample of 17- to 18-year-olds drawn from the same schools were also questioned. Differences in outlook between the two groups of high school seniors were related to corresponding changes by the youth and the parent panel. This made it possible to differentiate *period* effects due to changes in society from *life cycle* effects.

In the third study Dennis (1982b) like Jennings and Niemi, questioned school children and their parents at two points in time, separated not by eight years but by eight months, sufficient to assess the influence of the Presidential election campaign on party identification, issue awareness, political involvement and understanding. The age range of the Wisconsin sample, 11–17 years, was similar to that of Dowse and Hughes (1971).

## Sources of influence on adolescent party preferences

Social learning theories predict that, other things being equal, the influence of role models will be stronger where there is no previously established behaviour to be supplanted and where there is dependence on, as well as affection for, the model (Bandura, 1971). The family, as the primary socializing agent, has all the features required for exerting a strong influence on the child's political attitudes. How far this occurs in any particular case will depend on the political involvement of the parents, their agreement on matters politic as well as on the relation of child to parent. Where both parents are actively involved in politics, share the same political outlook and have good relations with their children, influence should be maximal, particularly where the wider community provides supporting cues.

Party preferences develop early: Dennis and McCrone (1970) found that in several countries by the age of 10 primary schoolchildren could accurately name the country's main political parties and express a preference for one. In the case of British schoolchildren 80% were able to do so.[4] The results from our longitudinal study were similar: 81% of the adolescents asked in the election year of 1951 for whom they would vote, declared their preference by naming a political party (Table 4.1).

TABLE 4.1

Hypothetical vote of the young men in 1951 at age 13 ($n = 246$)

| Vote decision | | | Would not vote/ | |
|---|---|---|---|---|
| Con | Lab | Lib | Could not decide | |
| 36% | 37% | 8% | 19% | 100% |

In 1951, our sample showed none of the Conservative bias in voting which characterized their voting as adults, especially from 1966 onwards. This is not surprising when we consider that not only were half the respondents' fathers manual workers but the parents' votes were evenly divided between the major parties (36% were described as voting Conservative and 37% as voting Labour). Fifty per cent of the fathers' and 54% of the mothers' choices were echoed by their sons.[5] The amount of agreement between parents and sons varied according to the parents' own choice. Where the parents had voted Conservative or Labour over 60% of the sons followed suit, while less than 20% did so where the parents had voted Liberal. This is hardly surprising. We showed in Chapter 3 how few of the Liberal voters in one election voted Liberal again in the next. Parents voting Liberal would be more likely therefore to provide contradictory rather than consistent cues for their children.

Acts of *omission* (not voting) had less of an influence than acts of *commission*. Where parents abstained, or their sons could not remember how they had voted,

[4]Jennings and Niemi (1974) found that, although the majority of second graders could correctly name the two main parties, less than half could describe what the parties stood for, compared with 85% among the eighth graders. Both Dowse and Hughes and Dennis rather surprisingly found that the percentage of children ready to express a party preference did not significantly increase with age.

[5]Parents' vote choice was obtained from the son in the interviews conducted in 1962.

their children were *no* more likely to abstain than were the rest of the sample. Instead, their votes were very evenly distributed across the whole spectrum (Himmelweit and Bond, 1974). Dowse and Hughes (1971) in Britain, and Jennings and Niemi (1974) in the United States obtained very similar results.[6]

Dowse and Hughes (1971) confirmed our findings that the degree of modelling varied with the parents' choice of party — it was highest for Conservatives and lowest for Liberals. They reported less parent–child agreement than we did. It may be that the agreement shown in our study is inflated since parental party preferences were based on recall with the bias towards consistency that this introduces (Himmelweit *et al.*, 1978; Särlvik and Crewe, 1983). On the other hand, recent studies, where this bias did not operate, also report less agreement. In the United States too parent–child agreement was lower in 1980 than in 1965. While Jennings and Niemi found that 57% of the 16- to 18-year-olds chose the same party as their parents, yielding a correlation of $0 \cdot 48$, in Dennis's study 15 years later the correlations tended to be lower between $0 \cdot 24$ to $0 \cdot 44$ (depending on the measures used) with a remarkably high percentage (58%) expressing no preference or opting for Independents. Dennis suggests that since his sample grew up in the 1970s the decline in strong party identification during this period in the electorate as a whole might well account for the lesser influence of parental example.

Ours as well as the two American studies examined the relative influence of mothers and fathers on vote preferences. Mothers were found to exert the stronger influence in the United States, in Western Europe and even in such a patriarchial culture as Japan, where Kubota and Ward (1970) found mothers' influence to be at least equal to, if not more dominant than fathers. It is an intriguing result[7] but its effect should not be overestimated since in our study 83% of the parents were reported to have voted the same way. But this need not always be so.

The mother's stronger influence might be due to closer emotional ties between mother and child as well as the greater amount of time spent together, i.e. her influence in the political domain might simply be one instance of greater all-round maternal influence. Alternatively, for the son to become aware that his mother's political orientation is different from his father's, both she and her husband need to be sufficiently politically involved to talk about her decision. In such a case, her stronger influence could be the result of the stronger salience that she, in comparison with the father, gives to political matters.

[6]By contrast Butler and Stokes' study (1974) yielded higher agreement between the respondent's recall of the parents' vote and his or her earliest party preferences. Both pieces of information were obtained in the same interview, which may have led to spuriously high agreement as errors in recall tend to exaggerate the consistency between past and present. This would be particularly marked among older members of the sample who had to cast their minds back over a quarter of a century or more. In our study, although unlike Jennings and Niemi we had to rely on recall of parents' vote, the adolescent's party preference were obtained at the time, that is 11 years earlier.
[7]We repeated the same analysis on the BES 1963–1970 panel, obtaining very similar results; again, the mother, where she was recalled as having expressed a preference for one party, proved the stronger influence.

Jennings and Niemi have examined these two hypotheses and found both confirmed: stronger party identification made imitation more likely and the degree to which this mattered was greater for the mother than the father.[8]

## THE INFLUENCE OF PARENTAL STATUS, SCHOOL AND NEIGHBOURHOOD: THE EFFECT OF CROSS PRESSURES

Children like adults take their cues and draw their experiences from many sources: school, their peers, the neighbourhood in which they live, and increasingly the mass media. As social learning theory predicts, modelling will be strongest where there is both consistency of cues over time and also consistency of cues from the different worlds on which the child draws, i.e. cross pressures should serve to reduce the parent–child agreement. We looked at the relationship between the adolescents' vote choice and the social class background of the family and at type and social composition of school attended.

The results (given in detail in Appendix 3, Table 6) were exactly what one would have expected: namely, more middle class adolescents (52%) than working class adolescents (26%), and more grammar school pupils (40%) than secondary modern school pupils (27%) opted for the Conservative party. These findings do not by themselves pinpoint the main sources of influence, since more middle class parents voted Conservative and more middle class children went to grammar school. To disentangle the relative roles of the various sources of influence we used multivariate analysis which would permit the study of the effect (on vote) of *each* of five sources of influence in turn, while holding all others constant.[9] Together the five sources of influence accounted for 20% of the variance, almost all (16%) was due to just one influence — mother's vote; the remaining 4% being due to father's preference in cases where this differed from the mother's.[10] The other three influences, the social background of the home, type and social class composition of the school, had no independent influence on choice of party. They came into their own only where there were cross pressures.

The other three studies found similarly that agreement on party identification accounted for more of the variance than did social class.

Several analyses were carried out to study the role of cross pressures.[11]

[8]Where the father was more partisan than the mother, 17% more sons imitated the father. Where the mother was more partisan than the father, the difference in the rate of imitation rose to 27%.
[9]The technique we used is known as Multivariate Nominal Analysis (MNA), and is described by Andrews and Messenger (1973).
[10]Sidanius and Ekehammer in Sweden (1979) carried out similar MNA analyses. There, too, parents' vote accounted for most of the variance, with mothers playing the more important role.
[11]Non-metric regression analysis (THAID: Morgan and Messenger, 1973) was used to detect interaction effects by dividing the sample into successively smaller and more homogeneous voting groups. Being non-metric, this technique isolates factors which might not be relevant across the board but have significance for a particular subgroup only.

TABLE 4.2                                                           *Longit. study*

Distribution of vote choice of adolescents from middle and working class homes, the groups
being further subdivided by father's vote

| Subjects vote at age 13 | Middle class father's vote | | Working class father's vote | |
|---|---|---|---|---|
| | Con (%) | Not Con (%) | Lab (%) | Not Lab (%) |
| Conservative | 67 | 36 | 14 | 37 |
| Labour | 13 | 36 | 60 | 30 |
| Liberal | 12 | 4 | 2 | 12 |
| Do not know | 8 | 24 | 24 | 21 |
| (*n*) | (47) | (47) | (73) | (78) |

Examples of their influence are given in Table 4.2. Where father's vote was
congruent with the dominant vote of his class, the sons echoed his choice in over
60% of the cases. Where it was not, no more than 37% did so.[12] Where father's
and mother's preferences differed, the social class composition of the school the
son attended helped to tip the scale; a homogeneous middle class school
environment provided a pull towards the Conservatives and away from Labour.
Hyman (1959) calls this type of influence "the tenor of a subsystem".[13]

There were also cross pressures at a subtler more interpersonal level. A number
of writers (like Orum, 1972 and Sears, 1974) have asked not why so many, but
why so *few*, young people dissociate themselves from the political stance of their
parents when in other aspects of life they seem to do so more frequently. Why
are politics so rarely used as a means of rebelling against parental authority? Is
it because in most homes politics are not sufficiently salient to provide a suitable
outlet? If no one cares, perhaps it might not be worthwhile to take an independent
stand. Our study permitted a partial test of this idea as we had data from each
adolescent about his father's interest in politics and the quality of parent–child
relations during this period (Himmelweit and Swift, 1971). We predicted, and
confirmed, an interaction effect: imitation was strong where the father was
interested in politics *and* relations with the son were good, but not where either
of these were poor.[14]

[12]This difference was statistically highly significant ($p\,0\cdot001$). Goldberg (1969) found a
similar reduction in his study of 17- to 18-year-olds in the United States.
[13]For details see Himmelweit and Bond (1974). Levin (1961), in a study of high school
students in Illinois, showed that where pupils' choice differed from that of their parents
it tended to be for the party preferred by the majority of their class mates. For the
educationally mobile, Dowse and Hughes (1971) suggest school serves to loosen identification
with parental values.
[14]In the MNA analysis, the independent variables were father's vote, father's interest in
politics and a measure of closeness of family relations. Linearly, these accounted for 14%
of the variance when predicting the adolescents' party preferences and for 18% where
allowance was made for interaction between the father's interest in politics and the son's
relations to his parents.

So far these results tell a consistent story. The parents of the men we studied played an important role in affecting the political decisions of their children, in the way suggested by Campbell *et al.* (1960). The degree to which this occurred varied with the party selected, with the salience of politics in the home and the quality of parent–child relations as well as with other aspects of the environment such as school and neighbourhood.[15]

Since the other three studies obtained in addition measures of political interest, knowledge and outlook, we could compare accuracy of children's knowledge of their parents' view and agreement with them, with their accuracy of and agreement with, parents' party preferences. The results were clear cut. Only with regard to party preference was accuracy high, on all other measures it was low as was the child's agreement with parental views. This is not really very surprising. Party preferences tend to be voiced at election times even in the least politically interested homes, but in very few homes are there discussions of political issues sufficiently explicit and consistent for these to make an impression. This does not of course preclude the likely possibility that parental influence may well be strongest in the general orientation parents transmit concerning the way people relate to others, instilling in their children certain priorities as to goals and means. These broad, rather diffuse, orientations would be difficult to capture in appropriate questions. Their influence would be indirect, rather than direct, and would vary by issue and context.

## Duration of effect of early influences

To see how long early influences continued to play a part in the years after the young men had come of age, we repeated the analyses, this time predicting the individual's first vote cast as adult (1959) and also his fourth vote 11 years later (1970).

Not surprisingly, parental influence declined. By 1959, parental example accounted for only 11% of the variance compared with the 20% obtained in adolescence. The results ten years later were almost identical. Figure 4.1 presents a detailed picture of parental influence across time. Using the adolescent's vote as the baseline, it plots for each of six successive elections, percentage agreement between sons and Conservative, Labour or Liberal parents. The extent of agreement varied between elections but throughout the period Conservative parents were imitated more often than parents voting Labour, and both were imitated more frequently than parents who had voted Liberal or had differed in their vote choice.

It would, of course, be misleading to assume from this discussion that agreement between parents and son's vote is necessarily the result of parental influence.

[15]A full account is presented in Himmelweit and Bond (1974).

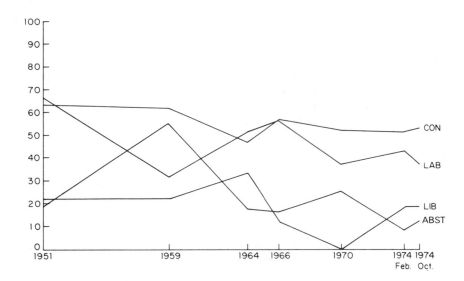

Fig. 4.1.   Percentage agreement between parents' votes and the sons' hypothetical vote at age 13 (1951) and their actual votes in the elections 1959 to October 1974. Longitudinal study: $n = 178$.

It is equally plausible that parents and their children, once they are adults, have similar experiences which move them independently to prefer the same party. We have no means of testing which of these explanations is the more valid, but we can make some assessment of parental influence relative to adult experiences by adding to the analysis the social class status (in terms of his job) of the voter at the time of casting his vote. Using the large and more heterogeneous Butler and Stokes sample of voters in the 1970 election, we found that parental example and social status each made a significant and separate contribution to the overall amount of variance in voting (22%) but of the two, parental vote was the more important.

Jennings and Niemi found among 16- to 18-year-olds agreement with parents' party identification and vote choice to be greater than with other measures of political beliefs but that such agreement dropped considerably once the children had become adult. As a result, in adulthood agreement with parents was no greater for vote and party identification than for other political beliefs, leading Jennings and Niemi (1981) to conclude

> Finally the partisanship and voting comparisons should lay to rest the notion that transmission of these characteristics is somehow different from that of the other attributes. (p. 93)

Parental influence can also show itself in other, more subtle ways, providing an extra *rootedness* thereby reducing the likelihood of the son becoming a floating voter.[16] In the case of the Labour voter, parental vote made a marked difference: 35% of floating Labour voters in the Butler and Stokes study had fathers who had voted Labour, compared with 70% of consistent Labour voters. Those who as adults changed from voting Labour to voting Conservative had, by comparison with other types of floating Labour voters, the largest percentage of parents who had voted Conservative and the smallest proportion who had voted Labour. In both studies, the mothers' influence was the more decisive on both stability and change. In the case of the floating Labour voter, only a quarter of the mothers had voted Labour.

## Cross pressures in adult life: the effect of inter- and intra-generational mobility

Butler and Stokes (1974), commenting on the elections of the 1960s, noted that while the social class of an individual was still strongly related to their voting ''the declining strength of association between class and party is one of the most important aspects of political change during this decade'' (p. 203).

Crewe (1983b), writing ten years later, found the decline if anything even more marked in 1979 and 1983. In Chapter 6 we examine the relative role played in the vote decision by a variety of social determinants including social class membership. Here our aim is complementary, namely to examine the factors, including parental vote choice, that modify or enhance the relationship — weak or strong in any given election — between social status and vote choice. We shall also consider the cross pressures set up by the individual's history of social mobility, its extent and timing.

Pomper (1975) describes two contrasting views concerning the relationship of social class and vote. The first view is represented by the Michigan model:

> social class is *a direct influence permanent in its effects, with little variation from one political context to another* . . . the dependent voter relies on a non-political characteristic, his economic position, to make electoral choices. (p. 43) (Our italics)

The second view, in line with our model, sees the influence of social class membership as indirect and variable:

> *While his class affects his life, its political relevance is indirect,* and it becomes salient only when he considers issues and policies which deal with economic matters. *The relationship between status and the ballot therefore changes with political influence such as the character of the election and the policy views of the citizenry.* (p. 43) (Our italics)

The first view would be substantiated if the relationship between social class membership and vote were strong and relatively invariant across elections. This is just what we did *not* find. Instead we found support for the second view: the

[16]In Chapter 3 we describe how we had divided the sample first into floating and stable major party voters and then in turn the floating voters by the parties to which they had moved. Appendix 3, Table 7a,b gives details of the relation of parental vote to vote stability and change for both our study and the BES 1963–1970 panel.

relationship between attitudes and vote was stronger and less variable across elections compared with that between social class membership and vote.

*Is the "responsive" voter merely responding to his background?* It might still be argued that we are just splitting hairs, since attitudes which predict vote are simply cognitive representations of the individual's social class membership. If this were so, it would follow that we should be able to predict accurately an individual's views on various political issues from knowledge of his social class and related structural factors. We put this to the test. Multiple regression analyses were carried out using measures of the social characteristics as independent variables, and 13 political issues which had differentiated well between voters as the dependent variables. For only six out of the 13 issues was prediction better than chance (Appendix 3, Table 8, column 1). The more highly educated held significantly more liberal views than the less well educated ($p < 0.01$). The middle class, compared with the working class, was more in favour of entry into the Common Market ($p < 0.001$), and more opposed to strikes ($< 0.02$) and trade union power ($p < 0.03$). The working class, in comparison with the middle class, was for more control of big business ($p < 0.001$) and for consultation of the work force before takeovers ($p < 0.01$).

Social factors, then, gave little indication of the men's political views, but they have an indirect influence by affecting their general orientation towards people and institutions (including authoritarianism) and the relative priorities assigned to different goals and values (as described in Chapter 2), which in turn affect political views. The men's degree of authoritarianism did indeed prove a significant predictor of nearly all the 13 attitudes we investigated; those high on authoritarianism were for strengthening the power of the police, for restricting student activism, demonstrations and strikes, and they were also opposed to trade unions. Those who gave high priority to societal goals wanted more control of big business and better social services, while those giving greater priority to personal success proved more restrictive — they were against liberalization of the law, against demonstrations, student activism and against trade unions. Views about trade unions, strikes and control of big business were best predicted by adding the individuals' background data to measures of their goals and values (Appendix 3, Table 8, columns 2 and 3).

We referred earlier to the individuals' outlook upon society as their "cognitive scripts". The broad orientations we have tapped reflect scripts indicating whether people value primarily success or find more satisfaction in concern with society, whether they are tolerant of ambiguity or rigid in their thinking (that is, inclined to see people in terms of in-groups and out-groups — the hallmark of those who score high on measures of authoritarianism). Once the individual has developed a particular script of his or her society, it is used to evaluate political issues and events.

The evidence we have presented here suggests that Pomper's *second* description fits the British electorate of the 1960s and 1970s. Social class provides one vantage point among many whose relevance varies across elections.

INTER- AND INTRA-GENERATIONAL MOBILITY

In discussing the adolescent's view of the parties, we argued that parental example would be influential not least because there were no established preferences to be displaced. This does not apply for subsequent reference groups. Although the political orientation derived from home might not be strongly held or well articulated, it is nevertheless likely to lessen the impact of subsequent experiences.

Abramson (1973) used Butler and Stokes' 1963 election survey data to study inter-generational mobility and party preference of male voters in Britain. He divided the men into four social status groups: the stable middle and the stable working class and two mobile groups: one upwardly mobile (of working class origin), the other downwardly mobile (of middle class origin). His results, summarized in Table 4.3, demonstrate that the frequency with which those of middle class origin see themselves as Conservative and those of working class origin as Labour was sharply reduced for the two mobile groups. For them, identification was more with the modal party of the voter's social class of *arrival* than of *origin*, regardless of whether the mobility was upward or downward. This finding contradicts the common assumption that inter-generational mobility benefits the Conservative party, because the upwardly mobile wish to identify with the party of the class to which they have moved, and because the downwardly mobile would be reluctant to give up the preference of their class of origin, seeing downward mobility as a temporary stage.

TABLE 4.3                                                                    *BES 1963*

Social mobility and partisan preferences among British men

| Social mobility | Non-mobile working class (%) | Upwardly mobile (%) | Downwardly mobile (%) | Non-mobile middle class (%) |
|---|---|---|---|---|
| Partisan preference | | | | |
| Labour | 68 | 29 | 51 | 14 |
| Liberal | 8 | 17 | 12 | 19 |
| Conservative | 20 | 50 | 32 | 60 |
| No party preference | 5 | 5 | 5 | 7 |
| Total | 101 | 101 | 100 | 100 |
| (*n*) | (480) | (175) | (65) | (124) |

From Abramson (1973): three respondents who favoured "other" parties were excluded from the analysis.

More important, however, than the social class of origin was the influence of early political socialization. When Abramson further subdivided each of the four groups by father's party preference, he found among the socially mobile groups that father's preference determined whether they voted more in keeping with their class of origin than that of arrival. Among the upwardly mobile working class, 86% of those with Conservative fathers saw themselves as Conservative compared with only 34% where the father had voted Labour. Indeed, in the case of the Conservative vote, social class of origin by itself had no effect: the upwardly mobile and the stable middle class voters were equally likely to vote Conservative.

The important role of early political socialization is further documented by the voting patterns of those whose fathers had expressed no preference. Comparing them with others with the same social mobility history we find that their vote choice falls somewhere between the vote choices of those whose fathers voted Conservative and those who voted Labour.

A problem with Abramson's study is that it draws on a wide age range whose mobility might have taken place at very different periods in their lives, making it difficult to distinguish between the effects of mobility and those due to changes in the life cycle and/or changes within society.

Our study remedies these deficiences and adds to the picture just presented. First, given the high degree of upward social mobility in our sample, we could look not only at working class mobility, but also at mobility *within* the middle class (from a low level routine white collar job to a more responsible upper middle class position). And, because all our voters were of the same age, we could look at the effect of mobility depending on its timing. Many of the men of working class origin in our sample acquired university and other relevant qualifications and as a result became socially mobile when they first entered the job market. Others achieved mobility much later, having first held working class jobs like their fathers before them. We compared the individual's vote choice at two points in time separated by ten years, 1964 and 1974.

Figure 4.2 charts the individual's social mobility across these ten years taking as starting point his father's social class (middle *v.* working class), followed by the son's achieved status at age 27 (1964) and then again ten years later at age 37 (1974). The resulting pattern is surprisingly clear, showing that:

1. There was no evidence of anticipatory political socialization as suggested by Goldberg (1969). Those who subsequently became socially mobile differed neither in their parents' nor in their own voting preferences as adolescents from those who remained solidly working class.

2. Inter-generational mobility made a difference, but the degree to which this occurred depended on the *time* at which the individual became socially mobile.[17] Between 1964 and 1974 the electorate as a whole moved away from Labour. While the shift away from Labour reflected the mobility pattern of the voters, it did not result in a corresponding increase of votes for Conservatives. This was the period

---

[17]While 68% of the solidly working class voted Labour in 1964, 55% did so in 1974. Among those who achieved social mobility early, 30% voted Labour in 1964 and 17% in 1974. For those who moved to a white collar job only in their thirties, the swing away from Labour was much smaller: 55% were Labour in 1964 and 25% in 1974.

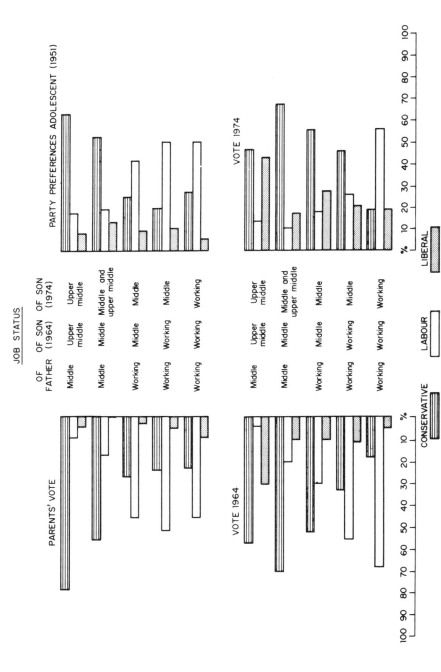

Fig. 4.2. Percentage distribution of votes of the longitudinal sample grouped by social status of father and job status at ages 27 and 37. The order is chronological beginning with parents' vote, followed by the man's party preference as adolescent and his votes in 1964 and 1974.

when the electorate as a whole lost confidence in the Conservatives, resulting in the large Liberal vote in 1974.[18]

*Party Identification:* One might argue that short-term strategic or reactive voting might account for the relatively low relation between class and vote choice and that party identification would provide a better measure of the influence of class. In 1974 we asked the men "irrespective of how you have voted in the present election, generally speaking, do you describe yourself as Conservative, Labour or Liberal, or do you not see yourself in that way?". Table 4.4 presents the distribution of replies for each of the groups. Party identification was no more class linked than the votes cast in the 1964 and 1974 elections. Three interesting findings emerged:

TABLE 4.4                                                                    *Longit. study*

1974 Party identification subdivided in terms of inter- and intra-generational social mobility patterns

| Social mobility | | | Percentage distribution of party identification | | | |
|---|---|---|---|---|---|---|
| Father's job | Own job at age 27 | Own job at age 37 | Con (%) | Lab (%) | Lib (%) | I do not see myself in this way (%) |
| Middle | U Middle | U Middle | 46 | 17 | 25 | 13 |
| Middle | Middle | Middle | 63 | 13 | 13 | 10 |
| Working | Middle | Middle | 57 | 16 | 11 | 17 |
| Working | Working | Middle | 35 | 25 | 10 | 30 |
| Working | Working | Working | 23 | 50 | 09 | 18 |

1. The middle class identified more with the Conservatives than did the working class with Labour. It will be remembered that more children imitated Conservative than Labour parental preferences.

2. Identification with the Conservatives was strongest not among the upper middle class, but among the middle and lower middle class and among those of working class origin who had achieved mobility early.

3. Party identification was least among the group who achieved mobility late. As many as a third were unable to identify with any party.

## Societal or period effects

Finally, evidence of period effects comes from the study of Jennings and Niemi which was specifically designed to differentiate between period and life cycle effects.

[18]In 1964 18% of the solidly working class voted Conservative and the same percentage in 1974. Of those who had achieved mobility early, 52% had voted Conservative in 1964, and 55% in 1974; of those who had achieved mobility late 33% voted Conservative in 1964 and 45% in 1974.

The 16- to 18-year-old populations of 1965 and 1973 differed with regard to several political beliefs they held — differences which were also reflected in changes in outlook of the parents. Here is just one example. The eight years included Watergate and Nixon's resignation. Not surprisingly, in 1973 the young were less respectful and trusting towards major institutions of the society and more cynical about the honesty and competence of office holders than the young in 1965. The difference existed in both age groups but was more pronounced for the young than for their parents.

Our study, on a more limited scale but extending over a longer period of time (12 years in all), also provides evidence of the influence of societal factors (Himmelweit, 1983).

In Chapter 2 we discussed the fact that changes in the individual's outlook, particularly with regard to the priorities attached to given goals, occurred in response to changing circumstances *in the individual's life*. It is generally held that as the individual approaches middle age, he becomes more authoritarian, less flexible and less tolerant. Yet the differences in the replies to the 10-item authoritarian scale across the 12 years were in the opposite direction. Moderately authoritarian to begin with, the men became significantly less so with time. This change, we suggest, says little about the men themselves, but a great deal about their responsiveness to the social climate.

The 1960s was a period of increased distrust of authority. In line with this trend, we found that in 1974 more people (67%, compared with 56% in 1962) disagreed with the statement that "the select few should be trained to lead the masses", and fewer agreed that "a good employer should be strict with his employees to gain their respect" (43% compared with 59%). The most marked change, and one clearly influenced by the Women's Movement, had to do with the position of men in the home. In 1962, the majority (53%) agreed that the husband should have the final say in family matters; by 1974 the majority disagreed (69%). Changes in the percentage agreeing with the statement "the father is the most important person in the house" tell the same story.[19]

The extent to which people subscribed to authoritarian statements varied by social class. In 1962 the working class were more authoritarian than the middle class but by 1974 there had been more substantial changes in the working class compared with the middle class, so that class differences were less significant. This provides neat support for Moscovici's (1984) theory of *social representation*.[20]

---

[19]For one item there was no change over time: "There will always be war, it is part of human nature" (49% and 55% respectively agreed). Hardly surprising, given than during this period there were several wars — in Vietnam, in the Middle East and in other parts of the world.

[20]This theory, a development of Durkheim's (1898) theory of collective representation, states that when a view of society and its relations, initially formulated by one group, becomes accepted by the majority of the society (through the influence of personal contact and the media), such a view acquires the characteristics of a social reality — it becomes a social fact.

Individuals are indeed responsive to the climate of opinion of the day even if that responsiveness takes time to become overt: their replies reflected the increasing liberalization of some of our laws and testified to the influence of the Women's Movement on the one hand but also to the diatribes of Enoch Powell about the dangers of immigration on the other. Thus, despite the fact that between 1962 and 1974 restriction on immigration had become much more severe, at both times the percentage of those who wanted still more restrictions remained the same. It is as if within the electorate a kind of snowballing occurs (whether progressive or reactionary in content) which, once started, is as difficult to stop as it is initially to arouse an apparently apathetic electorate to think about an issue, particularly when such an issue is removed from their everyday concerns.

## The global picture: direct and indirect patterns of influence

So far we have examined spheres of influences singly without placing them in a logically coherent sequence. Using the longitudinal study, we can move from a piecemeal to a more rounded picture locating the strength, duration and time of impact of the various sources of influence.

The statistical method we used to develop this picture was path analysis (Kerlinger and Pedhazur, 1973). This method can be used to determine whether variables which are *causally prior* on logical grounds — in this case on a time axis — act directly or indirectly through the influence of other variables. The model we set up was simple; it allowed every source of influence or variable to make itself felt on all voting indices, contemporaneous or subsequent in time, and also for all structural factors to affect all outlook and attitudinal measures. In addition, goals and authoritarianism were seen as potential influences on political attitudes. Using that principle, path coefficients were calculated to indicate the strength of each possible causal link in the model.[21] The higher the path coefficients the stronger the link.

We examined the effects of seven types of influence including outlook on economic, political and social issues.

1. *Parents' vote* choice.
2. The individual's *own vote choices* from the first election in 1959 to the fourth in October 1970. (A low score indicates a Conservative, a high score a Labour vote.)

[21]Where measures were repeated at various points in time, the earlier ones could influence later ones. A path coefficient is an index of the proportion of the variance of the dependent variable (indicated in Fig. 4.3 by the arrowhead of the link to which the coefficient applies) for which the variable lying on the other end of the link is directly responsible, that is, with the effects of all other variables partialled out. In Fig. 4.3, each path coefficient is expressed as a standardized regression coefficient.

3. *Structural factors:* parents' social class and the individual's social class status at age 25 (1962) and 8 years later at 33. (A low score indicates an upper middle class, a high score a working class job.)
4. *Educational indices:* type of secondary school attended. (A low score indicates attendance at a grammar school, a high score at a secondary modern.) Overall educational attainment. (A low score indicates a university degree or its equivalent, a high score absence of any educational qualification.)
5. *Three measures of general orientation to society:* a measure of authoritarianism and the relative priorities attached to two sets of goals: *personal success* (in terms of career and money) and *concern with society* (wanting to understand it, improve and change it). The same three measures were obtained in 1962 and 1970. (High scores indicate an authoritarian outlook and a high priority for the goal in question.)
6. *Liberal outlook:* a composite measure of five individual attitudes: to the abolition of capital punishment; to making the law on homosexuality less severe; respect for nuclear disarmers (in 1970 this was replaced by respect for protesters of the Vietnam war); and two attitudes to immigrants (one to do with restriction of entry, the other with attitudes to immigrants resident here). The same measures were obtained in 1962 and 1970. (A high score indicates a liberal outlook.)
7. *Politico-economic outlook:* a composite measure made up of four measures which, both in 1964 and in 1970, differentiated significantly between the voters for the different parties: attitudes to trade unions; to welfare provisions; and to comprehensive and public schools. (A high score indicates support for a Labour view on these issues, a low score for a Conservative view.)

Although we have listed these sources of influence under seven separate headings, this is merely for ease of presentation; the whole purpose of the exercise is to highlight the interweaving of sources of influences. Some have a direct, others an indirect, influence. Some exerted an influence in 1962 but not in 1970, their influence having been spent, while other influences mattered only when the individual got older. The results of the path analysis, shown in Fig. 4.3, indicate the direct and indirect paths of influence that we uncovered in the analysis.

The model presents a rather clear picture of the linkages involved.[22] It is drawn in such a way that like measures, repeated over time, occur on the same horizontal line. Looking at the bottom line first, we find that parental vote has a strong influence on the individual's first vote (1959) and that each vote in turn has an influence on subsequent vote; sometimes that influence is strong, as between 1964

[22]After computing the path coefficients we deleted small path coefficients from the figure since these may have constituted "noise". Kerlinger and Pedhazur (1973) point out that there are no formal criteria for determining the size of a path coefficient which should be left in the model. We chose a standardized path coefficient of 0·19 as minimum for including a path (such a coefficient is "significant" at the $p < 0·01$ level).

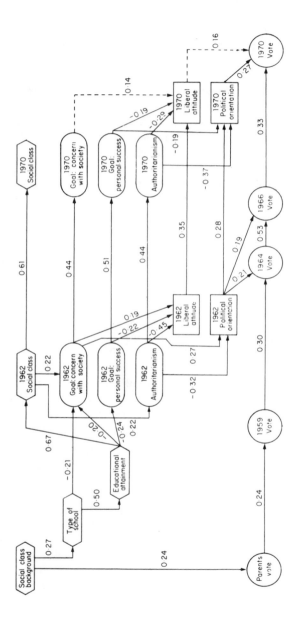

Fig. 4.3. Path analysis with vote choice 1970 as the dependent variable. This path analysis predicts the Labour vote and includes all those who voted in that election. (Longitudinal study.)

and 1966 or between February and October 1974, and at other times much weaker, as between 1959 and 1964.

The top line in Fig. 4.3 indicates the structural factors and shows the strong link between social background, type of school attended, subsequent educational attainment and social status at age 25 and 33. There is no *direct* path from the structural factors to vote choice (although the parents' vote was directly influenced by the father's social status). The influence is there, but it is *indirect*, via the individual's goals which in their turn affect his political outlook. The link to vote is from political attitudes.

The relation of structural factors to the goals and values appears at first sight paradoxical. On the one hand there is the close link between education and social status, yet both men in working class jobs and those with a university education gave a higher priority to goals related to social issues. The paradox is resolved if we look at the four individual goals subsumed under the summary measure *concern with society*. It would appear that the working class lays more stress on the first two (making the world a better place and changing society), and the better educated on the second two (feeling free to express myself and undertanding society). A university education might lead to a greater interest in understanding society and encourage the need for self-expression. But it is no lubricant for change, particularly since this particular group attached a high priority to personal success.

While education and the individual's position helped shape his orientation to society at age 25, social status at age 33 exerted no additional influence on such goals.

The two goals and the individual's authoritarianism influenced the individual's liberalism and political orientation. Concern with societal goals made for a liberal outlook while the need for personal success and authoritarianism were associated with an illiberal attitude to law and order, deviance and immigration. Authoritarianism and concern with societal goals also affected the individual's political orientation: the former made for a Conservative, the latter for a Labour orientation.

Eight years later in 1970 the pattern was much the same, except that this time emphasis on personal success aligned itself with authoritarianism and both influenced the individual in a Conservative direction. Although emphasis on personal success in 1962 was highly correlated with its emphasis in 1970, only in 1970 when the men were in their thirties did it have a direct influence on the individual's political orientation. This is in contrast with the *concern with society* which exerted its influence early when the young men were in their twenties. By the age of 33 its influence was spent. These changes mirror Turkle's (1979) comments about how a shift from attempts to seek fulfilment by changing society to one of concern with personal circumstances was typical of people of this age group through the 1960s in France as well as in the United States.

There was no link between liberal attitudes and vote; issues about law and order or immigration, though hotly debated, did not in fact sufficiently differentiate the policies of the two parties to influence vote. By contrast, the measure of political orientation influenced vote choice in 1964 as well as exerting an influence on subsequent vote.[23]

When we started the political study in 1962 we had less opportunity to sample a wide range of political attitudes than in later rounds since we had to catch up with what had been happening to the men since adolescence. In Chapters 5 and 6 we show that prediction of vote or classification of voters becomes more accurate the larger the range of issues sampled. We had a choice, either to include at each election the full set of cognitions we had obtained or else to restrict the analysis to those measures which had been asked in identical form in 1962 and 1970. We decided on the latter course as our concern was with delineating the pathways of influence rather than their strength. Had we used the full set, the findings reported in subsequent chapters suggest that the path coefficients between attitudes and vote would have been larger than those between vote and previous vote choice.

While complicated in detail, certain general features emerge from the path analysis. These are that the influence of structural factors on vote is *indirect*, operating through goals and values, which in turn exert their influence on the individual's attitudes to specific policy issues. Both the social context and the individual's own history have an effect. Different influences within this general pattern come to the fore at particular points in the individual's cycle, and at different historical moments.

What this path analysis, on its own, cannot tell us, however, is *how* attitudes about policy issues determine a person's vote. This is taken up in the following chapters where we examine *which* attitudes may be salient at given elections and how changes in these attitudes lead to vote change.

## Summary and implications

From our study and those to which reference has been made, certain general trends emerge:

1. Parental vote influences not only the individual's initial party preferences but continues to have some, though a decreasing, influence on subsequent vote and on the readiness with which the individual alters his vote in response to changing circumstances, including his resistance to the political perspective of his class of destination. The extent of parental influence varies with the extent to which the other socializing experiences provide supporting or conflicting cues, as well as with the parents' vote choice. Conservatives were imitated more than Labour voters and both more than parents who voted Liberal or abstained. Of the two parents, the mother exerted the stronger influence on the son.

2. There was no evidence of anticipatory socialization, either on the part of the parents' vote or as reflected in the adolescents' vote: those who became socially

---

[23]Confirmation of the pathways was obtained from a second path analysis in which the Conservative vote was predicted.

mobile were no more likely to vote Conservative in adolescence than were those who remained in the working class. Social mobility had an effect on vote depending on the time at which the mobility occurred.

3. The degree to which parents voted along class lines varied with the party; there was a stronger link between middle class status and voting Conservative than working class status and voting Labour. This trend was paralleled in the sons' voting as adults.

4. While in early adolescence there was greater modelling of parental behaviour than outlook, such behaviour was continued in adulthood only if the individual could back it by appropriate cognitive and attitudinal supports.

5. The importance of *cross pressures* when seeking to assess the role of different socializing influences was confirmed. Divergence in the political outlook of one parent or of both with those prevalent in school and neighbourhood in childhood tended to reduce the extent of modelling. Parental vote provided a *rootedness* or restraint on the influence of adult reference groups.

6. The term *political socialization* can usefully be extended to adults. Reference groups as well as the climate of the society exert an influence on adults as well as on the young.

The influence of social class membership will not only vary across domains but may wax and wane over time. In the 1960s there were great variations in attitudes and life styles within the different classes which overshadowed differences between the classes. Relative to earlier periods, there was a greater emphasis on people making individual choices rather than following the example of their group. The small effect of social class membership on vote we found may well be specific to the period under study. The extent of class-linked voting and hence the influence of social mobility on vote depends on the nature of the problems facing the country at election time. The relation of class to vote is therefore not an automatic one, as suggested by Campbell *et al.* (1960), but the result of a shared perspective generated by common problems. Such a relationship might, therefore, be election- and problem-specific and be "episodic rather than steady or steadily declining" (Pomper, 1975).

# 5

# Relevance of political attitudes to vote choice

So far we have shown that neither the individual's past voting record nor his social class and history of social mobility provide adequate indicators of vote choice. In this and subsequent chapters we examine the role of the individual's political attitudes in the decision process.

Basic to the "consumer model of voting" that we introduced in Chapter 1 is the assumption that people actively search for the party and/or candidate which seems most likely to implement policies which they favour and whose style of government they can respect. If all the parties are found wanting but they still wish to vote they will seek a *minimal-regret* solution, and vote for the party which offends their views least. Force of habit will affect the degree to which attitude-fit is relevant — the habit of avoiding a particular party being as significant as always voting for the same party. Such avoidance may be expressed as, "I have never voted Labour", or, "I could never bring myself to vote Conservative".

Two sets of conditions will have to be met in order to establish the validity of the "consumer model". The first requires that prediction from attitudes should be more accurate than that based on an individual's past vote and further that information about the voter's political outlook, when added to his or her voting record, will increase accuracy of prediction.

The second set of conditions concerns attitude-fit and attitude-shift. If the voting decision is crucially affected by the individual's outlook, it should follow that where there is a mismatch between the voter's outlook and that of the majority of voters for that party, sooner or later the individual will "defect", the probability varying according to past voting habit and the pressures that might be exerted from significant reference groups. Also, where people change their political views on salient issues, they should be more likely to change their vote in the direction of a party more in tune with their changed outlook at a subsequent election.

THE IRRELEVANCE OF INCONSISTENCY OF VIEWS

Blondel (1969) and Butler and Stokes (1974) argued that because the voter is inconsistent in his views his decision is only partially affected by them. As an example Blondel cited the fact that in 1959, when nationalization was a key issue in the Labour party's election campaign, those Labour voters who were indifferent or even opposed to more nationalization nonetheless voted Labour. Butler and Stokes pointed to two other types of inconsistency, one being a relatively low correlation among the voter's views on related political issues, and the other an inconsistency in the voter's views over time.

We maintain that these three types of inconsistency are not valid counter-arguments against the proposition that attitudes crucially influence the decision. The first argument, mismatch between attitude and vote choice, ignores the fact that in real life nearly all decisions are a compromise; there is a match for some issues and not others. Much must depend on the salience of the issue. RePass (1976) showed that when people were asked to identify what they considered to be the important problems, rather than simply being asked to respond to issues raised by the researcher, they were more accurate in identifying the parties' platforms *and* more consistent in voting for the party that matched their policy preferences. Indeed, as we shall show later, the role of saliency of an issue in the decision varies with the voters' beliefs that one party compared with the others is in a better position to ameliorate the problem or at least to effect some change.

Our model does not demand a logical connection between a voter's political views or require these to be consistent over time. The familiar gulf between theory and practice is particularly marked in politics and the implementation of a policy thought desirable on paper might turn out to have unexpected and unwanted side-effects which may cause the voter to think again. Also, some issues may be salient for the voter in one election but not in another, due to changes in the individual's circumstances (e.g. the question of comprehensive schooling assumes greater importance the closer the voter's own children come to entering the secondary school system) or in the type or severity of the problems facing the country at election time. In 1970 Enoch Powell's speeches made immigration an election issue despite both parties' efforts not to make it such, and in 1974 problems over housing and the health service once again gave nationalization a degree of salience it had not possessed for a decade. By 1983 72% cited unemployment as the most urgent issue facing the country. Inflation and industrial unrest, both key issues in 1974 and 1979, were less salient in the elections between 1964 and 1970. These seemed to us compelling reasons for sampling afresh the individual's views on a wide range of issues at each election.

In the sections that follow we shall first describe the relationship between attitudes and voting using our longitudinal sample and then present the results based on the representative British election study surveys.

## Longitudinal study

THE ISSUES STUDIED

In 1962 we re-interviewed the young men last seen as adolescents 11 years earlier. As we needed to update our information about them since leaving school we had less time than we would have liked for political questions. More issues were covered in 1970 and more again in 1974 where we added questions on specific policy options proposed in the election manifestos. Issues which in 1962 did not differentiate between the voters, and were not revived in subsequent election campaigns, were not repeated in the next round of questioning. This was necessary to make room for more current concerns and to ensure that in each round we asked sufficient questions about issues that mattered to the voters at the time. A full list of the questions, and how these were combined into composite measures, is given in Appendix 1. The reactions sampled were of three types:

1. *Evaluation of institutions*, e.g. trade unions, and their role in society. Example: "The way they are run now, trade unions do this country more harm than good." "Power without responsibility is a good description of trade unions today."

2. *Attribution of responsibility:* "The high level of unemployment is the result of workers' excessive demands", and alternatively, "Inefficient management and planning have led to the present level of unemployment".

3. *Reactions to specific policy proposals:* "Sell council houses to tenants"; "establish more comprehensive schools".

Butler and Stokes make a distinction between *position* and *valence* issues, the former being issues on which the electorate take a different stand and the latter concerns shared by the electorate as whole. However, another set of distinctions is more difficult to make: that between evaluation, attribution of blame, and policy proposals, not on semantic grounds, of course, but in terms of their significance for vote choice. The two parties may, for example, convey a different attitude towards institutions in the society, e.g. trade unions, without spelling out particular policy proposals that derive from the attitude. Or the underlying attitude may not be articulated and instead there are clear policy proposals which imply different attitudes between the parties, e.g. about the desirability of establishing more comprehensive schools. Nor does the electorate make the distinction. We found that on the subject of immigration, evaluation and policy proposals correlated highly; the same was true for law and order. Believing that stricter laws make for a healthier society correlated with wanting the death penalty restored and the power of the police increased, just as agreement with the statement that the so-called breakdown in law and order had been greatly exaggerated correlated negatively with these proposals.

As our main aim was to sample the individual's reactions to salient issues, whether these were policy proposals or evaluations of institutions or sections of the society, we selected the form of questions that seemed most appropriate and combined measures into a composite scale where replies to questions that might be subsumed under one broad heading correlated sufficiently highly.[1] This did not always happen: for example, we had expected answers to questions about trade union power and about strikes to be highly correlated. They were not, suggesting that in the electorate's mind these represented rather different facets of industrial relations.

The issues we questioned people on can be subsumed under the following headings:

1. *Selective education:* The abolition of grammar and public schools and the establishment of comprehensive schools (comprehensive schools were in their infancy in 1962).
2. *Industrial relations:* Trade union power and responsibility; management–employee relations; worker participation.
3. *Strikes:* The right to strike; the harm done by strikes; legal imposition of sanctions; voting by secret ballot; whether to cut benefits to strikers.
4. *Role of big business:* Questions on whether big business should be subject to more control, and whether mergers should be matters for management alone.
5. *Taxation:* Reducing company taxes and heavier taxing of the wealthy.
6. *Immigration:* Two questions were repeated in 1962, 1970 and 1974 about restriction of immigration from Commonwealth and colonies, and about the voters' reactions to immigrants already in this country. In 1970 and 1974 other questions on the same topic were added (whether the problems of immigrants had been exaggerated and whether it was wrong to control immigration to this country on the basis of a person's colour). In 1974 we also asked a question about Enoch Powell's proposal to encourage immigrants to return to their home country.
7. *Liberalization:* In 1962 we asked whether it would be right to make the law on homosexuality less severe, to abolish capital punishment and about attitudes to nuclear disarmers. By 1970, the law had been changed, so we asked then, and in 1974, whether it had been right to make the law on homosexuality less severe, whether capital punishment should be restored, and replaced the question about nuclear disarmers by one about protesters against the Vietnam war.
8. *Law and order:* By 1970 this had become an important issue. We included a series of questions on student activism, the right to demonstrate, violence at demonstrations, together with questions about increasing the power of the police and arming them. By 1974 student activism and demonstrations had become less important and fewer questions were asked about each of these issues.

[1]Composite measures are, of course, preferable to individual items, but there is a trade-off between thorough coverage of a few issues or a less thorough coverage of a larger number.

CLASSIFICATION OF VOTE ON THE BASIS OF ATTITUDES

Rather than weary the reader with exhaustive lists of all the items and the different responses, we present just one table (Table 5.1) to illustrate the mean evaluations in 1974 of 17 policy proposals by Labour, Liberal and Conservative voters. Although on nearly all items there were significant differences between the parties, the extent of the difference varied. On some policy options, like nationalization of building land, views were polarized: Labour voters saw it as a good thing, Conservatives as bad. On the other hand, the Conservatives took a neutral view on worker participation in industry, which was favoured by Labour. Reform of the electoral system, mildly favoured by both major parties was, not surprisingly, the only item on which Liberals came out as most in favour and as different from both groups. On almost every other item, the Liberals emerged, not as different from both groups, but as occupying a mid-position somewhat closer to the Conservatives than to Labour.

TABLE 5.1                                                             *Longit. study*

Mean evaluations of 17 policy options in 1974 by party preference ($n = 175$)

|  | Full | Con | Lab | Lib |
|---|---|---|---|---|
| 1. Abolish grammar schools | 3·82 | 4·52 | 2·39 | 3·78 |
| 2. Trust trade unions | 3·82 | 3·60 | 2·24 | 3·50 |
| 3. Subsidize foods | 3·06 | 3·45 | 2·12 | 3·22 |
| 4. Bring companies into public ownership | 3·84 | 4·48 | 2·34 | 4·07 |
| 5. Spend more on social services | 2·59 | 2·78 | 2·17 | 2·61 |
| 6. Heavier taxing of the wealthy | 2·93 | 3·42 | 1·93 | 3·00 |
| 7. Enforce equal pay for women | 2·27 | 2·51 | 1·85 | 2·28 |
| 8. Nationalize building land | 3·41 | 4·10 | 1·76 | 3·63 |
| 9. Worker participation in industry | 2·30 | 2·53 | 1·93 | 2·24 |
| 10. Reduce company taxes | 2·50 | 2·29 | 3·12 | 2·35 |
| 11. Keep private health service | 2·62 | 2·02 | 3·90 | 2·59 |
| 12. Sell council houses to tenants | 2·29 | 1·83 | 3·24 | 2·26 |
| 13. Ensure Britain remains in EEC | 2·30 | 1·96 | 2·88 | 2·26 |
| 14. Cut social security benefits to strikers | 2·06 | 1·54 | 3·37 | 1·94 |
| 15. Control wage increases | 2·53 | 2·35 | 3·10 | 2·46 |
| 16. Encourage immigrants to return to home country | 2·80 | 2·66 | 3·00 | 2·89 |
| 17. Reform electoral system | 2·32 | 2·52 | 2·56 | 1·85 |

Range of Scores: 1 = Very Good. 5 = Very Bad.

The mean responses to individual items tell us something about the role of attitudes, but not enough. Group means do not necessarily reflect the more idiosyncratic responses of individual voters, nor is the individual's attitude towards one or two issues sufficient to account for his vote; instead, it is an amalgam of reactions to many issues. To see how well such an amalgam of attitude measures can differentiate between Conservative, Labour and Liberal voters[2] we used a statistical technique known as discriminant analysis (Cooley and Lohnes, 1971). Such discriminant analyses offer other useful information:

1. A measure of overall accuracy of the classification in terms of the proportion of voters correctly classified as having chosen the party for which they had voted as an indication of how those misclassified were distributed over the other parties.

2. An indication of which particular groups were better "predicted" than others. Were attitudes, for instance, more important for the "prediction" of Labour than Conservative voters? Were the Liberals more readily misclassified?

3. A measure of which variables were important in discriminating between voters of different parties. In the discriminant functions underlying the classification of voters, each attitude item is assigned a weight. Some interpret the weight as a measure of the importance of the item in the discrimination.

4. An indication of how many "dimensions" are needed to discriminate adequately among voters of different parties. For example, are Liberal voters merely middle of the road on a single Conservative–Labour or "right–left" continuum, or is their attitude profile in some way distinct from those of the other two parties?'

5. Finally, the analysis provides for each voter an estimate of the posterior probability of his belonging to a particular group (i.e. voting for a particular party). These probabilities also express the degree to which each voter's attitudes reflect the mean attitudes of the voters for each of the three parties.

It is important, however, to bear in mind that a discriminant analysis is *not* a means of prediction but of discrimination between groups. By percentage correctly classified, we mean the percentage, for instance, of all Labour voters in the sample who were correctly identified on the basis of their attitudes alone. By contrast *real* prediction requires that the behaviour to be predicted is either not known in advance or does not form part of the analysis. In the case of the discriminant analyses, the actual vote cast is used as a criterion for optimizing the combination of attitudes that, in turn, will classify the same voters — of course if the attitudes measured were of little relevance, then few would be accurately classified. Such analyses therefore provide a kind of pseudo-prediction and are very useful for measuring the extent of the role played by attitudes in the decision.

Using attitudinal data obtained in 1962, 1970 and 1974, we carried out three sets of discriminant analyses to classify individuals on the basis of the votes they had cast in these years. The results shown in Table 5.2 indicate that in 1962 only 66% of the voters in the sample were correctly classified compared with as many as 78% in the 1970 and 1974 elections. As the number of measures we used was 12 in 1962, 14 in 1970 and 20 in 1974, we could not tell whether the improved accuracy of classification in the later elections was due to an increase in the number

---

[2]The analysis derives weighted linear combination(s) of the independent variables (in our analyses, attitudes), so as to maximize between-group, relative to, within-group differences. A stepwise discriminant analysis was used.

of measures, or because the 1962 sample were asked for an "as if" vote, "If there were an election tomorrow". This is quite different psychologically from making a choice, after a carefully orchestrated election campaign, which one backs with one's action.

TABLE 5.2                                                                          *Longit. study*

Voters correctly classified on the basis of three discriminant analyses carried out on hypothetical vote 1962, on vote 1970 and 1974. Attitude measures obtained in 1962, 1970 and 1974 were the independent variables

| | Percentage correctly classified | | | | |
|---|---|---|---|---|---|
| | Con | Lab | Lib | Total | *n* |
| Year | | | | | |
| 1962 (hypothetical vote) | 72 | 63 | 62 | 66 | 171 |
| 1970 vote | 79 | 78 | 65 | 78 | 180 |
| 1974 vote | 77 | 97 | 63 | 78 | 148 |

Number of measures used in the analyses: For 1962: 12; 1970: 14; 1974: 20

Of the *issues* which differentiated voters best, some recurred at every election, and others were highlighted during the campaign. Attitudes towards schools, for example, proved significant at each election, with Conservatives in favour and Labour either neutral or opposed to selective education. The power of the trade unions and attitudes towards them also made contributions each time. Details are given in Appendix 3, Table 9. In 1962, along with attitudes to schooling and trade unions, some class-related attitudes contributed. Labour voters agreed that the poor should be taken care of by the Government; the Conservatives remained neutral. Labour agreed that there is one law for the rich and another for the poor. Again the Conservatives were neutral. The Liberals on these issues came half-way between, with the exception of attitudes towards trade unions where their position was similar to that of the Conservatives. In 1962, attitudes towards Britain's possible entry into the Common Market also differentiated voters: while Conservatives and Labour were both neutral, it was the Liberals this time who were clearly in favour.

By 1970, welfare concerns no longer contributed significantly. Instead, views on labour relations and control of big business improved predictions over and above attitudes to schooling and trade unions. On schooling, Conservative and Labour voters now took clear and opposing stands, with the Liberals midway between the two. On the question of trade unions the Liberals were once again closer to the Conservatives. Control of big business was favoured by Labour voters and opposed by Conservative voters while the Liberals took a neutral position. Management–employee relations was the only issue where the Liberals were more positive than both Labour and Conservative voters.

In 1974 trade unions and schools were again important issues. For the first time, immigration became a significant predictor, although questions on immigration had been asked in 1962 and 1970 and Enoch Powell's speeches occurred at the time of the 1970 election. Other significant issues included nationalization, sale of council houses to tenants, and trusting the unions to honour the social contract. The pattern of attitudes evident in earlier analyses still held overall. Labour and Conservative voters tended to take opposing sides on these issues, while Liberal voters were in the middle.

In 1962 and 1970, a single dimension (discriminant function) was sufficient to describe the differences among voters, with Conservative and Labour voters at the two ends of the continuum and Liberals in the middle. These functions were defined by the attitudes described above. In 1974, with the introduction of a question on electoral reform, a second significant dimension was obtained which, however, accounted for only a small proportion of the variation among the voters. This second function, which differentiated Liberal from the other voters, was defined by only one issue, that of electoral reform.

## Confirmation of findings from the representative British election surveys

Analyses of the representative BES surveys, ranging from 1970, October 1974, 1979 to 1983, enabled us to examine the strength of the relationship between attitudes to issues and votes across the *whole* spectrum of the British electorate and across elections fought in different political and economic climates. While strict comparisons with the results from our study are not possible because of differences in the number, wording and content of the questions asked, the fact that each time attitudes differentiated well between the voters provides powerful confirmation of the generality of our findings and the usefulness of the model we propose.

The large scale surveys also made it possible to examine particular sub-groups by social class, sex and region and to see how well people's evaluation of the leaders of the parties differentiated between them by comparison with their evaluation of issues on which we had concentrated. In the BES surveys the respondents were asked how much they liked each of the three party leaders using a ten point scale and in 1983 instead, who would make the best and who would make the worst Prime Minister.

THE ISSUES SAMPLED IN THE BES SURVEYS OF 1974, 1979 AND 1983

In 1970, Butler and Stokes asked mainly about economic and social welfare issues (social services, strikes, trade unions and big business) and about immigration and the death penalty. In the later surveys, Särlvik and Crewe increased not only the number of issues covered but also the number of questions asked about each. In 1974 questions about the pace and direction of social and cultural change in society were added, covering modern teaching methods, challenges to authority and the treatment of lawbreakers. They also examined opinions about specific policy alternatives as to how wages should be settled, race relations improved and whether the government or the private sector were better placed to create employment. A trade-off question asked whether it was better to keep welfare services at the present level or reduce taxes. At the second stage of their panel study in 1979 Särlvik and Crewe dropped some questions, reworded others and added new ones to reflect concerns current at the time of the election.

In the BBC/Crewe 1983 survey, questions about many ongoing concerns (e.g. race relations, level of welfare benefits) were omitted to make room for current issues on proportional representation, and on defence concerning Cruise missiles and Polaris submarines. It also included a question on whether to allow a free vote on the death penalty. All three surveys contained a question about Britain's relations with the EEC; the emphasis given to that question varied depending on Britain's relations with the Community at the time.

TABLE 5.3                                                      *BES 1970, October 1974, 1979, BBC/Crewe 1983*

Percentage of voters correctly classified using discriminant analyses with attitudes as independent variables

| | Percentage correctly classified | | | |
| --- | --- | --- | --- | --- |
| Sample | Con (%) | Lab (%) | Lib (%) | Total (%) |
| BES 1970 | 71 | 56 | 32 | 61 |
| BES October 1974 | 69 | 76 | 49 | 68 |
| BES 1979 | 69 | 71 | 46 | 67 |
| | | | Alliance | |
| BBC/Crewe 1983 | 76 | 73 | 54 | 69 |

Table 5.3 gives the results of the analyses, showing that in every election about 70% of Labour and Conservative voters were correctly classified.[3] The overall accuracy of classification was reduced by the relatively poor differentiation of Liberal voters. This is not really surprising if one considers that the Liberal voters in one election are rarely the same as in another. People from both major parties turn to the Liberal party out of disaffection and are therefore unlikely to have as many attitudes in common as do the Labour or Conservative voters. As a result, within-group differences will be large. If we are correct, it should follow that by repeating the analyses, excluding the Liberal voters, accuracy of classification should markedly increase. Table 5.4 shows that this is indeed the case both in our and in the British election studies. Accuracy of classification increased by 20% to an impressive 88%.

[3]We should point out that the results of our discriminant analysis of the BES 1979 sample differ slightly from those reported by Särlvik and Crewe (1983, p. 286). Unlike them, we included attitudes to issues that had little univariate relation to vote since it is always possible that such issues might have an impact when taken in combination with others.

TABLE 5.4                    *Longit. study, BES October 1974, 1979, BBC/Crewe 1983*

Percentage of voters correctly classified using discriminant analysis with attitudes to issues as independent variables

|  | Percentage accuracy of classification | | |
|---|---|---|---|
| Sample | Con (%) | Lab (%) | Total (%) |
| Longit. study 1970 | 92 | 85 | 90 |
| Longit. study October 1974 | 96 | 97 | 97 |
| BES October 1974 | 91 | 87 | 88 |
| BES 1979 | 85 | 83 | 84 |
| BBC/Crewe 1983 | 89 | 86 | 88 |

Predictions for our sample tended to be more accurate than those for the large representative election studies. This is probably because of the greater homogeneity of our sample and because we had asked more questions than the large-scale surveys. Among the British election studies, accuracy was lowest for the 1970 survey. In this survey, fewer issues were tapped and the response categories were more restricted. The respondents could indicate only whether they were in favour or against a policy (three-point scale). In later surveys five- and seven-point scales were used. This made it possible, when there was a consensus that a given policy was good or bad, that the item could still differentiate between voters depending on the degree of endorsement or rejection.

In the studies concurrent with our own, several of the same issues were found to contribute to the discrimination among voters. In 1970, these were attitudes about comprehensive schooling, trades unions and big business. These issues made significant contributions again in 1974, as did views on nationalization, maintenance of social services, control of building land and redistribution of wealth. In the 1979 election, in addition to those found important in the 1974 election, opinions about the desirability of cutting taxes versus keeping social services, selling council houses, unemployment policies and abolishing the House of Lords played a role.

In 1983, not only did customary issues matter, such as nationalization and social services, but also views about proportional representation, relations with the EEC, about defence (Cruise missiles and Polaris submarines) and about ways of reducing unemployment.

## THE IMPACT OF ASSESSMENT OF PARTY LEADERSHIP ON VOTE CHOICE

To see how people's views about party leaders affected their vote choice, we carried out two kinds of discriminant analyses. The first used as predictors the respondents' views on the party leaders, and the second assessed what contribution attitudes on issues made to the accuracy of voter classification based on attitudes to the leaders (Table 5.5).

TABLE 5.5                                                                 *BES October 1974, 1979, BBC/Crewe 1983*

Percentage of voters correctly classified using discriminant analyses. Independent variables were (A) evaluations of party leaders and (B) evaluations of party leaders and issues.

| Sample | A Based on leader evaluations | | | | B Based on leader and issue evaluations | | | |
|---|---|---|---|---|---|---|---|---|
| | Con (%) | Lab (%) | Lib (%) | All (%) | Con (%) | Lab (%) | Lib (%) | All (%) |
| BES October 1974 | 77 | 81 | 69 | 77 | 79 | 84 | 71 | 80 |
| BES 1979 | 76 | 72 | 67 | 73 | 78 | 79 | 67 | 77 |
| BBC/Crewe 1983 | 82 | 73 | 52 | 73 | 83 | 75 | 71 | 77 |

Evaluation of party leaders alone discriminated effectively between voters, indeed better than attitudes to issues. Seventy-seven per cent of voters in the October 1974 and 1979 elections were correctly classified on the basis of their evaluations of the three party leaders, and 73% in the 1983 election, where evaluation was asked for in a rather different form. Interestingly, Conservatives were somewhat more accurately classified than Labour voters when their party was successful (1979 and 1983) and equally Labour voters were better classified in the October 1974 election when Labour won. Alliance voters were less well predicted than either of the other two parties in the 1983 election.

Adding attitudes to the assessment of party leaders increased the overall accuracy of classification by 3–4% (see Table 5.5). While in 1974 the improvement in accuracy was uniform across the three parties, in 1983 there was a big improvement in the prediction of Alliance voters compared with Conservative and Labour voters, when attitudes were added to the assessment of the leaders of the parties as potential Prime Ministers.

Since evaluation of leaders discriminates voters better than issues and since adding issues to party leaders yielded only a modest increment, should we conclude that attitudes matter little? We think not. Attitudes about issues and attitudes to party leaders are correlated; consequently the unique contribution to the prediction of vote by one or other set of attitudes will be small when the other set is held constant. As Särlvik and Crewe (1983) point out, the distinction between a party's policies and its leader is not always clear, as it is through the leader, as the party's "mouthpiece", that voters judge the parties' records and often learn about future policies. It therefore makes little sense to discuss the statistically independent effects of leaders versus issues when, in reality, these are intertwined in the voters' minds as part of their overall "image" of a party's record and prospects.

## DIFFERENCES BY SOCIAL CLASS, SEX AND REGION

We wanted to test some commonly held assumptions, namely that the middle class decides more on the basis of issues than the working class, and that men in general do so more than women. We were interested also to know whether different segments of the electorate would single out different issues in making their decisions. Table 5.6 gives the overall classifications of accuracy of vote for men and women and for the middle and working classes.

### Class differences

In 1974 there were no real differences between middle class and working class voters in the extent to which issues mattered. Generally, the same issues mattered to both, although the relative ordering of items varied somewhat.

In 1979 and 1983, issues seemed to matter marginally more for the middle class

TABLE 5.6                                        *BES October 1974, 1979, BBC/Crewe 1983*

Percentage of (A) men and women, (B) middle and working class voters correctly classified
using discriminant analyses with attitudes to issues as independent variables

| | Percentage correctly classified | | | |
| --- | --- | --- | --- | --- |
| | A | | B | |
| Sample | | | | Working |
| | Men | Women | Middle class | class |
| | (%) | (%) | (%) | (%) |
| BES October 1974 | 69 | 67 | 67 | 69 |
| BES 1979 | 67 | 65 | 72 | 63 |
| BBC/Crewe 1983 | 71 | 68 | 73 | 66 |

than for the working class voters. In 1979 72% of middle class voters and 63%
of working class voters were correctly classified.[4] The corresponding percentages
for 1983 were 73% and 66%. Although most of the same issues were significant
predictors for both classes, there were certain differences. In 1979, giving workers
more say and government control of building land were significant predictors for
middle class but not for working class voters, and in 1983 it was the issue of
reducing taxes versus government services which appeared to matter more for
middle class voters, with the working class being more concerned with the proposal
of a special tax for firms giving excessive wage rises.

## Sex differences

It has often been suggested that women's votes are influenced less by policies than
by the vote decisions of significant others in their immediate environment. If this
were so, political attitudes should predict their vote less well than for men. This
was not so. In the three elections, there were no consistent differences in the
predictive accuracy of attitudes for men and women. While in 1974 and 1983
there were also no differences in the issues that mattered, in 1979 nationalization
mattered for men but not for women.

## Regional differences

Because the class composition in the North, the Midlands, and the South-east
(including London) differs considerably, to control for possible class effects we
carried out separate analyses on the October 1974 and 1979 BES surveys for middle
class and working class voters within each general region. There were no striking
regional differences, either in the percentage of voters correctly classified or in

---

[4]Without extensive cross-validation of these discriminant analyses, we cannot be sure
whether these differences are reliable or due to random variation. Our results should
therefore be viewed as tentative.

the issues that differentiated voters. This is not to suggest that regional differences may not exist, but to bring these out would require a more fine-grained analysis of the respondents from the different regions than we were able to do.

Our own study and the analyses of the British election studies show that the first condition necessary to establish the validity of the consumer model is amply met: differences between attitudes define the different groups of voters, and do so with a high degree of accuracy.

## Prediction of future vote from past vote

To examine the second condition for the validity of the consumer model — that prediction from attitudes should be at least as high as prediction of future vote from past vote — we return to our longitudinal study. The influence of past vote involves more than the vote cast in one previous election, but concerns the entire voting history of the individual. The larger BES panel samples spanned too few elections or elections too close together (as in 1974) to examine how past voting history influences future choice.

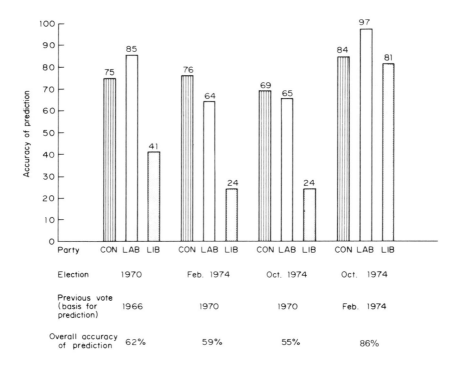

Fig. 5.1. Prediction of 1970 and 1974 votes from votes cast at the previous elections (longitudinal study).

We first looked at the relation between the votes cast in two successive elections. In 1970 only 62% were correctly classified on the basis of their previous vote and in February 1974 59%. These figures are lower than those obtained from attitudes. When up-to-date evaluation of issues by the electorate was used, prediction was greatly improved, so widening further the gap between ability to predict future vote from past vote and from the electorate's evaluation of issues (Chapter 9).

Figure 5.1 shows that only the October 1974 vote was as accurately predicted by the individual's February vote as by his attitudes — but then these two elections were exceptionally close together.

We found the same difference when using the BES 1974–'79 panel. Accuracy of classification of the 1979 vote by past vote was 71% compared with the 77% accuracy which we achieved using only the voters' attitudes to issues and to the party leaders.

One might rightly argue that even a strict habit model approach would not assume perfect correspondence between two successive votes, and that it would be more appropriate to take into account the individual's entire previous vote history. The longitudinal study permitted us to do just that. A discriminant analysis was carried out classifying the February 1974 voters on the basis of their past propensity to vote for the Conservative, Labour and Liberal parties (i.e. the number of times from 1959 to 1970 they had voted for each party). Table 5.7 shows that the accuracy of prediction (71%) was much better than that based on one election alone and better than true prediction from attitudes sought four years earlier (65%) but less good than prediction from up-to-date attitudes (78%).

If our aim had been solely to predict vote, we would have to conclude that full knowledge of an individual's past voting history comes close to being as good an indicator of that person's future vote as his attitudes. Such knowledge would, however, have to be based on data collected at the time of each election and not on recall because of the distortion that reliance on memory produces.

TABLE 5.7                                                                    *Longit. study*

Accuracy of classification of vote in February 1974 by (A) the individuals' voting history (1959–1970), (B) the individuals' voting history and 1974 attitudes

|  | Percentage accuracy of classification | | | |
| --- | --- | --- | --- | --- |
|  | Con | Lab | Lib | Total |
| (A) Voting history | 81 | 83 | 45 | 71 |
| (B) Voting history and 1974 attitudes | 87 | 93 | 59 | 80 |

## Prediction of vote from attitudes and voting history

To examine whether accuracy would be increased by adding measures of attitudes to a classification based on voting history, we carried out one further discriminant analysis on the 1974 vote.

As discussed earlier, past history classified major party voters well, but not Liberal voters, since they tended to be different individuals at each election. Adding attitudes to past voting history improved prediction considerably. The overall percentage of correct classification rose from 71% to 80% thus meeting the third requirement of our model, namely that attitudes should make a contribution over and above voting history. The gain was particularly marked for Liberal and Labour voters.

## Significance of attitudes — Summary and implications

The first set of conditions implied in the consumer model has been amply met. Attitudes matter more than past vote. Prediction based on attitudes proved better than prediction based on vote in the previous election. Apart from attitudes towards Britain's entry into the Common Market, we measured reactions to domestic issues: law and order, immigration, selective education, the power of trade unions and of big business; strikes, welfare, management–employee relations and nationalization. The large-scale and more up-to-date representative studies broadened their issue base to reflect changing political concerns and social mores. The differentiation of voters was usually achieved with just a few issues, those which met Butler and Stokes' three criteria: that people had to care about the issues, views had to be diverse and the parties had to take dissimilar stands recognized as such by the electorate. This was so for the power of the trade unions, of big business and the issue of selective secondary education, issues which in every election differentiated between the voters. Views on immigration did so in only one election, while those on law and order did not differentiate at all. The flogging Conservative appears to be as much a caricature as the Labour voter bent on nationalizing everything in sight.[5]

The results of the analyses showed why conversion from Labour to Conservative and vice versa was so rare: there were too many issues which separated the voters. Liberal voting was poorly predicted by a person's previous votes, and by their attitudes. The same was true of the Alliance voters in the 1983 election. They emerged as simply middle-of-the-road, moving *away* from voting for a particular major party rather than *towards* anything which might be identified as especially "Liberal".

As Särlvik and Crewe (1983) point out, this middle ground is not homogeneous, comprised of voters who share the same "centrist" attitudes, but rather of individuals who may fall closer to Conservatives on some issues and closer to Labour on others, but not necessarily on the same issue. To omit the so-called

[5]Some issues did not come to the fore, not because they failed to discriminate between the voters, but because they did not make an independent contribution. If attitudes to trade unions were highly correlated with attitudes to nationalization, only the one better able to discriminate will be included in the discriminant function, serving as a "delegate" for the cluster of attitudes which it represents.

centre parties from descriptions of attitudes characteristic of the electorate, as is often done, tends to exaggerate the degree of polarization of attitudes in the society. When we omitted the Liberals from the analyses, we could "predict" Conservative and Labour voters with close to 90% accuracy.

Attitudes have a significant and meaningful impact on vote regardless of the individuals' sex, class or place of residence. A few minor differences in the degree of accuracy of classification have been found across elections, but these may be due as much to the differential impact of a changing political and social climate and to the particular election campaign as to the individual voters. They may also reflect the researcher's decision which issues to tap and what questions to ask to gain insight into the complex cognitive map of the individual voter. The debate about the relation of attitudes to vote has for too long ignored two crucial aspects: the relevance of the issues studied to the circumstances of the voters and the need to develop measures that encapsulate the context and climate of problems within which a particular election is fought.

# 6

# Social determinants of vote choice

In the previous chapter we provided evidence for the important role that cognitions play in the individual's vote decision. Here we examine the role played by social determinants, first individually, then jointly and finally in terms of their importance relative to cognitive factors in vote choice.

We have already touched on one aspect of that theme in Chapter 4 on political socialization where we showed that although being middle class predisposed an individual to vote Conservative and being working class Labour, the extent to which this happened varied with parental vote preference, and where relevant, with the timing of the individual's social mobility. Social mobility on entry into the job market rather than later and having parents who voted Conservative accelerated the tendency to vote Conservative; late mobility or parents who voted Labour reduced it.

Here we look more closely at the extent to which a whole variety of potentially relevant social factors contribute to vote choice. To do so, we draw not on the small sample of the longitudinal study but on the two BES surveys of October 1974 and 1979 and on the BBC/Crewe survey of 1983. We shall examine how far such demographic factors as the individual's age, sex, education, social status, nature of employment (self-employed, employed in the public or private sector or being unemployed), home ownership and trade union membership provide perspectives on society that translate themselves into preferring one party to another.

Apart from age and sex which are clearly given, membership of the other categories we are considering is to varying degrees under the individual's control — some marginally or not at all (e.g. unemployment where a factory closes down), others more so (e.g. trade union membership). To take account of the reasons for the individual's placement in a particular category is beyond the scope of this book. Instead we assess the extent to which membership of a category is associated with particular political orientations.

## ͺographic factors

ͺeferred to Särlvik and Crewe (1983) for a detailed discussion of the ͺcmographic factors between 1959 and 1979, and to Crewe's (1984) analysis ͺ the 1983 election. Here, we shall restrict ourselves to selected salient features.

SOCIAL CLASS

It is worth remembering that the Labour party was explicitly founded to serve the interests of the working man. The first Members of Parliament returned by Labour constituencies were working men and, right to this day, the party has close financial, organizational and also inspirational ties with the trade union movement. The Conservative party too is linked to significant and powerful institutions: the City, commerce, industry and many of the professions, drawing from them financial support, members and views. Its links to institutions are less formal and explicit than those of the Labour party but perhaps no less close. It is only the Liberals, and since 1981 the SDP and the Alliance, who pride themselves on not being in the pockets of either industry or labour, and who claim that as a consequence their party would serve the whole nation more fairly.

Contrary to popular belief, class-based voting has never been very strong in post-war Britain. If it had, given that the electorate contains more working than middle class voters, Labour would have been continuously in office. As it is, since the war Labour and Conservatives have spent about equal time in government. In 1959 about 65% of the electorate voted in accordance with their class; by 1983 only half did so. In this decline in class voting, defection was more marked from the working class than from the middle class and became almost a rout in 1979, with a 15% increased vote for the Conservatives among the skilled working class and a 12% increase among the semi-skilled and unskilled.

Because this defection was so marked and also sudden, many commentators judged it to be a passing phenomenon. They attributed it to the voters' reactions to the "winter of discontent", in which the number and severity of strikes had shocked the electorate as a whole, and where Labour, despite its special relation with the trade union movement, had proved powerless. However, in 1983 there was no reversion to the Labour party; if anything, defection from it by the working class gained momentum. And this despite 3 ½ million unemployed, the deepening recession and the cuts in public expenditure — all factors which tend to hit the working class harder than the middle class.

In 1983, although the Conservatives lost some support in every social group, they did so more from the middle than the working class. Labour's loss was far greater, particularly from the working class with the Alliance's share of the vote in 1983 being extraordinarily even across the whole social spectrum, bearing out the party's claim to serve all classes. As Crewe (1984) points out, there was no indication whatever that the Alliance's supposedly middle class image deterred the working class. Its overall share of the vote was $25 \cdot 8\%$: among the professional and managerial class 26% voted for the Alliance, among the semi-skilled and unskilled 28%, and 26% among the unemployed.

## Type of employment

Consistent across elections is the high incidence of Conservative voters among the self-employed. Given the Conservative election promise to reduce the size and influence of the public sector, a promise repeated in 1983, one would have expected a veering away from the Conservatives within each social group by those employed in the public sector. There is some evidence that this happened, but only on a small scale: in 1983 the swing to the Conservatives among the public sector employees was 4%, compared with a 9% swing among their private sector counterparts.

## Unemployment

Unemployment made some difference in 1983, but only among the working class. The working class unemployed were the only group where defection from the Conservatives was larger than defection from Labour. The effect also showed itself in the level of support for Conservative policies among those who voted for the party within each of the four social class groups. In general, enthusiasm for the policies, their team of leaders and for their being best for ''people like me'' was high. But that enthusiasm was more muted among those who either experienced unemployment themselves or indirectly through some member of their family. This difference was more marked only when we looked at the percentage in each group who thought the Conservative party had the best team of leaders where there was a 15% difference in agreement between the employed and unemployment among the skilled working class and a 25% difference among the semi-skilled and unskilled. But taken all in all, the effect of unemployment on vote choice, contrary to all predictions, proved remarkably small.

## Trade union membership

This had the effect of strengthening the Labour vote up to 1979. In 1983, the swing to the Conservatives was twice as great among trade unionists as among non-unionists. As Crewe points out, this may have something to do with the increase in trade union membership among white-collar workers.

## Age and sex

Up to 1979, the young voted proportionately more for Labour than for the Conservatives. By 1979, that difference had disappeared and been reversed by 1983 when more of the first-time voters voted Conservative than Labour. Differences across the age scale were small except for the over-65 age-group, who still had memories of the Depression in the 1930s.

In every post-war election up to 1979, proportionately more women than men voted for the Conservatives. After 1979 the situation changed; fewer women than men moved to the Conservatives and more of these who had voted Conservative in 1979 defected in 1983. The result was a greater swing to the Alliance among women than men by former Labour and Conservative voters.

*Home ownership*

We have left home ownership to last because in 1983 this category clearly differentiated voters. Looking only at the percentage switching from Labour to Conservative, the picture is quite startling. Using the respondents' recall of their 1979 vote as the base line, Crewe (1984) found that while 21% of council tenants had moved away from Labour, twice that proportion did so among home owners. And the most telling statistic of all is that among those who had bought their home *since* 1979, as many as 59% of former Labour voters defected from Labour.

## Classification of vote choice by social determinants alone

As already mentioned, the various demographic factors are not independent of one another but are inter-related. Consequently it makes more sense to look at their joint contribution to vote choice. We did so for the October 1974, 1979 and 1983 surveys, using discriminant analysis. The overall accuracy of classification is given in Table 6.1 and the correct classification by type of voter in Appendix 3, Table 12. The results are quite clear cut. Social data alone do a relatively poor job: in 1974 overall accuracy was only 57%, by 1983 it had dropped to about half.

A subtler, interactive approach to the joint contribution made by social factors to vote choice was employed by Särlvik and Crewe on their 1979 sample. The analysis they used is one which permits a factor to make a difference to one category of people

TABLE 6.1                                              *BES 1974, 1979; BBC/Crewe 1983*

Overall percentage of voters correctly classified[a] using discriminant analysis. The independent variables were (A) structural data; (B) structural data and attitudes to issues; (C) attitudes to issues only

| Set of independent variables | Overall percentage accuracy of voter classification | | |
| --- | --- | --- | --- |
| | Elections | | |
| | 1974 | 1979 | 1983 |
| (A) Structural data only | 57 | 52 | 51 |
| (B) Structural data and attitude to issues | 69 | 66 | 71 |
| (C) Attitudes to issues only | 68 | 67 | 69 |

[a]Appendix 3 Table 12 gives the correct classification by type of voter.

but not to another. This type of "tree analysis" confirmed that among the variables included social class remained, however modestly, the most important differentiator.

Särlvik and Crewe isolated two groups who gave very solid support to their party: a middle class group where 70% voted for the Conservative party and a working class group of whom 70% voted for Labour, two groups which together represented no more than a quarter of the electorate. The faithful working class supporters of the Labour party were those who rented council homes, had at least one member of the family in a trade union, with either husband or wife working in the mining or manufacturing industries rather than the transport or service industries. By contrast, the middle class group that voted in large numbers for the Conservatives owned their own home and had no connection with any trade union. Conservative support in the middle class was weakest where there was some union tie, where people did not own their own home and had a reasonable, but not a good, standard of living. Of those, many supported the Labour rather than the Conservative party. The section of the working class from which the Conservatives drew their strongest support were non-unionized workers owning their own home and enjoying at least a moderate standard of living.

## Social versus cognitive determinants of vote choice

To examine the relative contribution of social and cognitive determinants, we carried out a second discriminant analysis including measures of attitudes as well as measures of social determinants. Adding measures of attitudes improved accuracy of prediction quite substantially, on a par with that achieved when classifying vote choice using attitudes alone. *Social data* per se *made hardly any contribution* (see Table 6.1).

These findings lend little support to the view originally expressed by Campbell and his colleagues in the 1960s, that "people think politically as they are socially" (Pomper, 1975). The reasoning behind this statement is that individuals become attached to the groups they join and follow their party preferences without necessarily sharing their views. If this had been the case, adding the individuals' cognitions should have made little difference.

Nor do people in the same social class group tend to hold similar views. If they did, our attempt to classify the 1979 sample in terms of their social class position, using their attitudes as independent variables, would have met with success. It did not. Only 41% were correctly identified using those attitudes to issues which had successfully differentiated between the voters for the three parties.

IMPLICATIONS

We have shown the extent to which the social basis of support for the Labour and Conservative parties has slipped over time, and that within any one social class there are great variations in the political views of its members. And it is these views on issues and party leaders that account for more than twice as much of the variance as all the social and economic characteristics (Särlvik and Crewe, 1983).

We have also seen that the Labour party in 1983 was no longer *the* party of the working class but only of a dwindling section of it; the working class ranges more freely across the political spectrum. It is too early to tell whether the accelerated defection from the Labour party in 1983 reflects a continuing trend begun in 1979 or a reaction to the 1983 election campaign, where Labour had the misfortune of an unpopular leader and displayed a disastrous lack of unity among its higher echelons right up to polling day.

That political views should play a far more dominant role than social characteristics fits nicely into our model of vote choice. It also says something of considerable significance about the electorate as a whole. It puts to rest many of the popular beliefs here and abroad about the stranglehold that class has on British society, and about the loyalty that each party can expect from individuals belonging to social groups which were originally closely associated with the respective parties.

In Chapter 3 we showed that parties have more difficulty in capturing the individual voter's support now that they cannot rely as much as formerly on strong party attachment. Here we show that the social bases of the parties' electoral support have also been substantially weakened. The political landscape is as ill defined and bewildering for the parties anxious to capture votes as it is for the voters seeking reliable guidelines. Both parties and voters have to focus increasingly on current concerns rather than rely on former loyalties.

# 7

# The life history
of issues: Attitude and
vote change

So far we have shown a close correspondence between individuals' reactions to issues and their vote choice. What is still lacking is evidence that the causal chain goes from attitude to vote rather than from past vote to attitudes, with individuals adjusting their reactions to those of the party *because* they have voted for it. To help establish the direction of the causal chain, we need to look at how attitudes and in particular attitude change relate to vote change. We shall first report on the analyses we carried out on the longitudinal sample, and then draw on the British election studies (Särlvik and Crewe, 1983).

The terms *attitudinal fit* and *attitude shift* are used frequently in this chapter. Each has been measured in a special way. Measures of an individual's *attitudinal fit* to each of the three parties is derived from the discriminant analysis procedure described in Chapter 5. Discriminant analysis allows one to determine how closely a voter's complex of attitudes matches or "fits" the mean profile of attitudes of Conservative, Labour and Liberal voters respectively. For each individual, using his or her attitudes, it calculates the likelihood of belonging to the Conservative, Labour and Liberal group of voters. These likelihood measures are called *posterior probabilities*: for each voter three posterior probabilities are obtained, one for each party, which together add up to unity. We have interpreted these measures as measures of *attitudinal fit*: the greater the probability of membership to a category of voters, the more closely the individual's attitudes resemble (or fit) the mean profile of the voters in that group. Measures of *attitude shift* were obtained by subtracting from the three posterior probabilities of the 1970 discriminant analysis the corresponding posterior probabilities of the 1974 analysis. The larger the difference between two probabilities of voting for a particular party, the greater the shift.

## Attitudinal fit and vote loyalty

On the basis of our model, the closer the individual's attitudes fit those of the majority voting for his party, the more likely he or she should be to vote for that party on the next occasion. Our prediction was confirmed (Table 7.1A). Dividing each group of voters in the 1970 election into those with good attitudinal fit (with a posterior probability of above $0 \cdot 50$) and the remainder, we found 74% of those with good fit voted for the same party in October 1974 compared with only 54% of those with poor fit.

TABLE 7.1A                                                                              *Longit. study*

Defection by attitudinal fit, 1970

|  |  | Vote 1974 | | |
| --- | --- | --- | --- | --- |
|  |  | Same as 1970 (remained) | Not same as 1970 (defected) | $n$ |
| Attitude | over $0 \cdot 5$ | 74% | 26% | 109 |
| fit 1970 | under $0 \cdot 5$ | 54% | 46% | 54 |

$x^2 = 6 \cdot 29$, df = 1, $p < 0 \cdot 02$

TABLE 7.1B                                                                              *Longit. study*

Defection by attitudinal fit, 1970, *stable* voters only

|  |  | Vote 1974 | | |
| --- | --- | --- | --- | --- |
|  |  | Same as 1970 (remained) | Not same as 1970 (defected) | $n$ |
| Attitude | over $0 \cdot 5$ | 82% | 18% | 72 |
| fit 1970 | under $0 \cdot 5$ | 60% | 40% | 30 |

$x^2 = 4 \cdot 39$, df = 1, $p < 0 \cdot 05$

For a more rigorous test of the prediction, we took only consistent voters, i.e. those who had voted for the same party throughout (Table 7.1B). Even in this group attitudinal fit made a difference. Those with poor fit were more likely to defect (40% compared with 18%). (The probability of obtaining such results by chance was less than $0 \cdot 05$.)

If the causal direction is from attitude to vote one would expect that attitudinal fit measures could be used, in addition to past voting record, to predict not only whether an individual will defect from the party he had voted for last time, but also the direction this defection will take. We therefore carried out a discriminant analysis to classify the sample in terms of their October 1974 vote on the basis of six predictor variables: three scores, each representing the number of times

TABLE 7.2                                                              *Longit. study*

Discriminant analysis prediction of vote 1974 from cumulative vote until 1970 and attitudinal fit in 1970

|              |      | Predicted vote | | | | |
|--------------|------|-----|-----|-----|-----|-----|
|              |      | Con | Lab | Lib | %   | n   |
| Actual vote  | Con  | 79  | 1   | 20  | 100 | 70  |
|              | Lab  | 2   | 85  | 12  | 100 | 41  |
|              | Lib  | 35  | 15  | 50  | 100 | 46  |

Overall correct prediction — 72%

the individual had in the past voted for each of the three parties, plus the three posterior probabilities from the 1970 discriminant analysis. The results were promising in two ways. Not only was the overall classification of 72% very satisfactory, with 79% of Conservatives, 85% of Labour and 50% of Liberal voters correctly identified, but also the variables which entered the prediction first, that is those which discriminated best between the voters, were, as we had predicted, the attitude fit measures and not the individual's past voting record (Table 7.2).

## Attitude shift and vote change

Shifts in attitude should lead to change in vote, provided the shift is significant enough to bring the individual's views closer to the views of those voting for a different party. For instance, someone once very much in favour of comprehensive schools whose enthusiasm has waned, may still hold views which fit better overall within the Labour rather than the Conservative party. On the other hand, someone who started out with middle-of-the-road attitudes which he then moderates still further, might find his revised attitudes more in tune with a party different from the one for which he had originally voted.

Consequently, having information about a person's *attitude shift* as well as about *initial attitude fit* should increase accuracy of classification of future vote. We investigated this through a discriminant analysis classifying voters in terms of their October 1974 vote, this time using nine predictors: three scores indicating propensity to vote for each of the three parties, three 1970 posterior probabilities and three shift scores representing the difference between the posterior probabilities obtained in 1970 and in 1974. The proportion of voters correctly classified was now 81% with as many as 93% of Labour voters correctly identified. For the first time, the Liberals were well predicted (69%).

In examining the order in which the predictor variables entered the step-wise discriminant analysis we found, as expected, that attitudinal fit entered first as the more powerful predictor, followed by attitudinal shift, with the individual's voting history playing a lesser role. Omitting voting history altogether and using only the measures of attitude fit and attitude shift reduced the proportion of voters correctly classified by only 4%. Details are given in Appendix 3, Table 13A, B.

If one's aim were to predict simply which individual will remain loyal or defect, attitude shift should play the decisive role and therefore enter the discriminant equation first. To test this, we divided our voters into two groups: those who voted the same way in 1970 and 1974 (regardless of the party for which they voted), and those who changed their vote in any way at all. A step-wise multiple regression yielded a multiple correlation of 0·47, accounting for 22% of the variance. As expected, all three shift scores entered the prediction equation first.

The picture presented so far is a very coherent one. It points to the importance of attitude fit to a party in influencing subsequent vote and to the significance of attitude change, allied to that initial fit, in predicting whether the individual will vote the same way or defect on a subsequent occasion.

TABLE 7.3                                                                                       *Longit. study*

Multiple regressions predicting change of vote 1970–1974 from change in four summary measures of attitudes 1970–1974[a]

| Groups to be predicted | Multiple correlation | First variable[b] entered in equation | Second variable entered in equation |
|---|---|---|---|
| Away from Con 1970 | 0·29 | Liberalism | Economic class relations |
| Away from Lab 1970 | 0·46 | Economic class relations | Selective education |
| Away from Lib 1970 | 0·40 | Economic class relations | Selective education |
| To Con 1974 | 0·37 | Economic class relations | Selective education |
| To Lab 1974 | 0·42 | Liberalism | Selective education |
| To Lib 1974 | 0·23 | Selective education | Economic class relations |

[a] Summary measures of attitudes to: (1) Economic class relations (attitudes to trade unions, strikes, and big business); (2) liberal issues (immigration, law and order); (3) selective education (grammar, comprehensive and public schools); (4) welfare (more spending on social services, concern about abuse of welfare).

[b] The two variables which added most to the prediction in order of importance.

It is equally important to know, for each type of voter separately, which issues contributed to the prediction of change. Using attitude measures obtained in 1970 and again in 1974, we computed for each voter four scores consisting of the sum of reactions to issues within the same domain.[1] A high score indicated answers in the Conservative direction, a low score in the Labour direction. We used the *difference* between the 1970 and 1974 score for each voter in multiple regression analyses to predict, separately for Liberal, Labour and Conservative voters:

[1] The four measures were: economic class relations (management–employee relations; attitudes to trade unions, strikes, secret ballots for strikes and control of big business); liberal outlook (attitudes to immigration, immigrants, law and order); selective education (comprehensive, public and grammar schools) and welfare (spend more on social services, concern over abuse of welfare).

*movement away* from the party for which they voted in 1970; and *movement towards* the party for which they voted in 1974. Table 7.3 shows that movement away from Conservatives was less well predicted than movement away from the other parties and, as one would expect, movement towards a different party was least well predicted for the Liberals.

In Chapter 5 we showed that attitudes to selective education, to trade unions and to big business predicted vote best. The analyses presented here, which use only scores indexing *shift* in attitude on these issues, further underline their importance, for it was changes in these two areas which best predicted movement away from, and towards, a given party. There was just one interesting exception, concerning movement away from Conservatives in 1970 and towards Labour in 1974. There a shift in attitudes towards liberalization of the law and immigration proved the most useful predictor. This was primarily because Mr Heath's 1970 election campaign was fought on the issue of who governs, with great emphasis being laid by the Conservative party upon the need for forceful leadership and the issue of law and order, including strengthening the power of the police.

## The social context of attitude and vote change: 1962–1974

Nine of the issues about which we asked voters for their attitudes in 1962 were repeated in 1970 and 1974. The questions dealt with views on issues concerning trade unions, selective schooling, liberalization of the law, immigration, management–employee relations and EEC membership. The repetition of these questions allowed us to look for changes in our sample's reactions to these particular issues over a period of 12 years during which much had happened in the country and to the people themselves. We investigated the relation of changes in individual voters' reactions about issues to changes in both the society and their own personal circumstances, as well as relating change in outlook to change in vote over the same period.

In the period between 1962 and 1974 capital punishment was abolished and the laws on homosexuality made less severe. New thoughts on selective schooling evolved with schools becoming more of a political issue. In 1971, Britain joined the EEC. With increasing numbers of immigrants (especially coloured immigrants) restrictions on entry tightened up and debates about immigration and the immigrants became more frequent and more heated. The early 1970s also saw an increase in confrontations between labour and management culminating in the miners' strike of 1974.

There were significant changes over time in the men's reactions to seven of the nine issues we studied. From 1962 to 1970, the men became more liberal in their outlook, while between 1970 and 1974 their attitudes remained the same or even became slightly more conservative. In response to the liberalization of the laws on homosexuality, many more came to agree that it was right to make the laws less severe (from 30% agreeing in 1962 to 68% agreeing in 1970). The sample's response to the abolition of capital punishment was more variable: the mean score did not change, but the variability of scores around the mean increased.

Despite the tightening of the laws on immigration, although the wish for more restrictions remained unchanged the men's attitude toward the behaviour of immigrants already in the country became significantly less prejudiced, particularly between 1962 and 1970. Management–employee relations were perceived as better in 1970 than in 1962, although the somewhat mistrustful attitudes towards trade unions remained. In the early 1970s which were leaner times economically, the number of strikes increased, with the country nearly brought to a standstill by the miners' strike in 1974. Not surprisingly, voters in 1974 saw relations between management and employees as full of conflict, with attitudes to trade unions becoming more negative.

In line with the changing attitude, at least of Labour politicians, to entry into the EEC, attitudes to the Common Market fluctuated considerably. Although initially favourable in 1962, by 1970 more of our sample were uncertain or opposed to Britain's entry. After three years' experience of being in the Common Market and perhaps also in response to the publicity leading up to the Referendum, the sample reverted to the more positive position they had held in 1962.

The secondary school system gained prominence as a political issue in the later 1960s. While many were opposed to or had no views on comprehensive schools in 1962 (30% had no views), by 1970 views had crystallized and attitudes had become more favourable, only to cool off again by 1974. The changes of attitudes toward public schools followed a complementary trend. The men were largely neutral on the issue in 1962, moved a little towards favouring the abolition of public schools by 1970, only to be opposed to their abolition four years later.

Not only did the individuals' attitudes change over time but the inter-relationship of responses changed as well. In 1962 schools were not an important political issue, and attitudes to comprehensive schools were not strongly correlated with attitudes to public schools ($r = 0 \cdot 12$) nor, indeed, with attitudes to other political issues. By 1970, schools had gained prominence as a political issue. As a result, attitudes to comprehensive and to public schools moved towards a closer (inverse) relationship ($r = - 0 \cdot 44$) and both, in turn, correlated with responses to other political issues. With the change during the 1960s of the relevant laws, homosexual practices among consenting adults became less an issue of public concern and the strength of the relation of this attitude to attitudes concerning capital punishment and immigrants decreased considerably by 1974.[2]

Class differences in attitudes were less clear-cut than one might have expected[3]

[2]In 1962 the correlations with attitudes to capital punishment and to immigrants were $0 \cdot 27$ and $0 \cdot 29$. By 1974 the correlations were $0 \cdot 14$ and $0 \cdot 19$.
[3]Although the middle classes were more in favour of joining the EEC and more opposed to trade unions than the working class, attitudes to selective schools were not as well defined. In 1962, it was the stable upper middle class who were least sure about comprehensive schools while everyone else was opposed to their establishment. By 1970 the balance had shifted with the middle classes more opposed than the working class, although this difference diminished in 1974, largely because the working class had become less favourably inclined.

and the men who were socially mobile during the 1960s and early 1970s did not appear to have changed their attitudes in line with their new status. Rather, their attitudes were more aligned with those of the social status group to which they had belonged in their early twenties.[4]

The pattern of results just outlined, far from supporting any "pure habit" or purely behavioural social learning theory of voting where attitudes espoused should be a corollary of one's class status or of one's voting behaviour, points once again to the important, mediating position of attitudes in determining vote.

## Change in party preference 1964–1974 and change in attitudes to trade unions and selective schooling

We selected three issues which our research had shown to be important predictors of vote — attitudes to trade unions, comprehensive and public schools — in order to discover whether individuals who had changed their party preference changed their views about these issues more than stable voters for the same party. We made two comparisons. The first, shown in Fig. 7.1, compares for each party those who *defected* between 1964 and 1974 with those who remained. The second comparison (Fig. 7.2) is by party "of arrival" and compares those who in 1974 *converted* to each of the three parties with the respective stable voters.

*Defections:* On the issue of selective schooling, those who defected from the Conservatives became more, and those who defected from Labour less, favourable toward comprehensive schools compared with the stable voters of the party from which they came. The same pattern was repeated for attitudes to public schools. On trade unions, too, the picture was as predicted — those who defected from Labour were more, and those who defected from the Conservatives less, critical than their stable counterparts.

The picture was less clear for *conversions* to Conservatives or Labour, except for attitudes to comprehensive schools where those who moved to the Conservative camp became more opposed to them while those who moved to the Labour camp became more disposed in their favour.

---

[4]To examine the effect of social mobility, we first divided the sample into five groups: three groups whose job status had not changed between 1962 and 1974 and who were holding upper middle class, lower middle class or working class jobs respectively; and two upwardly mobile groups who had moved between 1962 and 1974 either from lower middle to upper middle or from working class to middle class jobs. We then employed a repeated measures two-way (groups × times) analysis of variance which enabled us to investigate whether there were differences over time in the attitudes of the sample as a whole and, further, whether these varied depending on the social status and social mobility of the subjects. The results are summarized in Appendix 3, Fig. 1.

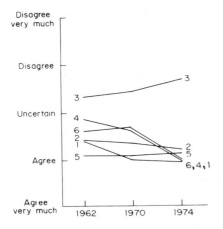

(a)    The way they are run now, trade unions
       do this county more harm than good

GROUPS
1. Consistent Conservatives
2. Con 1962; not Con 1974
3. Consistent Labour
4. Lab 1962; not Lab 1974
5. Consistent Liberals
6. Lib 1962; not Lib 1974

(b)    For establishment of comprehensive schools     (c)    Public schools    should be abolished
       (in 1974 changed to "more comprehensive
       schools should be established")

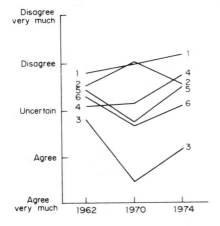

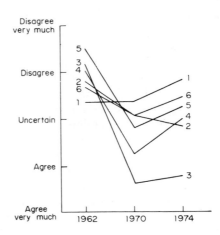

Fig. 7.1. Changes in attitudes over 12 years of *consistent* voters and those who *defected* (voting
for the party in 1962, but not in 1974) (longitudinal study).

Significant differences from two-way repeated measures analysis of variance:
(a) Groups: $p < 0.001$; Time: $p < 0.007$; Interaction: $p < 0.08$.
(b) Groups: $p < 0.001$; Time: $p < 0.001$; Interaction: $p < 0.001$.
(c) Groups: $p < 0.001$; Time: $p < 0.001$; Interaction: $p < 0.001$.

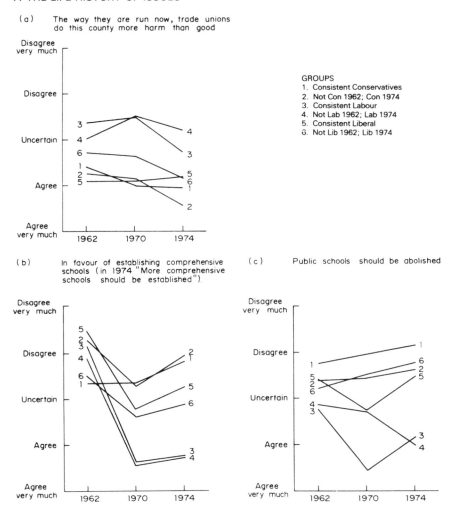

Fig. 7.2. Changes in attitude over 12 years of *consistent* party voters and those who *moved* to the party (voting for it in 1974, but not in 1962) (longitudinal study).

Significant differences from two way repeated measures analysis of variance:
(a) Groups $p<0.001$; Time: N/S; Interaction: $p<0.10$.
(b) Group: $p<0.001$; Time: N/S; Interaction: $p<0.001$.
(c) Groups: $p<0.001$; Time: $p<0.001$; Interaction: $p<0.001$.

## Opinion and vote change in the British election studies

Särlvik and Crewe (1983) present a rich description of the prevailing climate of opinion in the late 1970s and examine in detail the relationship between issues and vote change. Their analysis is complementary to our own, extending the study of the life history of issues to 1979. Despite using a different methodology to ours, they arrive at similar conclusions about the relationship of opinions to change in vote.

The Conservative party in 1979 offered an alternative economic strategy as an answer to the economic ills of the day. Särlvik and Crewe first discuss how shifts in opinion on economic issues could have contributed to the Conservative upsurge. They then pose the question of whether the Conservative victory was due not just to shifts in opinion on the economic issues, but also to a more general shift to the right among the electorate as a whole as a reaction to the rapid social and cultural changes of the previous decade.

The evidence the authors present is convincing. Much of the electorate was sceptical about the changes brought about by the permissive society. On issues ranging from the treatment of lawbreakers, the prevalence of pornography, to children's schooling and racial and sexual equality, the prevailing climate of opinion was moderately conservative rather than liberal or even radical. Between 1974 and 1979, there was a further move to the right on five of the seven opinions for which the authors had comparable measures. These included the availability of welfare benefits, changes in teaching methods and the reduction in Britain's military strength. On specific policy alternatives, the public also moved to the right, particularly with regard to nationalization and social welfare provisions. On these issues at least, Särlvik and Crewe found most of the electorate in the 1979 election to hold Conservative views, differing only in the degree to which they endorsed them.

The relation of opinion to vote change was examined in two ways. The authors first presented a detailed report on which particular issues contributed to vote change by examining the propensity to switch among voters in 1974 who were dissatisfied with their party's current position.

> For the Conservatives' and Labour's 1974 supporters the tendency was clear: those who sided with the other major party on an issue in 1979 were the most likely to change their votes; those whose 1979 opinions were in line with their 1974 party choice were the least likely to change. (pp. 251–252)

Their second approach was to compare divisions of opinion among party changers and stable votes, using a "balance of opinion" measure that indicated the extent to which the distribution of opinion on a particular issue was relatively more in favour of Conservative or Labour views. Among a number of interesting findings was the following:

> The balance of opinion on almost all issues among voters who switched away from the Conservative and Labour parties differed distinctively from the opinions of the remaining supporters of the party they switched from; and the farther they switched, the more they differed. Thus, for example, Conservatives who changed to Liberal were clearly less in favour of their party's stand on the issues than were the stable voters; but those who changed to Labour were even less likely to support Conservative policies and even more likely to side with Labour. (p. 255)

TABLE 7.4                                                                 *BES panel 1974–'79*

Defection of voter in 1979 by attitudinal fit to party voted for in Oct. 1974. Attitudinal
fit to (A) Liking of party, (B) Evaluation of party leaders, and (C) Attitudes to issues

| Attitudinal fit measures | Vote 1974 | | | |
| | Vote 1979 same | | Vote 1979 different | |
| | 1974 Attitude fit | | 1974 Attitude fit | |
| | good[a] | poor[b] | good[a] | poor[a] |
|---|---|---|---|---|
| A. Liking for parties | 84% | 58% | 16% | 42% |
| B. Evaluation of party leaders | 84% | 70% | 16% | 30% |
| C. Attitudes to issues | 82% | 69% | 18% | 31% |

[a]Good attitudinal fit denotes a posterior probability of 0·50 or above; poor attitudinal fit a posterior
probability of less than 0·50.

To see how far our findings (see page 94) that those with poor attitudinal fit
to the party for which they had voted were more likely to defect next time round
held for the electorate as a whole, we repeated the same analyses on the BES
1974–1979 panel. That survey made it possible not only to develop a measure
of attitudinal fit with regard to evaluation of issues but also two other measures,
one on liking for the three parties and the second on liking for the party leaders.
Our findings were confirmed. Table 7.4 shows that those with poor attitudinal
fit on any of the three measures were more likely to defect next time round,
compared with those with good attitudinal fit to the modal outlook of voters for
the party in 1974.

## Summary and implications

This chapter has explored the impact of attitudes and change of attitudes on vote
change in various ways. The weight of evidence suggests a causal link from
attitudes to vote and from attitude shift to change of vote. Using our own study
and the BES 1974–1979 panel study, we demonstrate that if an individual's
opinions do not closely fit those of the majority of voters for the party for which
he or she has voted, defection at the next election is more likely.

By examining in some detail changes in the outlook of the sample to such issues
as the Common Market, liberalization of the law, immigration, labour relations,
trade unions and selective schools, over a period of 12 years, we have also shown
that *attitude shift* is an appropriate, and not a random, reaction to the profound
changes that have occurred in society.

The debate about "genuine" attitudes and superficial or random responses,
referred to in Chapter 5, has centred for too long on an unwarranted assumption
that the consistent voters are those who have real attitudes. Given the inevitable
gulf between theory and practice, it seems natural that people should gain new

insights (and not everyone the same insight) from seeing a policy implemented which they have either favoured or opposed. If such insights were diverse, one would expect low correlations between one time period and another; in our case they were high between 1970 and 1974 and relatively low between 1962 and 1970. This was not only because the latter represented an eight rather than a four-year period but because up to 1970 changes in society were more marked on a wider variety of issues than between 1970 and 1974.

In order to decide whether an individual's views are genuinely held at a given period in time, the views should, where appropriate, find expression in behaviour. We have shown that this is so by being able to distinguish defectors from stable voters and by predicting very satisfactorily the direction of vote change. Those whose views changed the most tended also to change their vote, moving to a party more in tune with their changed outlook than the one for which they had voted so far, indicating the importance of matching views, and changes in these views, to what is happening in society.

# 8

# Perceptions and evaluations of parties' stands

The key link between attitudes and voting is the set of beliefs one holds concerning the parties' stands on various political issues. In deciding which way to vote it is not enough to be in favour of abolishing grammar schools: it is also necessary to know which party is most likely to implement such a policy.

Many political scientists have stressed the importance of a shared perception of parties' or candidates' stands. The mathematical model of electoral process proposed by Davis *et al.* (1970), for example, assumes that all citizens make identical estimates of a candidate's issue position. Merrin and LeBlank (1979) state:

> A finding that issues are an important component of the voting calculus carries with it the implication that the cause of democracy is thereby served. The voters would be deciding not simply between competing candidates for office, but between alternative courses of governmental action. *This would be the case, however, only if it is also found that voters agree on where the parties and the candidates stand on the issues and then match their attitudes with the objects of their issue concern.* (p. 65) (Our italics)

Rational choice models do not of necessity require that individuals be highly informed and accurate concerning parties' or candidates' positions. However, they *do* require that voters perceive *differences* between parties, and be able to locate these positions relative to their own and further that these social cognitions be shared by the electorate, irrespective of their own preferences. Evidence as to the voter's ability to make these differentiations has been conflicting. Campbell *et al.* (1960) found that in 1956 American voters were hardly aware of differences between parties on various issues. Even when the authors limited their sample to the "informed" segment of the population (i.e. those who held an opinion on a given issue) only 40% to 60% perceived any differences between the parties. The exceptions were issues to do with the New Deal where there was relative consensus about the parties' position.

Pomper (1975) and other investigators noted a growing political awareness in the American electorate during the period between 1956 and 1972. In Britain,

Butler and Stokes (1974) found that perception of party differences and agreement about their policies varied widely depending on the issue. In 1964, the Labour party was overwhelmingly acknowledged to be the party more likely to extend nationalization, with the gap between the proportion of the sample naming Labour and that naming the Conservative party as large as 84%, but on the issue of the Common Market it was only 22%. Differences over time were also apparent. In 1964, 69% of the electorate named Labour as the party more likely to spend more on pensions and social services. By 1970, only 48% did so. The proportion who found few differences between the parties on this topic had increased from 16% in 1964 to 29% in 1970.

How far was this due to a growing consensus on the part of the parties or how far to the tendency of voters to project their own views about policies they like on to the party they prefer? The degree to which projection of one's views can distort perception is indicated by Page and Brody's (1972) finding that in 1968 Republicans who were extreme doves in relation to the Vietnam war even saw Nixon as holding a similar view. Such bias does not operate as a general phenomenon.

Fishbein and Coombs (1974) showed that, among American voters, on many issues, though not all, perceptions of the parties' stands (in terms of Democratic, Republican and Independent candidates' positions) were relatively unaffected by respondents' party choices. Similarly, in a study of British voters in 1974, Fishbein et al. (1976) found that on most policy issues Conservative, Labour and Liberal voters were in relative agreement about the substantive positions taken by the three parties. Only with regard to broader issues, such as the likelihood of improving the economy, was there a systematic bias with voters believing that their party was better able to resolve these problems than the other parties.

In this chapter we consider first the views of our longitudinal sample on 21 policy issues and their perception of the parties' readiness to implement these policies were they to come to power in the October 1974 election. The 21 policy issues had been selected because they featured in one or other party manifesto or else had been given prominence in the media. We then explore voters' perceptions of parties' policy proposals in the 1974, 1979 and 1983 elections.

In the next chapter we show how individuals combine their views on policy issues and their perceptions of the parties positions on these issues in deciding which party to support.

## Evaluation of policies

In 1974, voters were asked to evaluate each of 21 key issues:

People differ in their views about the value of policies which have been suggested to help the country's problems. Please tick for each policy how *you* see it.

Table 8.1 presents the mean evaluations of each policy issue for the Conservative, Labour and Liberal voters in the 1974 election. Not surprisingly there were differences in the voters' views on many of the policy issues. For example, nationalizing building land was evaluated positively by Labour voters but negatively by Conservatives. Conservatives were in favour of keeping a private health service while Labour voters were opposed. Four policy issues, which are called *consensus* issues, were judged equally desirable by all voters. These were: stop unemployment rising; keep prices from rising too fast; make British industry more efficient; and hold mortgage rates down.[1]

A factor analysis of the voters' attitudes to the 21 issues yielded two factors. One factor represented the four *consensus* issues mentioned above, and the other, the 17 *non-consensus* or *policy* issues which were differently evaluated by the three groups of voters. Butler and Stokes (1974) call the former *valence* and the latter *position* issues.


TABLE 8.1                                                          *Longit. study*

Mean evaluation of 21 issues by Conservative, Labour and Liberal voters (October 1974)

| The issues | Con | Lab | Lib |
|---|---|---|---|
| *Non-consensus issues* | | | |
| 1.  Abolish grammar schools | 4·52 | 2·39 | 3·78 |
| 2.  Trust trade unions | 3·60 | 2·24 | 3·50 |
| 3.  Subsidize foods | 3·45 | 2·12 | 3·22 |
| 4.  Bring companies into public ownership | 4·48 | 2·34 | 4·07 |
| 5.  Spend more on social services | 2·78 | 2·17 | 2·61 |
| 6.  Heavier taxing of the wealthy | 3·42 | 1·93 | 3·00 |
| 7.  Enforce equal pay for women | 2·51 | 1·85 | 2·28 |
| 8.  Nationalize building land | 4·10 | 1·76 | 3·63 |
| 9.  Worker participation in industry | 2·53 | 1·93 | 2·24 |
| 10. Reduce company taxes | 2·29 | 3·12 | 2·35 |
| 11. Keep private health service | 2·02 | 3·90 | 2·59 |
| 12. Sell council houses to tenants | 1·83 | 3·24 | 2·26 |
| 13. Ensure Britain remains in EEC | 1·96 | 2·88 | 2·26 |
| 14. Cut social security benefits to strikers | 1·54 | 3·37 | 1·94 |
| 15. Control wage increases | 2·35 | 3·10 | 2·46 |
| 16. Encourage immigrants to return to home country | 2·66 | 3·00 | 2·89 |
| 17. Reform electoral system | 2·52 | 2·56 | 1·85 |
| | | | |
| *Consensus issues* | | | |
| 18. Stop unemployment rising | 1·98 | 1·54 | 1·80 |
| 19. Keep prices from rising too fast | 1·52 | 1·44 | 1·63 |
| 20. Hold mortgage rates down | 1·78 | 1·90 | 1·76 |
| 21. Make British industry more efficient | 1·21 | 1·27 | 1·26 |

Scores range from 1 ( = very good) to 5 ( = very bad).


[1]The issues were presented in a mixed order in the questionnaire, but have been rearranged in Table 8.1 to separate clearly consensus and non-consensus issues.

## Perception of parties' stands

The respondents were also asked to indicate for each issue in turn:

How likely would *each* of the three parties (Conservative, Labour, Liberal) have been to introduce the policies listed below had they won. Place a tick in the right column for *each party*.

(The five columns for each party read: "very likely", "likely", "in between", "unlikely", "very unlikely".)

All voters agreed that the Labour party was most likely (highest mean score), and the Conservative party least likely (lowest mean score) to abolish grammar schools, to trust trade unions, to bring companies into public ownership, to spend more on social services, to endorse heavier taxing of the wealthy, to enforce equal pay for women, to nationalize building land, and to create more worker participation. The Conservatives were seen by voters for all three parties as more likely than Labour to reduce company taxes, to keep a private health service, to sell council houses to tenants, to cut social security to strikers, to control wage increases, to encourage immigrants to return to their home countries and to ensure that Britain remained in the EEC. Liberals were seen as most likely to reform the electoral system. There was a striking agreement by all voters concerning the different parties' stands on the 17 policy issues.

There were only six issues on which there were differences in the way the voters of the three parties perceived a particular party's stand. In all six cases (marked by asterisks in Table 8.2) the differences were such that supporters of a party considered their party to be *less* likely to pursue policies to which it was committed in its manifesto than did the voters for other parties, and, conversely that the supported party was seen as less *unlikely* to pursue policies itself to which *other* parties were committed. Voters tended to see their own party as more flexible and "moderate", and the opposing parties as more dogmatic or extremist.

Turning to the four *consensus* policies (stopping unemployment rising; keeping prices from rising too fast, holding mortgage rates down; and making British industry more efficient), we find an entirely different picture. First of all, the voters were sceptical about the capability of any of the three parties to implement these policies. All parties were judged to be relatively unlikely to solve these problems, as can be seen from the high mean scores in this section of Table 8.2.

Yet within these *limits of inability*, there were systematic biases in voters' perceptions of the parties. Conservative and Labour voters saw their own parties as most likely (or rather as least unlikely) and the opposition as least likely to bring about the desired outcome.[2] Here we have evidence of the type of projection suggested by Markus and Converse (1979). The only agreement had to do with the in-between position assigned to the Liberals. On three out of the four issues,

---

[2]In some cases (marked by asterisks in Table 8.2) the differences were not only in ordering of the three parties but also in the degree to which each party was believed likely to implement a consensus policy.

the Liberal voters themselves concurred. Only in "making industry more efficient" did the Liberals consider their own party best.

## Evidence from representative studies

In the British election studies of October 1974 and 1979, respondents made judgments about the parties in a number of ways. For three *consensus issues*, concerning rising prices, strikes, and unemployment, they made retrospective assessments, i.e. indicated how well they thought the party in power had handled the issue and how well the opposition would have handled it had they been in power. For seven *non-consensus issues*, including nationalization, social services and relations to the EEC, respondents were presented with a scale of differing opinion positions on the issue and asked to indicate which view came closest to the Conservative party's position and which view closest to the Labour party's position. The same scale of opinion positions was used to obtain the voters' own views.

In the 1979 survey, Särlvik and Crewe included additional questions on policy proposals to do with taxation, unemployment, incomes policy, trade union legislation, Britain's relationship with the EEC, immigration and race relations. Respondents indicated their own policy preferences and also which of two policy alternatives for each issue came closest to the Conservative party's view and, in a separate question, which came closest to the Labour party's view.

Although the format of the questions concerning voters' own views and their perceptions of the parties' stands on the issues differed widely from those used in the longitudinal study, the distinction between consensus and non-consensus issues can still be made. On consensus items the findings were the same: in 1974 and 1979 Conservative and Labour voters saw their own party as better able to handle the problems of strikes, unemployment and inflation but once again were sceptical about any party's ability to make much of a difference. Särlvik and Crewe (1983) note that voters' confidence in their own party's ability was "tellingly qualified" (p.157).

Examples of non-consensus items were nationalization, trade union legislation the expansion or retrenchment of social services, and policy alternatives for job creation . On these non-consensus issues, voters of different parties disagreed as far as their own views were concerned, but agreed with one another on the relative positions taken by the Conservative and Labour parties.

Särlvik and Crewe noted that there were three issues on which the parties had changed their positions between elections or where the parties' stands on the issues were ambiguous. These were: incomes policy, Britain's role in the EEC, and race relations and immigration. On these issues there were hardly any differences in the voters' opinion according to their own party preference, but there was less (often far less) agreement concerning the relative positions of the Conservative and Labour parties. A comparatively large section of the voters was either unable to identify the parties' positions or saw no difference between them.

TABLE 8.2                                                              *Longit. study*

Mean perception by Conservative, Labour and Liberal voters of the perceived likelihood
of each policy being implemented by each of the three parties if they won

| The issues | The voters | Perception of the implementation by each party | | |
|---|---|---|---|---|
| | | Con | Lib | Lab |
| *Non-consensus issues* | | | | |
| 1. Abolish grammar schools | Con | 4·67 | 3·51 | 1·25 |
| | Lab | 4·68 | 3·70 | 1·88* |
| | Lib | 4·62 | 3·60 | 1·42 |
| 2. Trust trade unions | Con | 4·02 | 3·50 | 1·36 |
| | Lab | 4·25 | 3·48 | 1·78 |
| | Lib | 4·24 | 3·64 | 1·71 |
| 3. Subsidize foods | Con | 3·27 | 2·88 | 1·36 |
| | Lab | 3·78 | 3·13 | 1·58 |
| | Lib | 3·67 | 3·07 | 1·47 |
| 4. Bring companies into public ownership | Con | 4·25 | 3·45 | 1·35 |
| | Lab | 4·53 | 3·90 | 1·50 |
| | Lib | 4·60 | 3·84 | 1·38 |
| 5. Spend more on social services | Con | 2·46 | 2·31 | 1·68 |
| | Lab | 3·38 | 2·68 | 1·70* |
| | Lib | 2·98 | 2·47 | 1·60 |
| 6. Heavier taxing of the wealthy | Con | 3·91 | 2·83 | 1·35 |
| | Lab | 4·45 | 3·43 | 1·63 |
| | Lib | 4·11 | 3·04 | 1·73 |
| 7. Enforce equal pay for women | Con | 2·66 | 2·33 | 2·13 |
| | Lab | 3·15 | 2·60 | 1·88* |
| | Lib | 2·87 | 2·44 | 2·13 |
| 8. Nationalize building land | Con | 4·56 | 3·43 | 1·39 |
| | Lab | 4·78 | 3·80 | 1·53 |
| | Lib | 4·47 | 3·58 | 1·53 |
| 9. Create more worker participation | Con | 3·18 | 2·42 | 1·81 |
| | Lab | 3·98 | 2·30 | 1·85* |
| | Lib | 3·56 | 2·18 | 2·00 |
| 10. Reduce company taxes | Con | 2·18 | 2·68 | 3·85 |
| | Lab | 2·00 | 2·83 | 3·68 |
| | Lib | 2·11 | 2·67 | 3·82 |
| 11. Keep private health service | Con | 1·48 | 2·26 | 4·20 |
| | Lab | 1·43 | 2·00 | 3·43* |
| | Lib | 1·29 | 2·00 | 3·49 |
| 12. Sell council houses to tenants | Con | 1·65 | 2·35 | 4·15 |
| | Lab | 1·83 | 2·43 | 3·85 |
| | Lib | 1·96 | 2·42 | 3·85 |

TABLE 8.2 (*Continued*)

| The issues | The voters | Perception of the implementation by each party | | |
|---|---|---|---|---|
| | | Con | Lib | Lab |
| 13. Ensure Britain remains in EEC | Con | 1·32 | 1·87 | 2·80 |
| | Lab | 1·40 | 1·78 | 2·65 |
| | Lib | 1·36 | 1·53 | 2·62 |
| 14. Cut social security benefits to strikers | Con | 2·27 | 2·95 | 4·56 |
| | Lab | 1·73 | 2·80 | 4·18 |
| | Lib | 2·33 | 2·91 | 4·49 |
| 15. Control wage increases | Con | 2·14 | 2·18 | 3·86 |
| | Lab | 1·80 | 2·20 | 3·50 |
| | Lib | 2·00 | 2·04 | 3·82 |
| 16. Encourage immigrants to return to their home countries | Con | 3·39 | 3·79 | 3·95 |
| | Lab | 2·90 | 3·75 | 4·08* |
| | Lib | 3·29 | 3·51 | 3·84 |
| 17. Reform electoral system | Con | 3·68 | 1·44 | 4·00 |
| | Lab | 3·83 | 1·33 | 3·90 |
| | Lib | 4·09 | 1·53 | 4·29 |
| *Consensus issues* | | | | |
| 18. Stop unemployment rising | Con | 3·01 | 3·11 | 3·14 |
| | Lab | 4·10 | 3·18 | 2·10 | Con*[a] |
| | Lib | 3·62 | 2·89 | 2·73 | Lab* |
| 19. Keep prices from rising too fast | Con | 3·00 | 3·25 | 3·46 | Con* |
| | Lab | 4·05 | 3·30 | 2·65 | Lab* |
| | Lib | 3·51 | 3·11 | 2·93 | Lib* |
| 20. Hold mortgage rates down | Con | 2·07 | 2·64 | 3·08 |
| | Lab | 3·08 | 2·95 | 2·80 |
| | Lib | 2·56 | 2·60 | 3·00 | Con* |
| 21. Make British industry more efficient | Con | 2·25 | 2·61 | 3·43 | Con* |
| | Lab | 3:28 | 2·98 | 2·65 | Lab* |
| | Lib | 2·44 | 2·29 | 3·24 | Lib* |

Range: 1 = very likely, 5 = very unlikely.
*Indicates within a shared ordering that voters saw their own party as more flexible with regard to the implementation of the policy than did the voters of the opposing parties ($p0·05$).
[a]Where a party is named, this indicates that the ordering (as well as the flexibility within the ordering) differs depending on the voters' party choice.

On incomes policy and Britain's role in the EEC there was a tendency for voters to project their own views onto their preferred party. For example,

Conservative voters who themselves were in favour of incomes policy were more likely than others to believe that this was indeed the Conservative party's position on the matter, and those who were against were also particularly likely to believe that this was what the Conservative party stood for. (Särlvik and Crewe, 1983, p. 228)

On the issue of Britain's role in the EEC, in 1979 a third of the voters either perceived no differences between the parties' stands or were unsure on one or both positions. On immigration and race relations, the majority (61%) agreed that the Conservatives would be "tougher" than Labour, but as many as 30% either perceived no difference between the positions of the parties or else said they did not know where the parties stood. Little wonder since both parties had been at pains to downplay the issue!

A survey, conducted at the time of the 1983 election, brought further confirmation that the accuracy of perception of the parties stands varies with the issues and depends more on the party's ability or wish to spell out its position than on the voters' ability to perceive it. In a MORI poll conducted just before the election campaign began in 1983 the respondents were asked for their own views on 11 policies and also to identify the party associated with each policy (Worcester, 1983).

On widely publicized issues where the parties' stands were clearly stated, there was a high level of agreement in the perceptions of party policies among supporters of different parties. A majority of Conservative, Labour and Alliance supporters identified the basing of Cruise missiles in Britain as a Conservative policy and the cancellation of the decision to buy the Trident nuclear missile system as a Labour policy. Greater control over local council spending was also identified by the different supporters as a Conservative policy, while borrowing to finance an expansion of the economy was perceived by most as a Labour policy.

How far the voters' accuracy is affected by the explicitness of the parties was shown particularly clearly with regard to Britain's membership of the EEC. In the two previous elections Labour's stand had not been given wide publicity, in this election it had. Consequently in 1983 the Labour party was correctly identified as the party most likely to take Britain out of the Common Market, while in 1979 and 1974 a substantial proportion of the electorate had been unable to perceive any differences or did not know which party to select.

On less well publicized issues, many party supporters could not identify which party supported a particular policy. There was no agreement on which party would introduce income controls, a policy over which there had already been confusion in 1979. While reducing the power of the House of Lords was correctly viewed as a Labour policy, a large proportion (including 44% of Labour supporters) did not know whose policy this was. The number of people who correctly linked the abolition of metropolitan local authorities to the Conservative party was almost equal to those who did not know whose policy it was. While the introduction of import controls tended to be seen as a Labour policy, here, too, almost as many respondents could not name any one party.

Nor does the Alliance seem to have been sufficiently loud and explicit about wanting to introduce proportional representation. Although most of those who were able to link policy to party identified the Alliance with this policy, a staggering 51% had no idea which party favoured the policy: the highest percentage of "don't knows" among the 11 policies about which voters had been asked.

## Summary and conclusions

We have explored the two elements involved in the voters' decision; their own evaluations of policy issues and their perceptions of the different parties' stands on these issues. We were able to identify two broad types of issues. *Consensus* issues where there was agreement as to the desirability of the policy or outcome; and *non-consensus* issues which Conservative, Labour and Liberal voters viewed differently.

In deciding how to vote, it is not enough merely to have an opinion about different issues, it is also necessary to know the parties' stands. For an issue to have an impact, the parties' stands must be seen to differ. On *non-consensus* issues, voters of different parties perceived differences between the parties, agreed on the parties' relative positions, and did so accurately. On *consensus issues* voters agreed as to their desirability but tended to perceive differences between the parties' ability to handle the issue either in the past or in the future. Here the views of voters were partisan, each seeing their own party as best or least unable.

On issues where the parties had changed their stand between elections or where their positions were ambiguous, many voters were unsure as to the parties' views or perceived no differences between them. Among those who saw differences, there was a mild tendency to project their own views onto their preferred party.

The picture we have presented thus far is of a responsible and responsive electorate. Voters have opinions on various political, economic and social issues that change in response to political and social change. Their perception of the parties is also affected by the way the parties portray themselves. Where party stands are clear, voters accurately identify the party stand regardless of their own party preference. Where stands have changed, are ambiguous or not made explicit, many voters are unsure as to parties' policies or perceive no differences between the parties. The evidence, both in Britain and in the United States (Fishbein and Coombs, 1974), suggests that it is only on consensus or on ambiguous issues that voters' own views colour their perceptions of the parties' positions.

# 9

# Deciding how to vote:
# The consumer model

The various decision models of voting put forward by political scientists have certain characteristics in common. They are based on the idea of the "rationality" of the voter in that they assume that the voter wishes to maximize his or her expected utilities, that is, the advantages that might accrue from the opportunity of having competing choices. Voting masochists, out to select a party which would make matters worse, have no place in these models nor do voters who choose at random. All the models assume that the voter anticipates the futures offered by alternative choices but differ in terms of *the decision horizon* used by the voter, i.e. the point in the future beyond which the voter does not go when considering the consequences of selecting one party rather than another. Most models place the decision horizon *after* the outcome of the election. In the consumer model, we place it instead *at the moment of making the choice*. We shall show later that certain implications follow, depending on which decision horizon is used.

The consumer model comprises only part of a comprehensive model of vote choice, since it considers only a voter's current views and does not take into account the influence of background factors or past voting history. It is therefore a pruned down version (within the dotted square of Fig. 9.1) of the general model we outlined in Chapter 1.[1] In the latter part of this chapter we shall show what happens when we add to the voters' current views information about their voting history.

[1]Note that in Fig. 9.1 we have expanded the box which in Fig. 1.1 was labelled "political attitudes, beliefs and evaluations of parties and leaders" into their components to explain the genesis of the utilities and probabilities which are the inputs to the decision model. Toda (1976) describes how attitudes are functionally involved in the assessment of utilities through the use of a cognitive system which he calls "utility lookup for plans and situations"; Edwards *et al.* (1965), Pitz (1977) and Berkeley and Humphreys (1982) describe how cognitive probabilistic information processing systems function in the generation and articulation of beliefs.

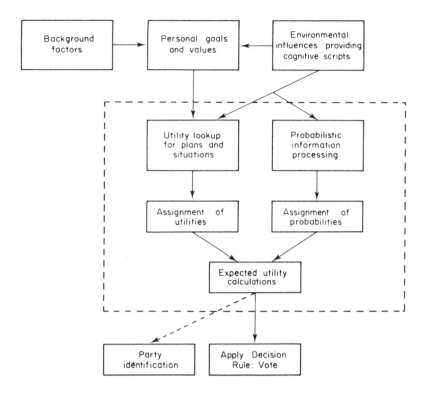

Fig. 9.1. The components of the consumer model are presented in the dotted square.

## Stage I: Why vote at all?

Turnout at elections varies considerably — during the period under study it was comparatively low in 1970, high in 1974 and returned to about the 1970 level in 1979 and 1983. By comparison with European·countries turnout in British general elections is low but by comparison with American Presidential elections it is high. There turnout is not much more than half the voting population. It is therefore no accident that the majority of explanations as to why people vote should have come from political scientists from the other side of the Atlantic. The most influential account of why people vote at all was given by Downs (1957, pp. 260–276).

In Chapter 1 we described how Downs' model was centred on the voter's economic rationality: a "rational" voter is someone who will vote *only* if the *expected utility* of voting rather than abstaining is great enough. Downs defines the expected utility as the difference in the utilities of the parties, *multiplied* by the probability that casting one's vote will affect the outcome of the election.[2] A person should therefore decide to vote *only* if the expected utility computed in this particular way is greater than the cost of voting (the physical inconvenience of going to vote, and the psychological cost of having to decide how to vote). Since the likelihood of a single person's vote affecting the outcome of an election is miniscule, all rational voters would abstain and all those who vote behave "irrationally". But this assumes that the model takes into account all the costs and utilities considered by the voter. Riker and Ordeshook (1968) point out that Downs' model omits at least one cost, namely guilt. This applies to those who have internalized the view that it is one's civic duty to vote, which is reinforced where significant others in their immediate circle do so. The model also omits the utility of the act of voting itself. Voting represents one of the very few occasions where a citizen is asked for his views, and being able to express them has an attraction in itself.

Ferejohn and Fiorina (1974) show that even if one ignores these additional reasons for not abstaining, the voter could still decide to vote while thinking along the lines suggested by Downs:

> If a citizen calculates according to the conventional analysis, he will decide to abstain. But all citizens will arrive at the same decision, therefore a smart citizen would vote and single handedly decide the election. And yet, other citizens would also follow this strategy, so maybe he should abstain after all. But if other citizens reason similarly, maybe . . . and so forth. (Ferejohn and Fiorina, 1974)

The Downsian voter would therefore vote because he could not predict whether his vote might not in the end be the one to make the difference. The trade-off here is the cost of voting against the regret of having been responsible for tipping the balance of the election in the unwanted direction, however remote that possibility might be in reality.

These considerations seem to suggest that the easier course is to vote rather than to abstain. Therefore, the minority who choose not to vote are likely to be those alienated from the system, those who see themselves as powerless anyway (we found that very few voters identified with this viewpoint) or for whom the cost of voting is unusually high (bad weather, working hours, ill health). Or voters might abstain if they saw little difference between the parties and therefore did not care who won the election.

Ferejohn and Fiorina characterize the original Downsian model as an *investment* decision; one accepts the cost of voting for the prospect of some future benefit. They see Riker and Ordeshook's addition to the model of the social desirability of the act of voting as having the effect of converting the model to a *consumption* decision. What is "consumed" is the "psychic pleasure" of pulling the lever of a United States' voting machine or, in Britain, of placing a cross on the ballot paper. The right to be the consumer is bought by the *cost* of voting, in the same

---

[2]This rather small probability is expressed as the probability of breaking or making a tie between the candidates. Downs' original model assumed only two candidates, later authors have tried to extend it to cover three or more candidates, but the calculations then became very complex.

way that the pleasure of consuming tomatoes (Ferejohn and Fiorina's example) is bought by the cost of their purchase. However, if this were all, there need not be any correspondence between a voter's outlook, his evaluation of the parties' stand and his or her party choice. Just putting a cross would be sufficient. Clearly this is not how the voter behaves.

## Stage II: Purchasing a vote or purchasing a party

In the polling booth, the voter selects a party to vote for. Yet if, following Downs, the voter takes into account the very low probability that his particular vote will affect the outcome, having set the decision horizon after the election, he is once more in an untenable position. While he may prefer one party over the others, this becomes irrelevant because his vote, one of millions, is unlikely to affect the outcome. What he can do is to decide to play safe, by adopting a *minimal regret* decision rule, as illustrated by the stickers which appeared on cars saying "Don't blame me, I voted Labour" a few months after the 1979 Conservative victory. However, from the responses to questions asked in our and in the British election study, there is little support for the use of a minimal regret rule. The majority chose a party either because they were attracted to what the party offered or because the party seemed "the best of a bad bunch", that is in both cases a preference was expressed, differing only in the degree of satisfaction with the available options.

The problems of why so many people choose to express their preferences through voting is resolved when the decision horizon is set, as we suggest, at the *actual moment* of voting. The voter then makes an appropriate "purchase" of a party among those offered, just as the consumer purchases tomatoes rather than any other vegetable on the stall. The voter here is primarily concerned with choosing a party and not as much as the other models suggest with the outcome of the election.[3] Problems to do with whether a party will actually achieve power consequent on this vote do not enter into consideration, as they lie over the horizon.

This is a consumer model not of *voting* but of *parties*: voting for a party "purchases" the party. The difference between these two perspectives is only one of emphasis. Strategic voting and the decision to vote Liberal are, of course, affected by the voter's assessment of the effect of his vote on the outcome, in reality a considerably inflated view of his role in the electoral process. If one exaggerates such beliefs, one can then believe (however irrationally) that one can bring about the implementation of a particular party's electoral platform merely by voting for it. Politicians help to foster this inflated view of the consequences of one's actions, hence perpetuating the myth, in Barthes' (1972) sense, of the power of the voter.

[3]Kelley and Mirer (1974) describe voting perceived in this way as "the simple act of voting".

## UTILITIES OF PARTIES

In a "consumer" model of parties, a choice has to be made on the basis of the relative preferences a voter has for each party. Brody and Page (1973), using data from two nation-wide opinion surveys conducted immediately after the 1968 US presidential election, found that the simple rule that a voter would choose the party whose *expected utility*[4] for him was higher than for the other parties, predicted better than a more complex rule which took also into account the relative strength of the preference.[5] Fiorina (1977) proposes that voters assess utilities of parties in terms of the promised change in the personal welfare of the voter that the party might bring about between this and the next election. But restricting the evaluation to changes in personal welfare is too limited. For some voters, the prestige of the country or the need to safeguard fundamental values concerning tolerance and justice might well be important in their evaluation of the policies, irrespective of whether this would bring about changes in the voters' personal welfare. Nor is it certain that people consider parties in terms of their possible performance between this and the next election. For many, conscious of the 13 years of Conservative or of the six years of Labour rule, time is not so clearly delineated. What criteria, then, do voters use in judging whether the promises the parties make will be implemented should the party come into power? Using the analogy once again of the purchase of goods, these promises are like the claims made by the manufacturers of products. In the case of the purchase of a car or a draught excluder, the firm's past performance in matching performance with claims enters into the assessment as does the realism of the claims themselves, e.g. that whatever the weather a car will not skid or a draught excluder will always keep out the cold. The same holds for assessment of future performances of the parties. In Chapter 8 we showed that for consensus policies, such as keeping unemployment down, or keeping prices from rising too fast, the voters' assessment of the parties differed only in the degree of their perceived *inability* to solve the problem.

While for a few voters the decision *not* to vote for a party may well turn on a single issue, e.g. not to vote for the National Front because of its racist stance, among the less extremist parties it is rare for one issue alone to determine the decision. Rather it is based on an amalgam of many issues. To test our model we therefore cast the net wide, drawing on issues listed in party manifestos and pre-election political commentaries in the mass media. The model received its first test in 1974, the final round of the longitudinal study. A set of questions was specially designed which addressed the 21 salient issues described in Chapter 8,

---

[4]Expected utility is the sum of the utilities of the various consequences of one's choice, weighted by their various probabilities of occurrence. In the consumer model, the voter decides as if the chosen party is purchased with *certainty* through the act of voting for it. So here we consider only the *utilities* of parties; probabilities do not enter into the model.
[5]The latter rule corresponds to Luce's (1959) beta response strength model.

four where evaluation consensus could be assumed but where the voters' perceptions about the parties' abilities to bring about the described state differed, and 17 where perceptions were the same but evaluations differed across voters for the three parties.

To compute an overall preference measure for each party, we needed to know the "part-worth" of a party to the voter on each of the 21 issues, that is the voter's perception of the direction and amount of change from the status quo (the present state of affairs) represented by the party's policy on the issue. We also needed a way of combining these part-worths into an overall measure of "total worth" or overall preference for each party. We used a simple additive model, from multi-attribute utility theory (von Winterfeldt and Fischer, 1975; Humphreys, 1977)[6] within which an issue possesses positive utility if it is either *desirable* and relatively *more likely* (or less unlikely) to be implemented by one party than any other, or *undesirable* and relatively *less* likely to be implemented by that party.

It follows that however much an individual cares about an issue, it will not enter the decision if he or she sees no difference in the likelihood of its implementation by the parties involved. On the other hand, the more an individual cares about an issue *and* the more definite his belief that it will or will not be implemented by one party rather than another, the stronger the influence of the issue on the decision. Into the decision, then, enter both the individual's attitudes and the parties' stand on the issue. In the MAUT model this is achieved by computing each individual's preference for each party's stand on each issue by weighting the perception of the party's expected performance on the issue by the evaluation of the issue, appropriately scaled in the way described below.

In the model, the voter's overall preference for a party consists of the sum of the 21 preference scores, on the individual issues. Expected utility theory predicts that the voter will vote for the party which has the highest overall preference score (Savage, 1972). Note that here attitudinal information is being used to *predict* the voter's decision *without* prior knowledge of how he has voted, something which is not possible in the case of statistical procedures such as the discriminant analysis employed in Chapters 5 and 6. It is therefore a *true prediction of the event* and *not merely a classification after the event*. This approach is of special significance *before* elections. Surveys of voters' views on issues and their evaluation of the parties' handling of these issues can then be used to make immediate predictions of how they will vote. Statistically based pseudo-prediction methods involve having to

[6]In this model each voter's "part-worth" perception of each party's policy on each issue was weighted by the voter's evaluation of the desirability of the issue.

Unlike statistically based procedures, such as multiple regression or discriminant analyses, this model does *not* require any parameter estimation or criteria variables, but it *does* require that the various issues rated be "utility independent" of each other. Utility independence does not mean that the ratings of issues have to be uncorrelated statistically, but only that the issues have to be separate in the voter's consideration when thinking about his or her personal welfare. Hence, we avoided asking overlapping questions about different policy issues.

wait until it is known how each individual actually voted in order to calculate
the statistical parameters for the prediction formula.

A rather full description of the method of computing the voter's preference score
for each party has been given to show that the procedure is simple and one in
which each voter's individual response to *each* issue has a role to play. The more
varied the issues sampled, the more likely then that they will cover those concerns
which affect the voter's decision making. In the other methods described in
Chapters 5 and 7 an issue played a part in the classification only if it was relevant
to many voters. The MAUT procedure, on the other hand, is *tailor-made to each
individual*— an issue may matter to one voter and be quite irrelevant to everyone
else. It is therefore a much more finely grained instrument for assessing the role
that voters' views play in their decision making.

TABLE 9.1

Direction of perceived change in personal welfare as a function of status quo, evaluation
of policy and perception of likelihood of party to implement policy

| Likelihood of party implementing policy | (i) Status quo "very bad" | | (ii) Status quo "neither good nor bad" | |
|---|---|---|---|---|
| | Evaluation of policy | | Evaluation of policy | |
| | bad | good | bad | good |
| very unlikely | 0 (status quo) | 0 (failed to realize opportunity) | + (avoided making things worse) | − (failed to make things better) |
| very likely | 0 (no worse than before) | + (made things much better) | − (made things worse) | + (made things better) |

Although the procedure is simple, it raises interesting questions about the scale
to be used for the voter's perceptions of parties' stands on issues. Which scale
is appropriate depends on how the voter sees the status quo (or the present state
of affairs with the policies in force at the time of the decision making). If he or
she perceives the status quo as *very bad*, then any policy even if only seen as bad,
rather than very bad, would be an improvement. However, if the voter sees the
status quo as *neither good nor bad*, but at some point in between, then only
policies which he or she evaluates as good would represent an improvement,
while those evaluated as bad (even if not as very bad) would make matters
worse. It follows that for the voters the effect on their preferences of a party
being likely rather than unlikely to carry out a policy will vary, not only with

the voters' opinions about that policy but with their overall assessment of the status quo.

Table 9.1 illustrates the consequences of these two different views of the status quo which generate two distinctly different MAUT representations of the consumer model of voting, both of which we tried on the voters' evaluations and beliefs.[7] We rejected *a priori* the third variant where the status quo is set at "very good" as this would imply an electorate considering itself to be living in the best of all possible worlds. Such an electorate would need to vote for the party which would upset things least by continuing as before.

## Test of the consumer model: prediction of the October 1974 vote based on the individual's cognitions using the longitudinal survey

Tables 9.2A and B compare the predictions made using MAUT with the actual vote choices made by the voters in the longitudinal study in 1974. The two tables differ in that the first table gives the results setting the status quo at *neither good nor bad*, and the second setting the status quo at *very bad*.

With the status quo set at *neither good nor bad* the model predicts Conservative and Labour voters exceptionally well (87% and 90% respectively) but only 57% of the Liberal voters, giving an overall percentage correct classification of 80%.[8]

Interesting differences between the results based on the two views of the status quo emerge. Using the view that the status quo was *very bad* Conservative were now as *poorly* predicted as the Liberals had been setting the status quo at *neither good nor bad*. Labour voters were now predicted slightly better and the Liberals strikingly so (correct prediction of 73%). Indeed the Liberals were now predicted better than Conservative voters, suggesting that Liberal voters had a more negative view of the status quo than the other voters in 1974, and a more positive views about the value of changing things. This supports our previous conclusion that Liberal voters (and occasionally Labour voters) look for policies that will "make

---

[7]In this MAUT model, voter's *perception* of each party on each policy issue forms a "part-worth" score (Kneppreth *et al.*, 1974), based on the likelihood of the party actually implementing the policy on a scale from 0 ( = very unlikely) to 4 ( = very likely). Relative scaling between these part-worth scores (c.f. Keeney and Raiffa, 1976; Humphreys, 1977), is achieved by employing the voter's policy *evaluation* rating as *scale factors*: running from $-2$ (very bad) to $+2$ (very good) when the status quo is set at "neither good nor bad", and from 0 to 4 when the status quo is set at "very bad". Each scale factor acts as a multiplicative weight for each of the three part-worth scores on the particular scale (one for each party) and the resulting *relatively scaled* part-worths are added across all policy issues to obtain the voter's overall preference for each party.

[8]When only Labour and Conservative voters are considered, the percentage correct prediction rises to 97% for both Labour and Conservative voters. This result, while very impressive, is not very useful in practice as it involves the exclusion *post hoc* of people who choose to vote for another party.

things better", whereas Conservatives are more intent on avoiding voting for policies that might make things worse. Himmelweit and Humphreys (1974) reported how in 1970 Liberal voters were the ones who agreed least with the statement "if you try to change things you only make things worse", while the Conservatives agreed the most. This difference in views of the status quo also characterized Liberal voters in 1979 and Alliance voters in 1983.

TABLE 9.2                                                                                                   *Longit. study*

Prediction of vote in October 1974 from attitudes and beliefs using MAUT with the status quo set at "neither good nor bad" and at "very bad"

A. Status quo set at "neither good nor bad"

|                  |          | Predicted vote | | | | | |
| --- | --- | --- | --- | --- | --- | --- | --- |
|                  |          | Con | Lab | Lib | % | n | |
| Actual vote 1974 | Con (%)  | 87 | 4 | 19 | 100 | 71 | Overall correct |
|                  | Lab (%)  | 2 | 90 | 8 | 100 | 36 | classification = 80% |
|                  | Lib (%)  | 30 | 13 | 57 | 100 | 40 | |

B. Status quo set at "very bad"

|                  |          | Predicted vote | | | | | |
| --- | --- | --- | --- | --- | --- | --- | --- |
|                  |          | Con | Lab | Lib | % | n | |
| Actual vote      | Con (%)  | 54 | 8 | 38 | 100 | 71 | Overall correct |
| 1974             | Lab (%)  | 3 | 92 | 5 | 100 | 36 | classification = 68% |
|                  | Lib (%)  | 3 | 25 | 72 | 100 | 40 | |

In any test of a model involving MAUT, special care must be taken to select appropriate issues, and to phrase the questions carefully. The computational procedures used are such that each item, appropriate or not, enters the preference calculation. Our results testify that we were successful in the selection of appropriate items. But did we need 21 items? Would a smaller number of well-chosen issues have done just as well? To establish whether this was the case, we repeated the MAUT analysis with the status quo set as "neither good nor bad", including perceptions and evaluations only of the *four* policy issues where there was a general consensus in evaluation across voters for different parties.[9] Here the MAUT predictions are made principally on the basis of the way voters perceive differences in the future capability of parties to deliver the goods. The resulting predictions of actual vote in October 1974 were 68% correct.

We then repeated the MAUT analysis, this time using four non-consensus issues on which there was no consensus on evaluation between voters for different

[9]Stopping unemployment rising: keeping prices from rising too fast; holding mortgage rates down; making British industry more efficient.

parties.[10] The resulting correct prediction was very similar (66%) to that obtained using the four consensus policies. Both predictions were considerably lower than the 80% correct classification based on a mixture of 21 consensus and non-consensus policy items, confirming the need to select an adequate and appropriate range of issues in applications of the consumer model.

## Further test of the consumer model: Prediction of the October 1974 and 1979 votes based on the individual's cognitions, using the British election studies

As described in Chapter 8, questions about evaluations and perceptions of policy issues were asked differently in the 1974 British election study. Questions addressing only five issues were suitable for the MAUT procedure. These were all questions about policies where evaluative consensus could be assumed (rising prices, strikes, unemployment, pensions and housing) and were asked purely in terms of the two major parties *past* record (e.g. how well Labour *handled* strikes; how well Conservatives *could have* handled strikes). On these five issues the voter was also asked how important the issue or policy was to him so we could, using an additive MAUT model, combine these assessments into estimates of the voter's view of the past performance of the parties. However, we had to restrict the analysis to Labour and Conservative voters only as no questions in this form were asked about the Liberals.

The results shown in Table 9.3 provide a 91% correct classification overall, better than the overall correct classification of voters by a discriminant analysis based on all the attitudinal measures obtained in that same survey (Chapter 5). These results confirm the general usefulness of the MAUT-prediction technique and with it the role that attitudes play in decision making.

Prediction of vote for two, rather than three, parties, particularly where the third occupies the middle ground, is of course easier. In the longitudinal study

TABLE 9.3                                                                *BES 1974*

Comparison of MAUT-based prediction of vote in 1974 and actual vote in October 1974: five *consensus* predictor items

|  | | Predicted vote | | | | |
|---|---|---|---|---|---|---|
|  | | Con | Lab | % | $n$ | |
| Actual vote | Con (%) | 83 | 17 | 100 | 631 | Overall correct |
| October 1974 | Lab (%) | 3 | 97 | 100 | 889 | prediction = 91% |

[10]The issues concerned the abolition of grammar schools, public ownership of companies, strikes and immigrants. These four items were selected as representing each of the four main clusters into which the 17 non-consensus policy issues fell.

we obtained for 1974 an 80% correct prediction including the three parties. Omitting the Liberals so as to make the analysis comparable to that of the British election survey just reported, the percentage correctly predicted rose to a remarkable 97%.

We were able to carry out the same analyses on the 1979 British election survey, where the same format of questions was used as in 1974. Indeed, three of the four consensus items were identical to those asked in 1974: rising prices, strikes and unemployment. For the fourth consensus item, a question about law and order was substituted for those on pensions and housing.

TABLE 9.4                                                                    *BES 1979*

Comparison of MAUT-based prediction of vote in 1979 and actual vote in 1979 based on four *consensus* issues

|  |  | Predicted vote | | | |  |
| --- | --- | --- | --- | --- | --- | --- |
|  |  | Con | Lab | % | n |  |
| Actual vote | Con (%) | 91 | 9 | 100 | 567 | Overall correct |
| 1979 | Lab (%) | 11 | 89 | 100 | 462 | prediction = 90% |

Ninety per cent were correctly predicted, almost identical to the 91% obtained in 1974. This time, however, Conservatives were predicted better than Labour voters. While this change may be due to changes in the electorate, it is more likely to reflect the inclusion of the law and order issue, an issue of greater relevance to Conservative than Labour voters.

In the 1979 (but not in the 1974) British election survey questions were also asked about *non-consensus* issues in a way which allowed us to apply a MAUT model in computing each voter's relative preference for each party. As described more fully in Chapter 8, the voter was provided with possible policies on seven issues: social services and benefits, taxes, nationalization, the Common Market, ways of improving race relations, incomes policy, and on the regulation of trades unions. On each issue, the voter was asked (1) which policy came closest to his or her *own view*, (2) which came closest to the view of the Conservative party, and (3) which came closest to the view of the Labour party. We took the policy closest to the voter's own view as that person's *ideal point*. We then scaled the voter's evaluation of the policies representing each party's view on the issue in terms of its distance from that ideal point: the closer the policy to the ideal point, the greater its utility (see Coombs, 1964; Dawes, 1972; Humphreys, 1977). As the voter was also asked how important each issue was in his or her decision, we could compute the relative preference for each party by summing the desirability scores over all issues, each weighted by the importance of the issue to that voter. Table 9.5 shows the accuracy of the resulting predictions.

This time Conservative voters were predicted less well than on the basis of their responses to consensus items (83% compared with 91% and Labour voters

TABLE 9.5                                                            *BES 1979*

Comparison of MAUT-based prediction of vote in 1979 and actual vote in 1979 based on seven *non-consensus* issues

|  | | Predicted vote | | | | |
| --- | --- | --- | --- | --- | --- | --- |
|  | | Con | Lab | % | *n* | |
| Actual vote | Con (%) | 83 | 17 | 100 | 379[a] | Overall |
|  | Lab (%) | 9 | 91 | 100 | 282[a] | prediction = 86% |

[a] Sample size is less than for the seven non-consensus items as in the analysis only those subjects are included for whom there were no missing responses. This eliminated a greater number of respondents compared with the analysis based on only four consensus issues.

somewhat better (91% compared with 89%), the same pattern of the Labour vote as in the longitudinal study being better predicted from non-consensus issues and the Conservative vote from consensus issues. The overall rate of prediction (86%) is not quite as good as the 90% we obtained for consensus issues. This may simply be a reflection of the difficulties we encountered in having to *construct* vote from the evaluative (desirability) ratings through making assumptions about their ideal points, rather than obtaining them directly as in our other tests of the MAUT model.

## Bringing in the parties' past

So far we have been working with the "pruned down" version of the cognitive model shown in Fig. 9.1, where the decision-making process is conceived as exclusively future-oriented: the voter starting from where he or she is now. Fiorina (1977) suggested that this model should be extended to bring in a voter's "past political experiences" (PPE), since:

> In making his voting decisions the citizen looks at the incumbent's performance, the alternative platforms of the incumbent and challenger and (perhaps) imagines a hypothetical past performance from the previous challenge. (p. 608)

Fiorina's solution was to split the model into separate PPE and "current issue concerns" components, the latter summarizing a person's "appraisal of the alternative future the parties promise him or her", corresponding to a "simple issue voting" model (Davis *et al.*, 1970). Fiorina wished to maintain the separate influence of the PPE component in line with Downs' (1957) argument for a "simple retrospective voting" model, on the grounds that parties' past actions provide a better indicator of their future actions than do their campaign pledges.

We consider such a distinction between past political experience and current issue concerns to be misconceived, being based, as Popkin *et al.* (1976) point out, on the excessive concern of those who studied "issue voting" in the United States with *accuracy* of perception of parties' stands, instead of studying the voter's perceptions of what parties might actually do (rather than say they would do) once in power. In forming his or her perception of the likelihood of a party implementing a particular policy once in power, a voter surely draws on *both* past political experiences and his or her knowledge of the parties' current statements. Hence a separate "PPE" component would be a redundant addition to a model of vote choice.

## Bringing in the voter's past

The path analysis of influences on vote choice we described in Fig. 4.3, indicated that structural factors (background, education, etc.) played an indirect role, but that there was a separate and *direct* link between a person's vote in a particular election and his or her pattern of voting in previous elections. Therefore, irrespective of whether the individual identifies with a given party, the habit of voting for a party should be included in a consumer model of voting, in the same way that "brand loyalty" is taken into account in other consumer models as a factor tempering the decision to switch allegiance to an apparently more attractive new product. Hence, in our cognitive model of vote choice we include a direct link between past voting records and vote choice. We give it less weight than the link between attitudes and vote since the influence of past votes on future vote varied considerably between elections, independently of the length of time between elections, and sometimes even bypassing the influence of vote of an intervening election. It also varied with the type of vote cast.

In Chapter 5, we showed how we could use a discriminant analysis to form an optimal classification of voters in our longitudinal study on the basis of weighted functions of their votes in previous elections. This assessment was, of course, made *post hoc*, as we could not form "predictions" through a discriminant analysis since we had to use the actual outcome (chosen vote) as a criterion. Using the individual's full previous vote history, 71% of the voters in the *February* 1974 election were correctly classified (Table 5.7). Table 9.6 shows what happens when the results from the February 1974 discriminant analysis are used to make "real" predictions about how the same men would vote in the following *October* 1974 election. Accuracy drops from 71% to 67%, quite a small drop, but probably atypical since

TABLE 9.6                                                                      *Longit. study*

Prediction of vote in October 1974 from voting history using weights from a discriminant analysis in which vote history was used to *classify* the February 1974 voters

|  |  | Predicted vote | | | | | |
|  |  | Con | Lab | Lib | % | n | |
|---|---|---|---|---|---|---|---|
| Actual vote | Con (%) | 76 | 7 | 17 | 100 | 71 | Overall correct |
| October 1974 | Lab (%) | 6 | 86 | 8 | 100 | 36 | prediction = 67% |
|  | Lib (%) | 38 | 27 | 35 | 100 | 40 |  |

the two elections were held within the same year and fought on similar issues in a similar economic climate. One would expect a poorer classification in cases where one is predicting forward to a more distant election, particularly in periods of greater social and economic change.

However, using MAUT the *October 1974 election was better predicted from the voter's cognitions than by the entire vote history of the men up to that date.* Despite this high degree of accuracy, it is still possible in theory that the inclusion of information about past vote history might improve *accuracy*. Kelley and Mirer (1974) indicate the circumstances under which past vote is likely to affect the decision, as follows:

> The voter canvasses his likes and dislikes of the leading candidates and major parties involved in an election. Weighing each like and dislike equally, he votes for the candidate toward whom he had the greatest net number of favourable attitudes, if there is such a candidate. If no candidate has such an advantage, the voter votes consistently with his party affiliation, if he has one. If his attitudes do not incline him toward one candidate more than toward another, and if he does not identify with one of the major parties, the voter reaches a null decision. (p. 574)

While we disagree with Kelley and Mirer's assumption that voters assign equal importance to each issue, their account has the advantage of setting out the conditions under which a person's party identification, or affiliation, plays a role, namely where for the voter the utilities of the candidates or parties are evenly matched. Brody and Page's (1973) analysis of American election studies showed this to be the case. Since there were hardly any voters in the longitudinal sample who in the 1974 MAUT analysis had equal preferences for more than one party we could not replicate these findings. But in any case, our assumptions about the role of past voting behaviour are different.[11] Our assumption is that the role of past behaviour in some form or another enters the decision process of *all* voters but that the degree to which this happens will vary with the individual. It will depend on the clarity of his preferences, on the consistency of his or her past behaviour and on the role of significant others in reinforcing or reducing that influence. It will also vary across elections depending on the historical context in which the elections are fought and on the saliency of the issues which separate the parties. Finally we expect it to vary with the type of voter. Other evidence we have presented suggests that the Conservatives are less issue-oriented than the other voters. We therefore expected that voting history would have a stronger influence on a Conservative than on a Labour voter. For the Liberals the influence of past voting history should be least, given that the majority of Liberal voters tend to be recruits to the party for one election only.

In order to examine these expectations, we "mixed" in various proportions the strength of preference for each party predicted for the voter by the MAUT-model (with status quo set at "neither good nor bad") with the strength of

---

[11]Note that this is a *behavioural* measure in contrast to the cognitive measures of preference for, or identification with, a party.

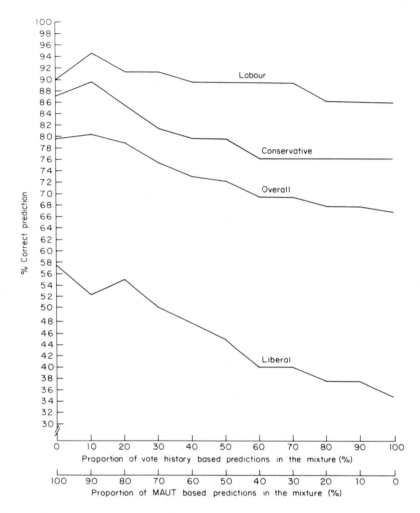

Fig. 9.2. Percentage correct classification of vote in October 1974 resulting from various mixtures of MAUT and vote-history based predictions (longitudinal sample).

preference predicted for the same voter by the vote-history model.[12] The results are shown in Fig. 9.2, which plots the effect of varying the combination of weights assigned to past voting habit and to the individual's cognitions about current issues. Two scales are provided on the horizontal axis. The first shows the percentage

[12]We used the February 1974 election as the criterion for the discriminant analysis with earlier votes as the predictors. Both sets of predictions were converted to standard scores (standardized over voters and parties), and then mixed using a weighted average technique.

weight given to vote history, running from 0% (left-hand side) to 100% (right-hand side); the second shows the corresponding percentage weight given to voters' cognitions in forming MAUT-based predictions, running from 100% (left-hand side) to 0% (right-hand side).[13] The vertical axis of the plot gives the percentage correct classification resulting from the particular mixture indicated along the horizontal axes.

Inspection of the figure shows that 10% weight given to past vote and 90% given to the MAUT predictions using social cognitions provided the best prediction of vote for that particular election. Table 9.7 gives the predictions based on this mixture. While the overall correct classification (80%) was the same as that based on MAUT prediction alone, for different types of voters the role played by past vote varied a good deal. For Labour and Conservative voters, adding a *small* proportion of vote history helped slightly, though less than we had expected for the Conservatives. By contrast (and this is what depressed the overall correct classification) prediction of the Liberal vote became poorer when their past voting was taken into account rather than ignored. Adding past vote was like laying a false trail.

TABLE 9.7 *Longit. study*

Classification of vote in October 1974 from a mixture of 90% MAUT and 10% vote-history prediction

| | | Percentage distribution of predicted vote | | | | | |
|---|---|---|---|---|---|---|---|
| | | Con | Lab | Lib | % | *n* | |
| Actual vote | Con (%) | 89 | 3 | 8 | 100 | 71 | Overall correct |
| October 1974 | Lab (%) | 3 | 94 | 3 | 100 | 36 | prediction = 80% |
| | Lib (%) | 32 | 15 | 53 | 100 | 40 | |

It is important to remember that the mixture involves predictions on the basis of vote history which were atypically apposite on account of the closeness of the February and October 1974 elections. As a general rule, we would expect past vote, as distinct from past voting history, to play an even smaller role than here in "improving" predictions based on the voters' cognitions. We were not able to explore this conjecture at the next election (1979) as the longitudinal study, spanning five previous opportunities to vote before the October 1974 election, finished then. The 1974–1979 British election panel study could provide information on only one previous vote (1974), which was not sufficient for scaled vote predictions based upon the individual's vote history.

[13]The two weights sum to 100% at every point. Where the weight given to vote history is 0%, the percentage correct classification is based entirely on the individual's cognitions, allowing no influence of vote history, and hence corresponds to Table 9.2; where prediction is based on vote history exclusively (100%) and no allowance is made for the individual's cognitions, the percentage correctly classified corresponds to Table 5.7.

## Methodological and substantive implications:
## How to predict how a person will vote

So far, we have shown that predictions (rather than pseudo-predictions) of how a voter will vote made using MAUT were more accurate than those made on the basis of either vote history or attitudes alone. But the success of the MAUT predictions depended crucially on being able to apply them within an appropriate structural representation of the way individuals formed the basis for their voting decision. For us, in constructing our 1974 questions for MAUT analysis, this involved selecting 21 policy issues (four where there was consensus in evaluation and 17 where there was not) on the basis of a content analysis of party manifestos and media presentations of parties' stands prior to the October 1974 election. Questions about perceptions and evaluations of these issues then had to be prepared in a manner which would elicit responses appropriate for use with a MAUT procedure.[14]

In Chapter 8 we gave details of these questions, and the scales used to elicit responses. We also reviewed there the ways in which questions had been phrased in the British election surveys of 1974 and 1979. Only a few of these questions were suitable for use within a MAUT model. In analysing the latter surveys we encountered uncertainties concerning the most appropriate way to re-scale respondent's evaluations and perceptions (particularly with non-consensus items) because of the way in which the response scales had been constructed in those surveys. The accuracy of MAUT-based predictions was high, but that obtained in the longitudinal study, when Liberal voters were omitted, was higher still — a remarkable 97%. If the questions had been asked in the 1974 and 1979 British election surveys in a way permitting a three-group discrimination including the Liberals, we would expect the accuracy of resulting predictions to fall considerably below those achieved in the longitudinal study which employed a comprehensive range of appropriately constructed questions.

In general, MAUT-based methods are unlikely to be of great use in the re-analysis of surveys originally carried out for other purposes since these may not contain appropriately constructed questions. MAUT comes into its own in the construction of new surveys where it is important to *predict* a person's choice on the basis of his or her perceptions and evaluations, before this choice is made. No *post hoc* statistical analyses are required before findings are presented. As we showed in Chapter 7 the salience of issues changes over time. It is therefore important to cover adequately the full range of policy issues which are potentially

[14]Fishbein had used a procedure which he called an "Intention model" (Fishbein *et al.*, 1976; Ajzen and Fishbein, 1980) in predicting vote on the basis of an additive combination of a person's attitudes and subjective norms relating to voting which in its *mathematical* form is similar to our (MAUT-based) additive composition rule. However, the Fishbein procedure is not, in the final analysis, comparable with ours as the questions about attitudes and beliefs to which the model is applied were not asked in a form which can yield material appropriate for combination within MAUT, even if re-scaled.

salient in an election campaign, not only because the individual's own past experience and present circumstances may colour which issues matter to him or her, and these might vary between voters, but also because the salience of issues changes in the course of an election campaign.[15]

MAUT was used here to *test* the validity of the consumer model of voting. Good use could also be made of this approach by carrying out a series of MAUT-based surveys during the period *before* an election to provide information about changes in the electorate's preference for one or other party, and *in the course of* an election campaign to monitor changes in the salience of issues and in the voter's perception of the relative capability of the parties in solving problems. Such changes could then be related to the conduct of the campaign or to particular political or economic events that surfaced at that time.

[15]The advantage of the tailor-made approach of the MAUT method of analysis is that it uses the respondent's personal assessment of the saliency of each issue.

# 10

# The structure of political attitudes: The nature of voting ideology

In the preceding chapters we showed that people's attitudes — their evaluation of institutions, issues and policy proposals — play a leading role in influencing vote choice and changes in that choice. We also showed that it was necessary to sample a wide range of issues so as to reflect adequately the voters' views and allow for differences in the salience of issues.

In this chapter we are concerned with a different, though related, question: that of the organization of these attitudes or the *cognitive maps* of voters' views about society. We shall examine whether issues are reacted to mainly as discrete entities or exhibit: "a configuration of ideas and attitudes in which the elements are bound together by some form of constraint or functional interdependence" (Converse, 1964). We therefore do not address ourselves to the debate on the nature of ideology itself or its primacy in society as illustrated by Aaron's statement that, "secular societies are today *founded* on ideas — on systems of ideas, on principles — *derived* from fact and from values all of which presume both institutions and ideas" (1977, p. 9, our italics).[1]

Instead, we are concerned here with the way in which values and views structure an individual's voting decisions and are themselves linked. In doing this, we shall consider three related propositions put forward by political scientists. The first is Bell's claim (1962) about the demise of ideology in advanced Western societies; the second Converse's claim that only the élite and not the mass public exhibits ideological or consistent thinking about political issues, and the third the claim that ideological thinking can be adequately expressed along a single, left to right political continuum. Our results do not support any of these claims.

Bell (1962) suggested that in the second part of the twentieth century in advanced Western societies such as Britain, "ideology" characterizes the thinking only of

[1] For a comprehensive review of the various critiques see Hall (1978).

disaffected minorities, students and intellectuals. Lipset (1977) similarly, but more mildly, claims that

> The "agreement on fundamentals", the political consensus of western society now increasingly has come up to include a position on matters which once sharply separated the Left from the Right. And this ideological agreement, which might be described as "conservative socialism", has become *the* ideology of the developed states of Europe and America.

True we found consensus on certain broad issues such as the need to keep unemployment and prices down, but there were more issues — related to goals as well as to means — where, contrary to Lipset's claims, there was no consensus among the voters for the major parties in Britain in the 1960s, 1970s and early 1980s.

The second proposition which we examine in detail below stems from a review of Converse of United States' electoral surveys from the 1950s. Converse concluded that, apart from a small élite amounting at most to a quarter of the electorate, the mass public had no coherent set of political beliefs which, however loosely defined, could be construed as a political ideology. Converse (1964) listed two criteria for establishing whether a group of people can be said to have an ideology. The first relates to the linkages or constraints between different beliefs and values and the second to their stability over time. Converse's concern here was less with logical constraints than with constraints experienced as such by the voter:

> Surprise has been registered at idea-elements brought together by such movements as Peronism and Italian Fascism by observers schooled to expect other combinations. Indeed, were one to survey a limited set of ideas on which many belief systems have registered opposite postures, it would be interesting to see how many permutations have been held at one time or another by someone, somewhere. Such diversity is testimony to an absence of any strict logical constraints among such idea elements, if any be needed. What is important is that the élites familiar with the total shapes of the belief systems have *experienced* them as logically constrained clusters of ideas within which one part logically follows from another. (1964, pp. 210–211)

We shall return to the question of the difference between the élite and the rest of the electorate later. Note that Converse sees the "experience of constraint" as emanating from (undefined) social sources. Idea elements, he points out, "tend to be diffused in 'packages' which consumers come to see as 'natural' wholes for they are presented in such terms" (p. 211). One such "natural" cluster for the United States electorate was described by Nie *et al.* (1976) as follows:

> A Liberal favoring greater welfare spending would be likely to favor a bigger and more active government, would be favorable to racial integration and would be an internationalist and not a militant anticommunist in foreign affairs. A Conservative would be expected to hold the opposite positions. (p. 23)

Converse (1964) took the size of the obtained correlations between attitudinal responses on a variety of domestic and foreign issues to indicate degrees of constraint, comparing an "élite" sample (congressional candidates) and a cross-sectional sample of the United States electorate in 1958. He found moderate correlations between responses on clusters of issues for the "élite" sample but only very low correlations for a cross-sectional or "mass" sample. He therefore argued that "constraints among political idea elements begin to lose range very rapidly when we move from the more sophisticated few towards the 'grass roots'; . . . we are contending that the organization of more specific attitudes into wide-ranging belief systems is absent as well" (pp. 228–229). Nie and Anderson (1974) suggest that this might be so because, "The mass public has neither the educational background, the contextual knowledge, nor the capacity to deal with abstract concepts that sustain an organized set of beliefs over a wide range of political issues".

By themselves low correlations are not, as Converse and others rightly point out, sufficient evidence of lack of ideological thinking. Consistency might still exist but *within* the beliefs of individual voters which cancel each other out when grouped data only are considered simply because the belief systems are not the same across voters. Alternatively, the constraints experienced by voters might either not be tapped through the issues sampled or else the questions might have been poorly worded reducing variance. Both these possibilities continue to be discussed.

## Changes in consistency in voters' beliefs between the 1950s and 1970s

Nie *et al.* (1976) compared correlations between responses to questions on a range of foreign and domestic issues which were included in surveys between 1956 and 1973 conducted by the University of Michigan Survey Center and the University of Chicago National Research Center. In line with the rise in issue voting during

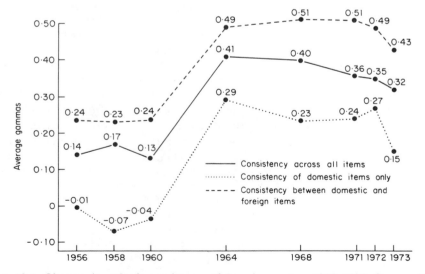

Fig. 10.1. Changes in attitude consistency of American voters 1956–1973. Source: Nie *et al.* (1976, Fig. 8.3).

this period they found increases in the linkages between issues for pairs of questions on domestic and foreign policy issues[2] (Fig. 10.1).

The graph shows that the average level of consistency among the mass electorate by 1964 had risen to, or even exceeded, that exhibited by the élite group of professional politicians studied by Converse in 1958. Possible reasons for this increase in attitudinal constraint were examined. Improved education was ruled out as a possible cause since parallel rises in overall constraint were found among the best as well as the least educated groups. The most likely explanation was an increase in the salience of politics among the public. The gamma coefficents increased both for the ''politically interested'' as well as for those who were not, but the gap between these two groups had widened over the years, leading Nie *et al.* to conclude that ''the combined impact of the rise in attitudinal consistency among those interested in politics and the increase in the numbers of such citizens accounts for a major proportion of the observed ideological constraint as a whole'' (p. 155).

In Britain, Butler and Stokes (1974) used the replies of the 1970 sample to study their level of ideological thinking. They included in the analysis only those who had expressed views on each of the issues sampled, excluding anyone who had no views on one or more issues or could not decide between the responses offered. Only 30% of the representative sample fulfilled the conditions for inclusion in the analysis. Butler and Stokes found that:

> Attitudes towards nuclear weapons were systematically tied to attitudes towards nationalization, as well as to immigration, the death penalty, big business power and the trade unions. People who opposed the recent level of immigration were more likely to be for the death penalty and against the power of the trade unions. Those who discounted for the importance of the monarchy were likely to accept nationalization, oppose the Bomb, accept recent immigration, condemn hanging and the power of big business and be tolerant towards the trade unions. (p. 320)

However, correlations among attitudes were sufficiently low, even with this atypical sample, for the authors to conclude that while ''there is a mild tendency here for opinion to organize along left–right lines which would be recognised by political insiders . . . by the standard of elite opinion the tendency is very mild indeed'' (p. 320).

The debate as to whether there has or had not been an increase in ideological thinking continues. Some, prompted by Achen (1975) but challenged by Niemi and Weissberg (1976), suggest that the increase is a methodological artifact resulting from an improvement in the scope and type of questions asked over the various surveys in the series.

Whether this is so or not, what seems strangely lacking in the debate is a careful

[2]The questions were drawn from five ''issue areas'': size of government, welfare, integration, welfare for blacks, and the cold war. The linkages between issues were measured by average tau-gamma coefficients. Converse (1964) originally opted for the tau-gamma coefficent (Goodman and Kruskal, 1954), rather than the more familiar product moment correlation coefficient ''because of its sensitivity to constraint of the scales''.

study of the social and political reality in which the opinions were sought. This is particularly necessary where responses to the same issues are compared across time and differences in the size of the correlations between issues taken as evidence of changes in the political sophistication of the electorate. Such assessment ignores the fact that issues have a life history of their own, moving in and out of the arena of party politics and political debate.

Since we had asked the men in our longitudinal study for their views on three separate occasions, in 1962, 1970 and 1974, using identical questions on many issues, we could examine changes in the correlations of one issue with others.[3] Following Converse and Nie, we calculated tau-gamma coefficients for pairs of issues at each point in time and computed average coefficients for the four "liberal" issues separately for 1962, 1970 and 1974. These concerned the abolition of capital punishment, making homosexuality among consenting adults no longer a criminal offence, restricting the entry of immigrants and views about immigrants already in this country.

In 1962 the average tau-gamma coefficient was $0 \cdot 33$, by 1970 it had risen to $0 \cdot 46$, only to drop back to $0 \cdot 39$ by 1974. We suggest that the differences in the size of the coefficients reflect changes in the political and social scene more than changes in the voters. The increased overall linkage between views, as reflected in the higher coefficient in 1970, was due to salience given to the law and order and immigration issues in the 1970 election and the subsequent decrease in overall linkage between 1970 and 1974 to the removal from the arena of debate of liberal issues of the change in the law on homosexuality.[4] This resulted in lowered correlations with the other three "liberal" issues.

The idea that we are dealing here with changes in the political scene rather than changes in the ability of voters to conceptualize gains further support when we consider the changing relationship between attitudes to comprehensive schooling and other issues over the same period. In 1962, comprehensive schooling was not a major political issue. Indeed, few such schools existed in Britain and as many as 30% of our sample had no views about them. For the remainder they were unrelated to other political views and even to attitudes to the abolition of public schools.[5] By 1970, comprehensive schooling had come to the fore as a

---

[3]The men's interest in politics (ranging from moderate to low) had not increased between 1962 and 1974, and their education had already been completed by 1962.

[4]Soon after 1962 Parliament, going against public opinion, abolished capital punishment and the law making homosexual practices between consenting adults a criminal offence. Capital punishment continued to feature in debates on law and order but the abolition of the law on homosexuality was little mentioned in subsequent years. The men came to accept this particular change in the law but not the abolition of capital punishment.

[5]For readers not familiar with the British educational system, comprehensive schools are non-selective schools proposed, and implemented, to replace selective secondary schooling in the public sector. Public schools are selective, independent fee-paying schools in the private sector.

party political issue. Once this happened the correlation with attitudes to other political issues (trade unions, restriction of immigration, capital punishment, as well as attitudes to public schools) became substantial, increasing even further by 1974.[6]

These examples illustrate the importance of the social context and of the life history of issues and the stance taken by the parties as sources of variation in the linkage that the electorate establishes. In any case what justification is there to express ideological "constraint" in terms of average correlations between responses to sets of questions? Nie *et al.* (1976), discussing the data shown here in Fig. 10.1, warn against over-interpretation, pointing out that there is not only no logical consistency between the answers to different policy proposals (as between a dovish attitude to the Vietnam war and a wish for faster school integration) but also that what is placed on the same side of a liberal–conservative continuum is relatively arbitrary. *De facto*, "attitudinal consistency" or "degree of constraint" represents the extent to which respondents line up their responses with what Converse (1964) calls the liberal–conservative "ideological dimension of judgement or yardstick", elevated to criterion status largely because it

> has been highly serviceable for simplifying and organizing events in most Western politics for the past century . . . on which parties, political leaders, legislation, court decisions and a number of other primary objects of politics could be located. (Converse, 1964, p. 214)

We tried to use this yardstick in specifying the direction of coding responses to the nine issues we used to construct our measure of attitudinal constraint. For issues like capital punishment, homosexuality, immigration and schooling, it was easy to make conventional liberal–conservative distinctions. For trade unions and management–employee relations, we could identify one response with *Conservative party* opinion, but the opposite response was by no means "liberal" in the sense used by ideologues in the United States, but was merely opposed *historically* as being consistent with longstanding *Labour party* policies. The final issue, that of the Common Market, was particularly tricky. We finally coded it in terms of wishing to join being "Conservative", as that was consistent with Conservative party policy in 1970 and 1974 (and to a lesser extent in 1962). The result was that in 1962 a "Conservative" attitude of wishing to restrict immigration was *negatively* correlated ($r = -0.29$) with the "Conservative" desire to join the Common Market (which would have the consequence of increasing immigration from other European countries). The "inconsistency" here is not in the minds of the electorate, who in fact perceived quite accurately an "inconsistency" in Conservative party policy from the standpoint of the (politically "élite"?) liberal–conservative yardstick.[7]

---

[6]The tau-gamma coefficient between attitudes to the abolition of public schools and the introduction of comprehensive schooling was insignificant in 1962 ($-0.07$). By 1970 it had risen to $-0.56$ and remained so in 1974 ($-0.60$). The correlation with attitudes to trade unions, insignificant in 1962 ($0.03$), became significant by 1970 ($0.23$) and increased further by 1974 ($0.35$).

[7]Note that if the direction of scoring the Common Market issue were changed other "inconsistencies" would arise.

## The structure of political attitudes

In any case linkages between two sets of beliefs are by themselves insufficient evidence that the individual's cognitive map of views is a structured one *across* a range of social and political issues — each view representing one ''idea element'' of a political ideology. Despite the importance Converse (1964) attached to the notion of structure, he soon gave up the search for it on the grounds that the correlations among beliefs of the public were so low that there was no point in applying factor analysis or similar techniques to detect a non-existent underlying pattern.

Most research workers took Converse at his word and did no more than compute the degrees of linkage between pairs of attitudes. The few who ventured further and used a multivariate approach obtained results which suggested that Converse (1964) might well have been too pessimistic. For example, Stimson (1975), using principal components factor analysis, found meaningful dimensions along which political attitudes could be studied, for all voters regardless of their educational level. In one way the results also provided support for Converse's view in that a *superordinate* dimension was found only among the attitudes of the most highly educated group.[8]

In our search for structure, we adopted a two phased approach. First, like Stimson, we used principal components factor analysis to identify families of attitudes and then, using multidimensional scaling analysis, mapped the families of attitudes so as to represent the voters' cognitive maps.

## Structures of attitudes within the longitudinal study

FAMILIES OF ATTITUDES

Principal components factor analysis with oblique rotation was carried out[9] to see whether voters' attitudes clustered on interpretable dimensions and if so on

---

[8]Among Stimson's lowest ability group, dimensions isolated by the principal components analysis were clearly separated according to topic: racial issues loaded with other racial issues, economic issues with other economic issues. Among the more educated the first dimension accounted for more of the overall variance with items loading on it drawn from different domains. Consistency in responses was therefore not solely due to the superficial similarity of the content of the attitude items.

[9]For readers not familiar with factor analysis, this technique involves looking at the matrix of intercorrelations among all items under consideration in the attempt to extract factors which more or less represent ''families'' (a family is a set of items which are relatively highly correlated with each other and relatively poorly correlated with items outside the family). Our concern was not so much to look for factors orthogonal to one another but to look for order across domains. To the extent that there is a single underlying ideological dimension guiding responses, we would expect the factors describing various ''families'' of attitudes to be correlated.

how many, as well as to search for the presence of a superordinate conservative–liberal dimension corresponding to Converse's (1964) concept of an ideology. The 1974 round of questioning provided the richest set of attitudinal data, consisting of 37 items.

A five-factor solution accounted for 51% of the variance. The results after rotation are shown in Appendix 3, Table 14, together with the matrix of correlations between the rotated factors. Factor 1, which alone accounted for 28% of the variance, correlated with Factor 4 (0·55) to form a *"supra-family"* of attitudes to issues which customarily feature in Conservative and Labour disputes, i.e. to do with the British educational system, with public ownership, with rich–poor relations and with the relation of labour to big business (including the role of the trade unions and welfare provisions).

A second and separate supra-family (centred on Factor 2) grouped items relating to immigration policies and attitudes to immigrants, linking these to "law and order" issues, including such items as "stricter laws make for a healthier society" and "a large number of people abuse the Welfare State".[10]

This "law and order" supra-family resembles Converse's (1964) description of the liberal–conservative continuum. The existence of these two relatively *separate* supra-families explains why we had difficulty in expressing "attitude constraint" using the yardstick of a *single* continuum. This means that there were sections of the British electorate in the 1970s who held "liberal" views on economic issues while at the same time holding "conservative" views on matters of law and order and immigration, and vice versa. We shall show later that it is the juxtaposition of these two continua that successfully differentiates between voters for the Conservative and the Liberal party (Chapter 10).

We repeated the factor analysis using the panel's 1970 responses to 32 attitude questions. Twenty-two of the questions were the same as those asked in 1974, but in the 1970 round we had more questions about student unrest, law and order and demonstrations since these had been dominant issues of the day. The similarity of the results of the two factors analyses was striking.[11]

SUPRA-FAMILIES AND SUB-FAMILIES OF ATTITUDES IN 1970 AND 1974

These two-factor analytic studies indicate the continuing existence of *two* supra-families of attitudes. Each of these groups together comprise smaller clusters of

[10]While organizing several attitudes, it played a poor second to the first supra-family which groups items on a continuum which in Britain has historically separated class interests and Labour–Conservative policies.
[11]Again with 5 factors 51% of the variance was accounted for. Three (highly correlated) factors constituted the law and order supra-family with responses to questions on law and order, demonstrations, student unrest and immigration loading on these factors. Factors 2 and 4, largely independent of the other three factors, represented the economic and class related supra-family we had also isolated in the 1974 analysis.

attitudes whose inter-relations are close but intricate, with a few items falling between the two or right outside. Figure 10.2 gives a schematic representation of the relation between the families of attitudes in 1970 and 1974 and the way they organize into the two supra-families.

Families of attitudes grouped within the first major family (the left-hand side of Fig. 10.2) concern class or economic issues: public ownership (of building land, companies; abolition of private health service, etc.), trade unions (their powers; can they be trusted? are they harmful?), strikes (the need for legal sanctions; social security benefits to strikers, etc.) big business (should it be controlled, more heavily taxed, etc?). They also include attitudes to selective secondary schooling.

Families of attitudes grouped within the second supra-family (the right-hand side of Fig. 10.2) concern law and order, the need for stricter laws and increase in the power of the police, etc., views on capital punishment and the law on homosexuality as well as on immigration (should it be restricted? should it be controlled on the basis of colour, etc?).

Between the two supra-families of attitudes lie the responses to three sets of issues:

> Attitudes to *student unrest* were related both to law and order issues and to the first supra-family that comprised attitudes about the educational system and class interests.
>
> Attitudes concerned with the *social services* also divided into two groups. Views on how much should be spent on pensions and services fell within the first supra-family while views on whether too many people abuse the Welfare State related in the voters' minds more to concerns about law and order (in 1974 much more than in 1970).

Attitudes to three issues lay right outside both supra-families: the perception of management–employee relations; views about the need to reform Britain's electoral system;[12] and attitudes towards the Common Market. We shall say more about this later.

## COGNITIVE MAPS SHARED BY VOTERS

Once we had evidence for the existence of separate supra-families of attitudes, we sought to describe their relations to one another in a geometric space forming a cognitive map. In this map each attitude is represented by a point in space, and the distances between these points are so arranged that small distances indicate close linkages, and vice versa. This means that closely linked attitudes are

[12]The "need" to reform Britain's electoral system was the only issue to distinguish the platform of the Liberal party from the platforms of the (larger) Conservative and Labour parties. "Reform" means a change to proportional representation which would ensure that the number of Liberal voters was reflected by a larger number of Liberal Members of Parliament.

Fig. 10.2. Structure of political attitudes (longitudinal sample).

| SUPRA-FAMILY I: Political-economic | | | | | | SUPRA-FAMILY II: Liberalism | | |
|---|---|---|---|---|---|---|---|---|
| Secondary Schooling | Nationalization | Big Business | Trade Unions | Cause of Unemployment | Strikes | Law and order | Liberalization of the Law on: | Immigration |
| Attitudes to public, grammar and comprehensive schools | Building land | Subject to more control | Do more harm than good | Workers' excessive demands | No restrictions | Breakdown exaggerated | Capital punishment | Problem exaggerated |
| | Keep private health service | More consultation before mergers | Power without responsibility | Inefficient management | Legal sanctions | Need for stricter laws | Homosexuality among consenting adults | Further restriction of entry |
| | More companies to be nationalized | | Trust social contract | | Secret ballot | Increase power of police | | Encourage return to home land |
| | Sell council houses to tenants | | | | Cut benefits to strikers | | | |
| | | *Close to cluster I* | | *Classes I and II* | | *Closer to cluster II* | | |
| | | *Taxation* | *Students* | *Social Services* | | *Demonstrations* | | Control of entry on basis of colour wrong |
| | | Heavier taxing of the wealthy | Genuine grievance | Spend more on pensions and social services | | No patience with demonstrations | | Prejudiced against immigrants in this country |
| | | Reduce company taxes | Opposed to student violence | Many abuse welfare state | | Right to demonstrate important, not to be interfered with | | |
| | | | Right to express views (questions asked in 1970) | | | | | |

*Outside any cluster*

Assessment of management–employee relations (from trust to open warfare)
Need for electoral reform
Assessment of Britain's membership of the EEC

With suitable reversal of items depending on their wording, SUPRA-FAMILY I was scored in the Labour and SUPRA-FAMILY II in the Conservative direction with the items that lay between being allotted to either Labour or Conservative depending on their closeness to one or other Supra Family. Two items which fell outside either group on: conflict between management and employee and the desirability of electoral reform were added in the format in which the questions had been asked (see Appendix 1).

represented by disctinct clusters of points. Non-metric multi-dimensional scaling was used to construct these maps (Schiffman *et al.*, 1981). [13]

We used the results of the factor analyses to determine the direction in which items should be coded. The set of issues which had to do with nationalization, education, trade unions, strikes, big business, taxation, and unemployment (the first supra-family in Fig. 10.2) were coded so that a high score reflected a Labour response. [14] Those issues grouped in the second supra-family dealing with law and order and immigration were coded so that a high score reflected a ''Conservative'' response.

Coding according to these specifications provides us with an opportunity to check the consistency of voters' attitudes defining the structures shown in the maps. If the ''supra-families'' represent genuinely different schemata and are not just an artifact of the factor analytic procedure, then two separate clusters of attitudes, one corresponding to each supra-family, should appear as distinct areas. Lack of consistency, on the other hand, would result in a generally amorphous structure.

We carried out multidimensional scaling analyses, [15] one of replies to 33 questions in 1970 and one of replies to 37 questions in 1974. In each case the measure of ''goodness of fit'' of the distances between the points on the map to the original data indicated that the responses were adequately expressed by maps drawn in two dimensions only. [16] These are shown in Figs 10.3 and 10.4.

In both figures the horizontal axis divides the attitude items into the same two supra-families. On the right we find the economic and class-related items neatly split into sub-clusters dealing with nationalization, strikes, trade unions, educational system, and so on. On the left we find law enforcement concerns, again divided into sub-clusters concerning immigration, liberalization of the law, law and order, and demonstrations.

The core of the first main cluster relates to attitudes towards trade unions and strikers. [17] The centre of the law enforcement cluster has to do with views on immigration.

To relate these clusters of attitudes to vote choice, we included in the analysis four variables describing each person's cumulative vote for each of the parties

[13]Such ''cognitive maps'' can also be obtained through factor analyses from the loadings or projections on to factor axes. Non-metric multidimensional scaling analysis has the advantage over factor analysis in that it makes fewer assumptions concerning the nature of the data. It attempts to translate higher similarities (correlations in our case) to smaller distances, but not necessarily to preserve the relative magnitudes of the similarities. In other words, it attempts to provide monotone, rather than linear transformations from correlations to distances. For further clarification, see Green and Rao (1972).
[14]For example, for the item ''Trade unions do this country more harm than good'', disagreement was coded as high.
[15]See Kruskal *et al.* (1973) or Lingoes (1973) for the appropriate computer programmes.
[16]The stress values were 0·15 for the 1974 and 0·12 for the 1970 data.
[17]Attitudes to the assertion that ''workers' demands led to unemployment'' lie in this cluster and not within a separate unemployment cluster (attitudes to the opposite claim, in 1974, ''inefficient management led to unemployment'', lie outside the economic cluster).

and his cumulative abstentions from the first vote cast in 1959 until his fifth and sixth in the elections of 1970 or 1974.[18] These four variables, of course, correlate negatively with each other since a person who voted many times for one party cannot also have voted as many times for another party. The points representing these variables must therefore fall well apart from each other in a two-dimensional map. What is important, though, is not that they fall apart but that they fall exactly where they should on the assumption that the voter's perceptions of the parties' stands on issues guides his vote choice. Propensity to vote Labour lies at the *very centre* of the items coded in the "Labour" direction. Propensity to vote Conservative, on the other hand, is located close to, though not *in* the centre of, the items coded in the "Conservative" direction, suggesting that Labour voters have a more tightly knit ideology than Conservative voters. This result is in line with other evidence, presented in Chapters 8 and 9, showing that the Labour vote, compared with the Conservative vote, is more ideologically determined.

In 1974, the cumulative abstention and cumulative Liberal vote scores lay at right angles on the map to the horizontal dimension defined by Labour and Conservative votes. The picture for 1970 was very similar. Both abstentions and Liberal vote scores fell outside both attitude clusters. Only attitudes towards reforming the electoral system and cooperation between management and employees lay anywhere near the Liberal vote position.

While in 1970 the Labour vote was located near the sub-cluster of educational items, by 1974 it was closest to the "trade unions" sub-cluster, probably because the controversy over comprehensive schools was not as salient a party political issue in 1974 as it had been in 1970. In 1974 the most salient issue was the confrontation between the Miners' Union and the Conservative Government.

The position of the item concerning Britain's membership of the EEC is interesting. It was coded in a "Conservative" direction following that party's policy in the 1970s in favour of joining the EEC. Yet it was only in 1974, after Britain's entry, that it fell within the Conservative space. In 1970 it was closer to the "Labour" cluster, reflecting the fact that it was a *Labour* Government under Harold Wilson (1964–1970) which had tried hard to bring Britain into the EEC.

## Multidimensional scaling analysis of attitudinal structure: 1974 and 1979 British election studies

The 1970 and 1974 multidimensional scaling analyses from the longitudinal study, together with the factor analyses discussed previously, show that political attitudes are coherently structured in relation to one another rather than discrete or random. However, since the sample of the longitudinal study was not representative of

[18]Each smallest space analysis was conducted twice, once with, and once without the inclusion of cumulative votes. As inclusion of cumulative vote did not change the attitudinal structure, we show only the results including these variables.

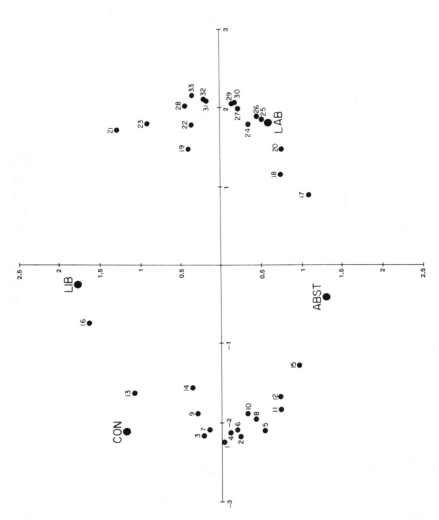

Fig. 10.3. Two-dimensional structure of 33 attitude measures obtained in 1970. Multidimensional scaling (longitudinal sample).

*Issues in direction of high scores*

1. Capital punishment should be restored.
2. Disagrees that right to demonstrate more important than law and order
3. Many people abuse the welfare state.
4. Government should further restrict immigration from Commonwealth and colonies.
5. Does not respect people who oppose the Vietnam war.
6. Problem of immigrants not exaggerated.
7. Stricter laws make for a healthier society.
8. No patience with demonstrators.
9. So-called breakdown of law and order not exaggerated.
10. "Give an inch will make a mile" applies to immigrants in this country.
11. Not wrong to control immigration on basis of colour.
12. Not wrong that coloured people born in this country treated as outsiders.
13. Government should not spend more on pensions and social services.
14. Power of the police should be increased.
15. Wrong to make the laws on homosexuality less severe.
16. Management–employee relations cooperative.
17. Until big business subject to more control, prices will continue to rise.
18. Voting to strike not by secret ballot.
19. Take over bids and mergers not matter for management alone.
20. Public schools should be abolished.
21. Britain should not enter the Common Market.
22. Disagrees that student violence, however mild, ever justified.
23. Students have right to express views on political matters.
24. No government restriction on the right to strike.
25. More comprehensive schools.
26. Grammar schools should be abolished.
27. No legal sanctions to control strikes.
28. Students have a right to more say in the running of their colleges.
29. Power without responsibility not a good description of trade unions today.
30. Disagree that trade unions today do more harm than good.
31. Students can complain about way they are taught.
32. Student unrest because of genuine grievances.
33. Students who take part in sit-ins should not have their grant suspended.

*Cumulative vote* for: Conservatives = Con
Labour = Lab
Liberals = Lib

*Cumulative abstentions* = Abst

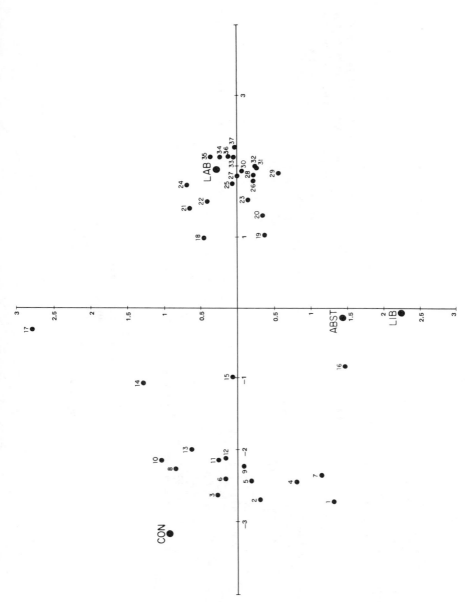

Fig. 10.4. Two-dimensional structure of 37 attitude measures obtained in 1974. Multidimensional scaling (longitudinal sample).

*Issues in direction of high scores*

1. Against subsidizing essential foods.
2. So-called breakdown in law and order not exaggerated.
3. Restore capital punishment.
4. Against spending more on social services.
5. Many people abuse the welfare state.
6. Problem of immigrants in this country not exaggerated.
7. Government should not spend more on pensions and social services.
8. Power of police should be increased.
9. Restrict immigration from Commonwealth and colonies.
10. Not wrong to control immigration on basis of colour.
11. Encourage immigrants to go home.
12. "If you give them an inch, they take a mile" applies to immigrants in this country.
13. Stricter laws make for a healthier society.
14. Management–employee relations cooperative.
15. Wrong to make the law on homosexuality less severe.
16. Good to reform our electoral system.
17. Remain in the Common Market.
18. Against introducing statutory wage control.
19. Present level of unemployment due to inefficiency of management.
20. Big business should be subject to more control.
21. Against reducing company taxes.
22. Voting to strike not by secret ballot.
23. No restrictions on the right to strike.
24. Trust trade unions to honour the "social contract".
25. Heavier taxing of the wealthy.
26. Abolish public schools.
27. Nationalize building land.
28. Abolish private health service.
29. Against selling council houses to tenants.
30. Bring more companies into public ownership.
31. Abolish grammar schools.
32. All schools should be comprehensive.
33. Wrong to impose legal sanctions to control strikes.
34. Disagrees that trade unions do the country more harm than good.
35. Unemployment not due to workers' excessive demands.
36. Wrong to describe trade unions as having "power without responsibility".
37. Not to cut social security benefits to strikers.

*Cumulative vote* for: Conservatives = Con

Labour = Lab

Liberals = Lib

*Cumulative abstentions* = Abst

the British public, but biased towards higher than average levels of education, it could still be argued that these results merely confirm Converse's (1964) contention that ideological consistency is found only among the better educated. To see how far our results might generalize across all sections of the electorate, we carried out a multidimensional scaling analysis on the responses to 24 attitude questions given by the October 1974 representative sample of the British election study. We included items dealing with the same issues covered in the 1974 round of questions in the longitudinal study (nationalization, social services, law and order, education, and so on) and other items to do with military cuts, aid to developing countries, and decentralization of state power.[19]

The results of this analysis are shown in Fig. 10.5. Once again a two-dimensional map adequately represents the structure underlying the responses to these items (stress = $0 \cdot 20$). Despite the differences in the sample and in the content of the items the similarities between the 1974 results for the British election study and our longitudinal study are marked.[20] Attitudes once again fell into two major and distinct clusters, one reflecting the more traditional party political "class-related" concerns, and another which encompasses law and order and immigration items.

In both cases attitudes to law and order and immigration clustered more tightly than did those within the economic and "class-related" cluster, and attitude to Britain's membership of the EEC fell outside the two main clusters. The close ties between attitude and vote choice were confirmed by the location of Conservative and Labour vote positions close to, or within, the two main clusters of attitudes. The Labour vote was located practically at the centre of the items coded in a "Labour" direction while the Conservative vote here too was located more towards the periphery of items coded in a "Conservative" direction, replicating the position of the cumulative votes for these parties in our panel study.

The Liberal vote once again fell between the two main clusters of attitudes on the horizontal axis (but at a different position on the vertical axis). There were few issues where the Liberal party took a position opposed to both the major parties.[21]

Figure 10.6 shows the structure resulting from a multidimensional scaling analysis of the responses to 25 attitude questions answered by the 1979 British election sample. While the overall structure closely resembles that of 1974 and also scales adequately in two dimensions (stress = $0 \cdot 17$) there are some changes in detail. Attitudes towards policies on government spending (on welfare, the military, social services etc) remained close to the Conservative vote position, but those relating to the "law and order" cluster of issues became less close between 1974 and 1979.

---

[19]Attitudes towards military cuts and the decentralization of power were coded in a "Conservative" direction, while a question on aid to developing countries was coded in a "Labour" direction.

[20]The same was true when we compared the respective factor analyses.

[21]Questions about electoral reform were not included in the British election study, the one issue clearly identified with the Liberal party. This is why the Liberal vote lies outside any attitude cluster or item.

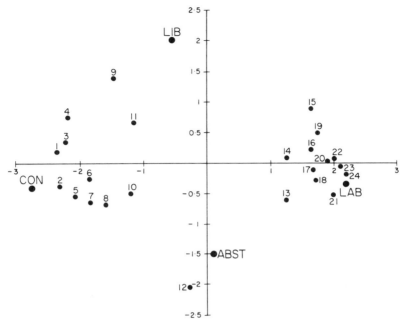

Fig. 10.5. Two-dimensional structure of 24 attitude measures analysis. Multidimensional scaling, BES 1974.

*Issues in direction of high scores*

 1. Welfare benefits gone much too far.
 2. Reduction of military strength gone much too far.
 3. Cut back on social services and benefits.
 4. Should not increase cash for National Health Service.
 5. Police should be firmer in handling demonstrations, sit-ins.
 6. Too little respect for authority.
 7. Attempts to ensure equality for coloured people in Britain gone much too far.
 8. Desirable to send coloured immigrants back to their country.
 9. Staying in the Common Market is a good thing.
10. Should take tougher measures to prevent crime.
11. Should not go easier on people who break the law.
12. Extent of strikes depends on government.
13. Good to decentralize power to the regions.
14. Big business has too much power.
15. Government should increase foreign aid.
16. For voluntary wage control.
17. Increase state control of land for building.
18. Spend more money to abolish poverty in Britain.
19. More industries to be nationalized.
20. Give workers more say in the running of their place of work.
21. Modern methods in teaching children not gone too far.
22. In favour of redistribution of wealth.
23. Establish comprehensive schools in place of grammar schools.
24. Trade unions do not have too much power.

|  |  |
|---|---|
| *Vote in 1974* for Conservatives | = Con |
| Labour | = Lab |
| Liberals | = Lib |
| *Abstentions in 1974* | = Abst |

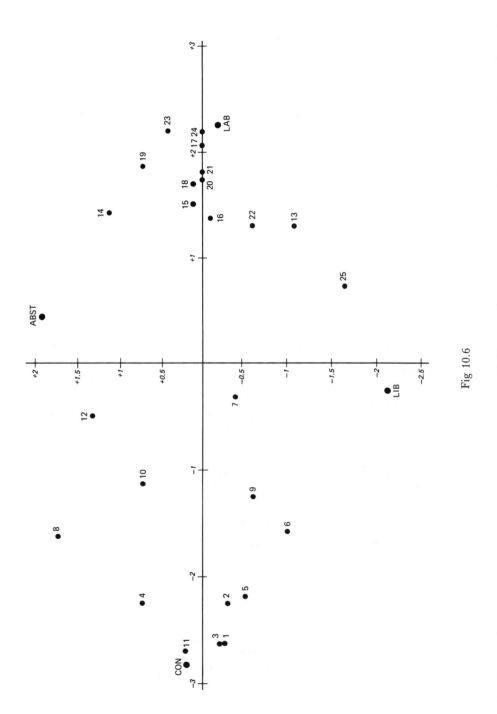

Fig 10.6

One issue which had become increasingly salient during the late 1970s was the increased use of nuclear power in the generation of the country's electricity supplies. Dislike of any expansion characterized the Liberal vote position better than any other. Throughout the 1970s, both the Labour and Conservative parties had been committed to nuclear power (the Conservatives more aggressively so). The absence of a firm policy on maintaining nuclear power on the part of the Liberals may thus have attracted those disaffected with the nuclear prospect.

## Differences in ideological consistency by educational level

Despite the clarity and stability of the multidimensional scalings, there remained the possibility that in smallest-space analyses conducted on attitudinal data from

---

Fig. 10.6. Two-dimensional structure of 25 attitude measures. Multidimensional scaling analysis, BES 1979.

*Issues in direction of high scores*

 1. Welfare rights gone much too far.
 2. Reduction in military strength gone much too far.
 3. Cut back on social services and benefits.
 4. Reduce taxes rather than keeping up government services.
 5. Challenging authority gone much too far.
 6. Recent attempts to ensure equality for coloured people in Britain gone much too far.
 7. Desirable to send coloured immigrants back to their country.
 8. Britain should be more willing to go along with the economic policies of other countries in the Common Market.
 9. Should give stiffer sentences to people who break the law.
10. Desirable to give council tenants the right to buy their houses.
11. Desirable to allow companies to keep profits to create more jobs rather than government spending tax money.
12. Government should set firm guidelines on salaries and wages.
13. Big business has too much power.
14. Government should give more aid to poorer countries in Africa and Asia.
15. Increase state control of land for building.
16. Spend more money to get rid of poverty in Britain.
17. More industries should be nationalized.
18. Give workers more say in the running of their place of work.
19. Modern methods in teaching children not gone nearly far enough.
20. Desirable to redistribute wealth.
21. Desirable to establish comprehensive schools in place of grammar schools.
22. Should put more money into the Health Service.
23. Trade unions do not have too much power.
24. Should not be stricter laws to regulate the activities of trade unions.
25. Should not go ahead with further expansion of nuclear power industry.

| | |
|---|---|
| *Vote in 1979* for Conservatives | = Con |
| Labour | = Lab |
| Liberals | = Lib |
| *Abstentions in 1979* | = Abst |

samples of all educational levels, the displayed structure was largely determined by the "ideologues" within the sample, the "inconsistencies" of the remainder serving to depress the average level of the correlations on which the analysis was based. The low stress coefficients for the two-dimensional solutions which we obtained made this unlikely. However, there could be differences in the way (rather than the extent to which) people who had continued their education to different levels structured their political attitudes.

We started by repeating the principal components factor analysis for different sub-samples to see if we could replicate Stimson's (1975) finding (for a United States' sample) discussed earlier in this chapter that at lower levels of cognitive ability certain families of attitudes exist but no supra-families.

Using the attitudinal data from the 1974 British election survey described above, we divided the sample into four groups, according to their educational level, following the criteria used by Alt et al. (1975, 1976):[22] those who had left school at or before the minimum school leaving age; those who had left school after the minimum school leaving age; those with some further education; and those with a university or equivalent education. Unlike Stimson we found that the number of factors did not decrease with increasing levels of education.[23] The amount of overall variance accounted for by the first factor was higher among those with a university education compared with those with no further education but the differences were slight[24] (variance rose from 16% to 22%) with more issues loading on the first factor.

There is evidence therefore of "supra-family" groupings at all levels of educational ability (contrary to Stimson, 1975 and Converse, 1964), and rather weak evidence in support of Converse's contention that "élite" groups' views are more tightly structured.

[22]Alt et al. (1975) used an individual differences multi-dimensional scaling approach (INDSCAL), to explore differences in cognitive structuring among different educational levels in the British electorate. They were interested in discovering the dimensions underlying perceptions of differences between the Conservative and Labour parties, and whether groups differed in the importance or salience they attached to the various dimensions. They identified two broad dimensions on which people differentiate the two major parties: (a) an image dimension, where individuals distinguish between the style and the performance of the parties; (b) a dimension which reflected a policy orientation, where individuals distinguish items with a high policy content. Examination of the salience attached to these two dimensions revealed that the highly educated members of their sample were less image conscious and more policy conscious in discriminating between the parties than were those with little education.

[23]Only between those with some further education and those with a university education was there a small decrease in the number of factors needed to describe their attitudes (from 8 to 7).

[24]The items that loaded on the first factor for those who left school at or before the minimum school leaving age included some, but not all, of the items in the supra-family grouping traditional party political concerns and class-relations in Fig 10.2 — nationalization, education, social services, trade unions, and labour relations. For the highly educated group only, this factor included *also* items identified with the second supra-family in Fig. 10.2 namely immigration, race relations, and law and order.

However, since in Britain educational level is confounded with class position, the differences found may reflect *different ideologies* rather than simply increased consistency within a shared ideological framework.

## IDEOLOGICAL DIFFERENCES AT DIFFERENT EDUCATIONAL LEVELS

We examined the possibility of *differences in ideology* (as opposed to differences in ideological consistency) across educational levels by repeating for our longitudinal study the multidimensional scaling analysis of 33 attitudinal measures, this time dividing the sample by educational level.[25] The similarity in the patterning was striking. The polarization of the two supra-families, and even the division into sub-clusters within each family, was as clear for each sub-sample as it was for the total sample. Even the locations of votes were similar in that the Liberal vote and abstentions for each group fell more or less between the Conservative and Labour vote position.

But there were some differences. At the high educational level, Liberal vote and abstention fell very close to each other, indicating that for this group a Liberal vote represented primarily a protest vote against the major parties while at the low educational level the Liberal vote came closer to the Conservative position.

For all educational levels, the Labour vote fell more centrally into one attitudinal cluster than did the Conservative vote in the other. Among the better educated the Labour vote was closest to items dealing with the educational system, among those with little education closer to trade union items. The immigration cluster was always at the heart of the "Conservative" region but it was the law and order issue which was closest to the Conservative vote, particularly among the least educated.

These analyses show how the voting ideologies of groups of voters of all levels of education in Britain in the 1970s were clearly structured around two supra-families of attitudes. The differences between the structure of attitudes at the various educational levels represent not so much different degrees of cognitive organization, in an abstract or "intellectual" sense, as differences in the salience of particular issues which reflect the interests of voters who occupy, for reasons correlated with their level of educational attainment, different positions within society.

## Changes in the structure of attitudes between 1962 and 1974 (longitudinal study)

Having shown how attitudes were structured in a stable way around two supra-families in 1970 and 1974 among the élite as well as the mass public, we can now turn

[25]We did this for 1970 attitudes only, because the 1974 sample was too small to be divided into three meaningful educational groups. The three educational groups were: high education level (all those with at least some University or College education), medium educational level (some "O" and/or "A" levels, but no further education), low educational levels (no school or further education qualifications).

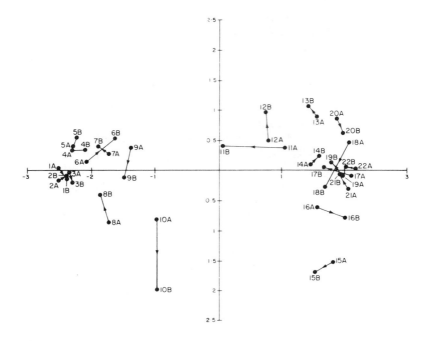

Fig. 10.7. Changes in attitudinal structure, 1970–1974, 22 issues. Multidimensional scaling (longitudinal sample). A = 1970, B = 1974.

*Issues in direction of high scores*

1. Disagrees that the way they are run now trade unions do this country more harm than good.
2. "Power without responsibility" not good description of trade unions.
3. There should be no legal sanctions to control strikes.
4. Abolish grammar schools.
5. More comprehensive schools (all should be comprehensive).
6. No restriction on the right to strike.
7. Abolish public schools.
8. Disagrees that voting to strike should be by secret ballot.
9. Big business should be subject to more control.
10. Management–employee relations full of conflict.
11. Britain should not join (leave) the Common Market.
12. Wrong to make the law on homosexuality less severe.
13. Not wrong to control immigration on the basis of colour.
14. "If you give an inch, they take a mile" might apply to immigrants in this country.
15. Wrong to spend more on pensions and social services.
16. So called breakdown of law and order not exaggerated.
17. Further restrict immigration from Commonwealth and colonies.
18. Stricter laws make for a healthier society.
19. Problem of immigrants in Britain has not been exaggerated.
20. Increased power of police.
21. Many people abuse the welfare state.
22. Capital punishment should be restored.

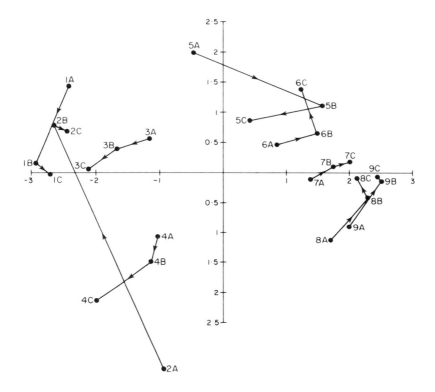

Fig. 10.8. Changes in attitudinal structure; 1962, 1970, 1974, nine issues. Multidimensional scaling (longitudinal sample). A = 1962, B = 1970, C = 1974.

*Issues in direction of high scores*

1. Disagrees that way they are run now trade unions do more harm than good.
2. Wants more comprehensive schools (all schools to be comprehensive).
3. Abolish public schools.
4. Management–employee relations full of conflict.
5. Britain should not join (leave) the Common Market.
6. Wrong to make the law on homosexuality less severe.
7. Agrees that "If you give them an inch, they take a mile" might well apply to immigrants in this country.
8. Restrict (restrict further) immigration from Commonwealth and colonies.
9. Capital punishment should not be abolished (should be restored).

to Converse's second criterion for establishing whether a group of people can be said to have an ideology: the stability of their attitudes and their structure across time.

Many of the questions asked in 1970 were repeated in 1974; nine of these had also been asked in 1962, making it possible to examine changes in the position of these questions over a 12-year span.

CHANGES BETWEEN 1970 AND 1974

We carried out a multidimensional scaling analysis of the sample's responses to 22 attitude questions repeated in 1970 and 1974. Figure 10.7 shows the position of the items at the two points in time. The structure previously obtained separately for 1970 and 1974 attitudes was also obtained here with the pairs of points constituting attitudes towards the same issue in 1970 and 1974 usually close together, affirming the stability of the structure over time.[26]

The one notable exception is the relative position of the attitude rejecting Britain's membership of the EEC which moves from the Conservative cluster in 1970 to a "neutral" position in 1974. Given that the Labour Government was pushing Britain towards the EEC until 1970 and then opposed membership when the Conservatives held office, it is not surprising that voters had a similarly unstable view on this issue, particularly since Britain joined the EEC only after 1970.

CHANGES BETWEEN 1962 AND 1974

The multidimensional scaling analysis of the nine questions repeated in 1962, 1970 and 1974, which yielded 27 points (nine for each time period) shows that, with two exceptions, attitudes towards the same issue between 1962 and 1974 formed a cluster of their own (Fig. 10.8). Where there was change it was orderly, with the position of the attitudes in 1970 lying between those of the same attitude in 1962 and 1974.

The two exceptions have already been mentioned: attitude towards comprehensive schools had very recently been introduced on the political scene, and moved to the place one would expect from reading the parties' manifestos in 1970, and 1974. The second exception is once again the attitude to membership of the EEC already discussed.

## Changes in the structure of attitudes between 1974 and 1979 (British election panel)

Sixteen similarly worded questions about political attitudes were asked of the same voters in the panel study which linked the British election surveys of 1974 and

[26]The direction and extent of the movement between 1970 and 1974 is indicated by the arrow connecting each pair of points.

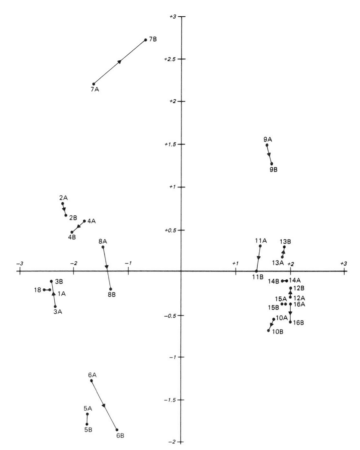

Fig. 10.9. Changes in attitude structure, 1974–1979, 16 issues. Multidimensional scaling, BES panel 1974–1979. A = 1974, B = 1979.

*Issues in direction of high scores*

  1. Welfare rights gone too far.
  2. Reduction of military strength gone too far.
  3. Cut back on social services and benefits.
  4. Challenging authority gone too far.
  5. Attempts to ensure equality for coloured people in Britain gone too far.
  6. Desirable to send coloured immigrants back to their country.
  7. Desirable to go along with the economic policies of other countries in the Common Market.
  8. Should give stiffer sentences to people who break the law.
  9. Government should increase foreign aid.
 10. Increase state control of land for building.
 11. Spend more money to get rid of poverty in Britain.
 12. More industries should be nationalized.
 13. Give workers more say in the running of their place of work.
 14. Desirable to redistribute wealth.
 15. Desirable to establish comprehensive schools in place of grammar schools.
 16. Trade unions do not have too much power.

1979, making it possible to carry out multidimensional scaling analyses to chart the changes in structure in these voters' cognitive maps between 1974 and 1979. The results are shown in Fig. 10.9. The stability of this structure is even more striking than that obtained in the corresponding analysis of the longitudinal sample (Fig. 10.7). In the second half of the 1970s, changes in the way the voters structured their political attitudes were the exception rather than the rule. This suggests that the marked reduction of support at the polls for the Labour party in 1979 was associated with changes of voters' perception of the *desirability of the Labour party's traditional policies in practice* rather than to a change in perception of the place of those policies in the political arena.

There were only two changes of any magnitude between 1974 and 1979; concerning attitudes in favour of (1) "sending coloured people back to their country" and (2) "going along with the policies of other EEC countries". Both became less closely associated with voting for the Conservative party, but in different ways, reflecting the treatments of these issues in the 1974 and 1979 election campaigns. In 1974, Edward Heath, the outgoing Conservative Prime Minister, dissociated his government from the policy of repatriating coloured people, yet this issue was often raised, notably in the media coverage of speeches by Enoch Powell who was then a prominent member of the Conservative party. In 1979, Mr Powell stood as a candidate in Northern Ireland, and media attention concentrated on his views concerning the failure of both Conservative and Labour policies with respect to the Irish question. Repatriation was an issue relegated to the platforms of parties like the National Front and British National Party, commanding little electoral support and media coverage.

In 1974, Mr Heath was strongly committed to support for policies formulated within the EEC. The views of those Conservatives politicians opposed to or less enthusiastic than the Prime Minister on this issue received little coverage in the media. In 1979, on the other hand, the misgivings of Margaret Thatcher, the new leader of the Conservative party, about unconditional support for EEC policies were echoed in the Conservative party's manifesto and in speeches by Conservative leaders reported in the press and on television.

## Overview

In summary, our multidimensional scaling analyses of the structure of British voter's political attitudes between 1962 and 1979 satisfy the second of Converse's criteria in showing stability of attitudes across time except for those items where there were specific policy reversals or where an issue was catapulted into, or out of, the political arena.

This brings us back to the opening theme of this chapter: that one cannot express a voting ideology simply in terms of degrees of "attitudinal constraint" on a single ideological continuum, nor ignore the life history of issues. We have shown the importance of careful analysis of the voters' cognitive map of political issues which are shared by voters at a particular point in time. It is only by examining *the location and movement* of attitudes towards salient political issues in relation to each other and to vote choice that we can begin to understand the voters' ideology in any *dynamic* sense.

In discussing ideology as a cultural system, Geertz (1964) claimed

> There are currently two main approaches to the study of the social determinants of ideology: the interest theory and the strain theory. For the first, ideology is mask and a weapon; for the second, a symptom and a remedy. In the interest theory, ideological pronouncements are seen against the background of a universal struggle for advantage; in the strain theory, against the background of a chronic effort to correct sociopsychological disequilibrium. In the one, men pursue power; in the other they flee anxiety. As they may of course do both at the same time — and even one by means of the other — the two themes are not necessarily contradicted.

While Geertz' two themes should not be equated with the two supra-families we have identified, it may well be that both aspects of the social determinants of ideology which he indicates feature in the voters' shared "cognitive maps". Such maps represent the voters' collective *responses* to the social and political climate of their society.

# 11

# The middle ground:
# The Liberal and the Alliance voters

Liberal voters have made appearances throughout the book, flitting in and out of the Conservative and Labour camps, more fickle and less predictable than voters for the two major parties. In this chapter we draw the strands together. In Part I we examine the characteristics of Liberal voters across elections. In one way our longitudinal study is particularly well suited for this exercise because it covers so many elections. On the other hand, since in any one election there are relatively few Liberals, the sample is too small for a reliable assessment of their views, so here too we extend the analysis using the British election studies, particularly the 1974–1979 panel and the survey at the time of the 1979 election, which was the last election the Liberals fought on their own.

In Part II, we examine the Alliance voters to see how far what we have learnt about the Liberals across seven elections applies to the Alliance voters at their first election. To do so, we needed to repeat several of the analyses on the 1983 sample. To avoid repetition, their results have been included in the tables presented in Part I, even though they will only be discussed in Part II.

## Part I: The Liberal voters

The longitudinal study began and ended with a Liberal upsurge. We carried out the first interviews in 1962, soon after the famous Orpington bye-election, which many saw as the beginning of a Liberal revival and to which our sample responded enthusiastically, with as many as 25% saying they would vote Liberal if there were an election tomorrow. The study ended in October 1974, the year of another Liberal upsurge, this time of majestic proportions. In the 1974 election, the Liberals gained a 19% share of the vote and close to four million new voters[1] — one million more than the increase in the number of Conservative voters in 1979, which was their largest increase since World War II. Had there been proportional representation, the Liberals would have had 121 seats instead of 14.

Both times, the revival was short-lived. Two years after the initial interviews in 1964 only 10% of the young men in our sample voted for the Liberals, and as many as three out of four of the 1962 would-be Liberals made a different choice when it came to the test in 1964. Similarly, in 1979 the Liberals' share of the vote — two million less than in 1974 — dropped from 19% to 14%.

After each revival, the drop in popularity was large. But it still benefited the Liberals in that it created a new baseline of voting for the Liberals. Their share of the vote in 1964, though much less than had been expected, was 11% compared with only 6% in the previous election, and remained above 6% in every election since. Equally the drop of 5% of the share of the vote between February 1974 and 1979 still left the Liberals with a larger share than in any election since 1945.

Even in the volatile electoral climate of the past 20 years, with see-saw like changes in government, the Liberal voters stood out as far more changeable than any other. Between February and October 1974, 15% of the Conservative and 12% of the Labour voters changed their vote. Among the Liberals as many as 31% did so. And of the 58 would-be Liberals in our sample in 1962 only three voted consistently for the Liberals in the three subsequent elections (1964–1970), while four times their number voted consistently for the other two parties. Why should this be?

What is it about the Liberal party which at times enables it to sway the electorate so powerfully that it can produce increases in vote far larger than have been achieved by either of the two major parties during the same period? And equally, what is it that makes the momentum gained so ephemeral?

The way the question is put suggests that we need to ask what it is in the Liberal party's policies and electoral campaign which attracts large additions to the core of its faithful, and equally, what draws the newly converted away from that party. This presupposes a sizeable core of faithful Liberals (relative always to the overall size of the Liberal vote) which new voters join and others leave. But is there a solid core of faithful supporters? When we looked at the voting history of the 178 men in our sample over the five 1964–1974 elections (including the two elections with the massive Liberal gain) only three men had voted consistently for the Liberals and a further three had done so four times and abstained once — a tiny number. It might be argued that we studied voters at the beginning of their voting career where one would not expect to find many consistent Liberals. Consistency of voting, especially for a minority party, may take time to establish. We therefore also looked for the consistent Liberal voters among the Butler and Stokes panel: of the 750 men and women only 10 had voted for the Liberals consistently at each of the four elections 1959–1970, and a further two had done so three times,

[1]In our sample, 27% voted Liberal in the February and 23% in the October 1974 election.

abstaining once. This analysis confirms that there was and probably is not a sizeable core of faithful Liberal voters. In both studies, there were as few consistent Liberals as there were consistent abstainers.

Some constituencies regularly return a Liberal candidate, but these are the exceptions. Loyalty there has been built up because of special historical or geographical circumstances or because of trust in particular individuals. Our concern, however, is not with these exceptions but with the electorate across the country. It was among them that we looked for the voters who consistently preferred the Liberals to the other parties and found too few to account for the Liberal voters in any of the elections.

The Liberal voters in one election are rarely the same people in another. Each election produces a new crop of Liberals thrown up by the vagaries of the two main parties. This makes the paradigm, appropriate for discussing the changing fortunes of the Conservative and Labour party, inappropriate when discussing changes in the fortunes of the Liberal party. A more appropriate paradigm is one which looks, not so much at what attracts the voter to the Liberal party, but rather at what draws the voter away from the party for which he or she had previously voted. *The Liberal vote is a vote of disaffection; it represents movement away from a party rather than movement to the party; it is a vote signifying departure rather than arrival.*

The view we offer of the genesis of the Liberal vote in any given election is not one which would commend itself to the Liberal party. They might rightly argue that the tiny group of consistent Liberal voters in our samples severely underestimates the many convinced Liberals that exist in the country who simply do not vote for the Liberals either for strategic reasons, or because they cannot do so in those constituencies where there is no Liberal candidate. They also rightly argue that the number who would vote for the Liberals cannot be established until there is proportional representation, since many would be deterred from voting for them for fear of wasting their vote. Butler and Stokes (1969) asked the Conservative and Labour voters in the 1964 and 1966 elections whether they had ever considered voting for another party, and those who had, whether they had considered voting for the Liberals. Accepting that such statements are likely to be overestimates, the authors added half their number to the number of those voters in constituencies with no Liberal candidate who said they would have liked to have voted for the party had it been possible. On the basis of these calculations Butler and Stokes estimated a 23% and 25% Liberal share of the votes for the two elections in the 1960s. In 1979, when every constituency had a Liberal candidate, Särlvik and Crewe (1983) asked a differently worded question, namely:

> If you had thought that the Liberals would have won a lot more seats in Britain as a whole, how likely is it that you would then have voted Liberal? (Very likely; Not very likely; Not at all likely).

Twenty-nine per cent of Conservatives and 28% of Labour voters said they would very likely have done so. Had they all voted Liberal, the overall share of the Liberal vote would have been 34%, a figure falling not "much short of proportional representation in Parliament, even under the present electoral system'' (Särlvik and Crewe, 1983, p.290). The authors rightly urge caution; there is a big difference between intention and action. But it is worth remembering that what seemed a projection of an impossibly large share of the vote in 1966 actually came to pass when the Liberals and the SDP joined forces in 1983.

No one can forecast what might happen under a different electoral system, particularly since such a system would be established only if there were profound changes in the fortunes of the major parties, i.e. if the political scene were to be transformed. While the number of "true" Liberal voters is anybody's guess, what we can do, however, is to look more closely at the outlook and attitudes of the Liberal voters in each of the elections[2] to examine whether the premise put forward earlier, that the Liberal vote is a vote of disaffection rather than support for Liberal policies, can be substantiated.

Whether intention or preference is translated into action depends not only on the strength of an individual's views, but also on the presence of *rootedness factors*. There are four such factors: (1) early political socialization; (2) for the party to be firmly anchored, i.e. it requires a strong social or regional base; (3) the habit of voting for the same party repeatedly; (4) identification with the party for which the individual votes.

The longitudinal study showed that on all four counts Conservative and Labour voters proved more firmly rooted to their party than were the Liberals. (1) Only 20% of those adolescents whose parents voted Liberal said they would vote the same way, compared with the 60% overall who echoed their parents. (2) Relative to the Liberals, the voters for the main parties have a firmer social and regional base, even though its strength is declining. (3) The extreme volatility of the Liberal voter has made it unlikely that many would build up a habit of voting for the party. (4) Finally, as Table 11.1 shows, fewer Liberals compared with Labour and Conservative voters identified with their party, and the strength of their identification was weaker: only 13% were strong identifiers compared with as many as one in four among the voters for the other parties. Indeed in 1979 30% of those who identified with the Liberals actually voted for another party, due either to tactical voting on the part of the potential Liberal voter or to an identification with "liberalism" rather than with the Liberal party.

## THE LIBERAL VOTERS' ATTITUDES TO THEIR PARTY

There is other evidence to suggest that the relation of the Liberal voter to the Liberal party is less a love match than a marriage of convenience. For example, when in 1974 and 1979 the voters were asked to indicate how much they liked

---

[2]That is, all those who voted Liberal in a particular election, irrespective of whether they did so in any preceding or subsequent election.

TABLE 11.1                                                                *Longit. study*

Indicators of rootedness in the preference for a party

| I | Political socialization | | Parents voted | | |
|---|---|---|---|---|---|
| | | | Con (%) | Lab (%) | Lib (%) |
| | Percentage of men as adolescents who expressed same vote preference as | | | | |
| | | Mother | 63 | 65 | 20 |
| | | Father | 61 | 62 | 13 |

| II | Consistency of vote across two adjacent elections | Type of voters | | |
|---|---|---|---|---|
| | | Con (%) | Lab (%) | Lib (%) |
| | *From:* | | | |
| | 1959–1964 | 57 | 77 | 45 |
| | 1962 intention to 1964 vote | 70 | 79 | 22 |
| | 1964–1966 | 86 | 85 | 41 |
| | 1966–1970 | 75 | 58 | 41 |
| | 1970–Feb. 1974 | 68 | 74 | 74 |
| | Feb. 1974–Oct. 1974 | 84 | 86 | 70 |

| III | Party identification 1974 | Vote cast October | | |
|---|---|---|---|---|
| | | Con (%) | Lab (%) | Lib (%) |
| | Percentage who identified with the party for whom they had voted | 87 | 74 | 42 |

each of the three parties (using a 10-point scale), the mean rating by the Liberals for their party was less than that of the devotees of the other two parties for theirs.

Even more pertinent were the Liberals reactions when asked which party they thought would be best at handling particular problems.[3] While the majority of Labour and Conservative voters judged their own party to be best, there was not a single issue on which the Liberal voters preferred the Liberal party. For some issues, they preferred the Conservatives and for others the Labour party. Even amongst the few who had voted Liberal in 1970 as well as in 1974, less than half chose their own party.

Nor was the picture any different in 1979. The Liberal voters did not consider their own party to be best at handling the major problems like inflation, taxation, unemployment, industrial relations or law and order. In 1979 Labour voters were

[3]The problems referred to were the Common Market, legal control of wages, influence of communists in the trade unions, nationalization and social services.

less sure of the superiority of their own party compared with 1974, but, by comparison with the Liberals, they were their party's staunch supporters (Butler and Kavanagh, 1980).

So far we have considered a variety of factors which explain the special volatility of the Liberal vote. But such volatility does not necessarily mean that an individual who chooses to vote Liberal once, or even twice, might not do so because he or she has a distinctive set of attitudes which attract him or her, however fleetingly, to the Liberal party. If so, even though the Liberal voters in one election are not the same individuals in another, they might still share a common set of attitudes and an outlook that would differentiate them from the voters for the two other parties.

## Comparison of the attitude profiles of the Liberal voters with major party voters

In our study the first thing to note is that with regard to most attitudes or responses to particular policies, the Liberal voters' views were more moderate than those of the Conservative or Labour voters. On economic issues their views tended to be closer to those of the Conservatives; on liberal issues closer to those of Labour voters. Well over 60 comparisons were made.

Using Butler and Stokes' distinction between *position* and *valence* issues, the Liberals were middle of the road on both. This, however, does not preclude the possibility that in the structure of their beliefs and attitudes, or shared cognitive maps, the Liberals might not differ from Conservative and Labour voters.

In election campaigns Liberal politicians made the point that while Labour is for trade union power and against the power of big business, and the Conservatives for big business and against trade unions, the Liberals accept no such divide. Instead they are against excessive power of any institution whether labour of management. In 1974 Crew (1977) found that more Liberal than Conservative or Labour voters considered both trade unions and big business too powerful.

Also the Liberal party has been at pains to emphasize that both Labour and Conservative policies are divisive and seriously underplay the degree of cooperation that exists in the country. If these views were reflected in the Liberal vote, this might well result in a distinctive profile of attitudes less polarized than those of Conservative and Labour voters whom we have shown to be sharply divided on many issues.

The discriminant analyses of the large-scale surveys reported in Chapter 5 showed not only that a considerable percentage of Liberals were misclassified as either Conservative or Labour, but that on issues which differentiated the voters, the Liberals did indeed occupy the middle ground: opposed to nationalization, they were less keen on privatization of existing nationalized industries, while critical of the unions, they were less hostile to them than the Conservatives; and more critical of big business but less so than Labour voters. The list is endless.

Särlvik and Crewe derived from a discriminant analysis of the 1979 data with attitudes as independent variables and vote choice as dependent variable, an average scale position for the attitudes of each type of voter. These scale positions ranged from + 4 expressing positions on the right of the continuum to − 4 expressing those on the left. The differences in the mean scale positions support the story told so far: the Conservative voters had a positive mean value, the Labour voters a negative mean value, and the Liberals one close to zero.[4] Figure 11.1 represents the approximate party position of the vote at each point of the scale (Särlvik and Crewe, 1983). Not only is the Liberal voter centrally placed (a little more to the right than to the left) but also there are many Conservative and Labour voters who hold moderate views, a potential source of support for a centrist party, given favourable conditions.

The most telling evidence that the Liberals had no distinctive attitude profile or "ideology" comes from the multidimensional scaling analyses discussed in Chapter 10. Our sample and the Crewe sample each yielded two distinct attitude clusters: those voters with a high propensity to vote Conservative being located close to one cluster of attitudes and those with a high propensity to vote Labour close to another. Those with a high propensity to vote Liberal (as well as the abstainers) had neither a distinctive cluster of attitudes nor were they located close to either party but were midway between, mostly on their own (Chapter 10, p.147). The position of the Liberals and the abstainers was very similar. The only item in 1970 close to the position of the Liberals (Britain's membership of the EEC) had no link with either the Conservative or Labour "ideology". In 1974 and 1979

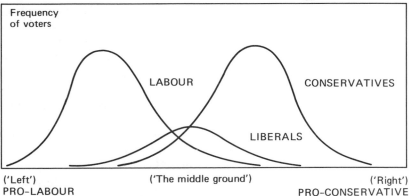

Fig. 11.1. The Labour and Conservative modes and the shared middle ground. *Note:* The figure shows the approximate party division of the vote at each point on the scale. The total number of voters at any given point is of course equal to the sum of the numbers of Conservative, Liberal and Labour voters at that point. Source: Särlvik and Crewe (1983, p.287).

[4]The mean value for Conservatives was + 0·69, for Labour − 0·92 and for the Liberals − 0·15.

electoral reform occupied a similarly isolated position. The fact that the Liberal vote occupied much the same position as abstentions within this multidimensional space suggests that the decisions to abstain and to vote Liberal have similar roots.

In 1974, Alt *et al.* (1975) carried out an individual differences multidimensional scaling analysis (INSCAL) using measures of the voters' attitudes to policies and their evaluation of the style or image of each of the three parties. The analysis yielded two dimensions. The first was an *image dimension* or style of government and related to the voters' perception of each of the parties (extreme *v.* moderate; divides *v.* unites; bloody-minded *v.* reasonable; good for one class *v.* good for all classes). The second dimension related to their views on *policy issues* (Common Market, nationalization, social services, strikes, wages, pensions, etc.). Having isolated these two dimensions, the authors then ascertained for the different groups (Labour, Conservative, Liberal and abstainers) the dimensions important to them. Conservative voters stressed the policies dimension and Labour voters both policies and images equally. The Liberal voters were the only group for whom the image dimension alone was salient, i.e. the Liberals and also the abstainers reacted more to the general impression the party made on them than to their views on specific policies. These results, along with the scaling analyses reported here, lend support to our premise that the individual votes Liberal less because of the attraction of Liberal policies than because of his or her disaffection with the other parties.

By and large, Liberal voters return to the party from which they came, so much so that until 1979 voting for the Liberals was viewed as an alternative to abstaining, and not as a halfway house in a journey from Conservatives to Labour or vice versa. In 1979 this was no longer the case. Quite a number of those who had voted for the Liberals in 1974, having come from Labour in the previous election, moved over to the Conservatives in 1979; others made the journey in one fell swoop, moving from Labour straight to the Conservatives.

So far we have shown that on the basis of their attitudes the Liberals do not differ from the voters for the major parties and that Liberal voters are drawn from, and move to, both parties apparently with equal ease, their numbers and composition being determined by the government of the day and by the vagaries of the two major parties.

Two questions remain to be answered; first, how is it possible for the Liberal party to provide such a convenient resting place for voters whose past voting patterns suggest that they hold rather divergent views? Why is the Liberal party all things to all men? And secondly, a question not unrelated to the first, what propels the Conservative and Labour voters to move away from their party towards the Liberals?

To answer these questions we sought to learn more about the attitudes of the Liberal voters by comparing them, not simultaneously with both major parties as we had done previously, but with each of the two parties in turn.

Table 11.2 shows that when we compared the Liberals in this way they were almost as well predicted as were the Conservative or Labour voters. The issues which differentiated best between Liberals and Conservatives had to do with the

TABLE 11.2                                    *BES October 1974, 1979, BBC/Crewe, 1983*

Percentage accuracy of classification of (A) *Conservative versus Liberal* and (B) *Labour versus
Liberal* voters in the October 1974, 1979 and 1983 elections, using the voters' views on
issues as independent variables (discriminant analyses)

| Election sample | (A) Percentage accuracy of classification between Conservatives and Liberals | | |
|---|---|---|---|
| | Conservative (%) | Liberal (%) | Overall (%) |
| October 1974 | 73 | 67 | 71 |
| 1979 | 76 | 67 | 74 |
| | | *Alliance* | |
| 1983 | 79 | 76 | 77 |

| Election sample | (B) Percentage accuracy of classification between Labour and Liberals | | |
|---|---|---|---|
| | Conservative (%) | Liberal (%) | Overall (%) |
| October 1974 | 78 | 78 | 78 |
| 1979 | 73 | 67 | 72 |
| | | *Alliance* | |
| 1983 | 76 | 75 | 75 |

power of big business, the redistribution of wealth, the buying of council houses
by tenants, and with workers having more say in industry. Differences between
Liberals and Labour related to their attitudes to trade unions, nationalization,
comprehensive schooling, and whether private companies or government would
be best for creating jobs. There were two issues in which the Labour voter lagged
behind the Liberal voter: the first had to do with electoral reform and the second
with policies towards equality for women.

These analyses indicate that Liberal voters hold some attitudes which come close
to those of the Conservatives and others which are closer to Labour. Liberal voters
are not simply pale versions of the typical Tory or Labour voter. Rather they
are people who have a less polarized view of society and its institutions and who
react to individual issues rather than to the political package of which the issues
form a part. In the case of selective education, for example, they were *for* the
establishment of comprehensive schools and *against* the abolition of public schools.
They were *against* the way trade unions conducted their affairs but were *for* some
control of big business and in favour of worker consultation.

For the disaffected Labour voter the Liberal party has the attraction of being
less tied to the sacred cow of the Labour party without being blatantly Conservative
about big business or seemingly antagonistic to the workers. For the disaffected
Conservative, the Liberal party offers a view of the economy not too dissimilar
from that of the Conservatives but with the added attraction of being more liberal
and humane. The potential Liberal, it would appear, shies away from the

extremism of either party: in the Labour party such extremism tends to be linked to such issues as nationalization, the role of the trade unions and of big business; and in the Conservative party to the issues of immigration and law and order.

Many of the transient recruits to the Liberal party are there because they have reacted adversely to the stridency of either party. Such stridency is less noticeable between elections in the daily conduct of the parties in either government or opposition than at election times when it may surface in the manifestos and in the speeches and reactions of politicians during the campaign.[5] It makes good sense, therefore, as was shown in Chapter 9, that the ex-Conservative or ex-Labour voter votes Liberal out of fear of, or dislike for, what he or she believes their own party might do in the future rather than out of disapproval of what that party has done in the past.

It follows that by comparison with Labour and Conservative voters, knowledge of the voters' attitudes to issues which were salient at one election would not be of much help in predicting who will vote Liberal at the next, not because the potential Liberal voter changes his mind more than other voters, but because his decision depends on the gulf between the voter's attitude and those of the party for which he tends to vote. And it is this difference which changes over time, depending on the conduct and above all the electioneering of the parties concerned.

Comparison of predictions of our sample's 1974 vote from measures of attitudes obtained in 1974 with those from measures obtained at the time of the 1970 election revealed a great deal about the three types of voters. For the Conservatives who, as we have shown elsewhere, tended during the period of our study to be less issue-sensitive than Labour or Liberal voters and more influenced by past voting habit, past attitudes proved a better predictor than current reactions, but neither was very good. For Labour voters, prediction was high with both past and present attitudes playing an equal role. The pattern for the Liberals proved different again. Predicting their vote on the basis of attitudes that had been salient for making such a decision at the last election was no better than tossing a coin. On the other hand, knowledge of the individual's current attitudes predicted accurately three out of four Liberal voters.

Given these very different results, we tried to see whether our predictions would improve if we added to the present (each person's perception of current issues) the past, i.e. his attitudes as measured four years earlier. We found that Conservatives were best predicted by giving a weight of 80% to past attitudes and 20% to current views. Labour voters were almost equally well predicted by any mixture of past and present, and the Liberals solely by their views about current issues, thus confirming that Liberal voters tend to decide largely on the impression they form in the course of the electoral campaign itself. This explanation is in keeping with our finding that the Liberal voter made up his mind significantly later than the voters for the other parties. These results may seem at first sight

[5]Enoch Powell's speeches in 1970 and again in 1974 forced both parties to speak out about issues neither had wished to form part of their electoral platform.

paradoxical when compared with our conclusion that there is no such thing as the typical Liberal voter.

The paradox resolves itself once we accept that the individual who finally votes Liberal is, in many respects, the comparative shopper *par excellence*. However, his shopping is guided more by dislike for products he had bought in the past than enthusiasm for the one he finally selects. It should follow that those Labour and Conservative voters who are potential defectors (i.e. those with poor attitudinal fit) should be searching for more information about the parties than those not in doubt.

To test this view, we divided the 1970 Labour and Conservative voters respectively into those with poor attitudinal fit (below $0 \cdot 50$)[6] and the remainder, asking each voter how much he had learnt from television about the politicians of each of the three parties (their personalities, views on current affairs and the principles they stood for). Table 11.3 shows that *more* of those with poor attitudinal fit, compared with those with good attitudinal fit, thought they had learnt a lot about the personalities of the politicians of their *own* party. For Labour, the difference between the two groups was 29%, for the Conservatives 21%.

On the other hand, *fewer* among those with poor fit, compared with the other voters for their party, thought they had learnt a lot about the principles or views on current affairs of the politicians of their own party and those of the opposition.

TABLE 11.3                                                               *Longit. study*

Percentage of 1970 Conservative and Labour voters (subdivided by attitudinal fit to their party) who said they had learnt a lot from television about the politicians of each of the three parties: (A) Their personalities; (B) Their views on current affairs; (C) The principles they stood for

| About the politicians of the three parties | Percentage who had learnt a lot | | | |
| | Conservative | | Labour | |
| | Poor fit | Good fit | Poor fit | Good fit |
|---|---|---|---|---|
| A. *Their personalities* | | | | |
| Conservative politicians | *51* | 30 | 32 | 23 |
| Labour politicians | 47 | 33 | *56* | 27 |
| Liberal politicians | 16 | 20 | 33 | 15 |
| B. *Their views on current affairs* | | | | |
| Conservative politicians | 33 | 45 | 20 | 42 |
| Labour politicians | 15 | 18 | 20 | 35 |
| Liberal politicians | *22* | 10 | *33* | 19 |
| C. *The principles they stood for* | | | | |
| Conservative politicians | 39 | 38 | 16 | 27 |
| Labour politicians | 18 | 15 | 24 | 23 |
| Liberal politicians | *24* | 10 | *33* | 23 |

[6]A description of the method of arriving at poor or good attitudinal fit is given in Chapter 3, p.45).

Instead, and this is the interesting finding, in all four comparisons more of the potential defectors, compared with the others, thought they had learnt a lot about the Liberal politicians' views on current affairs and the principles they stood for. These results concerning the potential defectors to the Liberal party, supports the view of Alt *et al.* (1975) and our own that it is the image, style or personalities to which the potential Liberal voter is sensitive. Like the comparative shopper he wishes to be reassured or have his doubts confirmed about the purchases made in the past, and to examine the positive features of an alternate brand, before deciding whether or not to change.

So far we have shown what propels the Liberal voter away from his customary party. We now need to examine what makes it so easy, when dissatisfied, to move to the Liberals rather than abstain or stick it out. There are two answers. First, most people prefer to vote rather than abstain; habit, normative pressure and a sense of civic duty all play a part in this. The second answer lies in the way the Liberal party presents itself to the public. Few people read election manifestos and the specific proposals and promises they contain. Most voters therefore learn about the Liberals from television. Liberal party leaders in the post-war elections have tended to put forward, not specific proposals, but a general message which has become increasingly attractive to the voters of the two major parties, namely that the divide in society is magnified by the parties for their own ends and that the Liberal party, through a pragmatic and caring approach, can bring about effective cooperation. It is a message of hope embodied in the slogan ''People count''. As we have shown elsewhere, the attraction of the party is built on the echo these sentiments evoke rather than on a consideration of the party's policies.

Since the message of the Liberal party has not changed much from one election to another, although their share of the vote has, we used the results of our analyses to examine the conditions which would favour a high vote. On the day of the February 1974 election, we published a forecast[7] based on our longitudinal study in which we predicted a considerable gain for the Liberals and specified the conditions under which such gain should occur. We were proved right, confirming that an increase in the Liberal vote is more likely when:

1. The two main parties indulge in mud slinging and stridency, particularly in the last few days of the election.

2. The Liberals refrain from attacking the main parties on issues which might alientate potential supporters who, as we showed earlier, still hold many of the views of the party from which they intend to defect. That is when the Liberal party remains low key, presenting itself in terms of a general approach rather than in terms of specific proposals. This makes it easier for voters from different parties to *project* onto the Liberals those features they would wish their own party to have, without becoming aware that this choice implies foregoing others which they value.

[7]Himmelweit and Humphreys. The Liberal Floater (*New Society*, February 28, 1974, **27**).

3. The Liberals emphasize their readiness to collaborate on broad strategy or on specific issues with either Labour or Conservatives. This permits each voter — ex-Labour or ex-Conservative — to think that by voting Liberal he will not desert his own party's *policy* but add to it a much needed flexibility, since it is the party's *rigidity* which he or she dislikes.

4. As election day approaches, public opinion polls reflect a rise, or at least not a decline, in the members intending to vote Liberal. This signals to the potential Liberal voter that he is one of many and so reduces his anxiety about a wasted vote, especially important since our studies have shown that Liberals and abstainers make up their minds much later than other voters.

5. The constituency is marginal. The voter's belief that the Liberal candidate has a good chance is important and this may well be affected not only by the opinion polls but also by the level of activity of the candidate and the local party, especially in the last crucial days before the election.

All these conditions were met in the 1974 election, which yielded a massive increase in Liberal votes. They were not met in 1979 when the Liberal share of the vote dropped from its all-time high of 19% in February 1974 to 14% in 1979. There were a number of reasons for this drop: first, as Butler and Kavanagh (1980) have pointed out, "both parties moved carefully on the issue of extremism . . . and because the main parties did not indulge in slanging, there was less scope for the Liberals to appeal to the moderate centre" (p.333). Secondly, the Labour–Liberal pact during the latter part of the Labour government brought home to potential voters that voting Liberal was not just a way of expressing disaffection but might mean supporting another party's policies with which the voter was in disagreement. As Freud has shown, projection works best where the individual or the organization is shadowy rather than distinct. Thirdly, the fact that over six million votes for the Liberals in 1974 yielded only 14 Liberal MPs may have alerted voters to the enormous difficulty of translating Liberal votes into effective political influence given the current electoral system. This demonstration was particularly relevant for those Conservatives who had either voted Liberal in 1974 or wanted to do so in 1979, making them aware that only by voting for the Conservatives could Labour be ousted. Trend analyses have shown that whenever a Labour government is in office, the Liberal vote in the following election drops; Conservatives return to the fold to be in a better position to remove the Labour government. And finally, in 1979 there was, after the "winter of discontent", a wish for a change; hence the appeal of the Conservatives' claim to provide a radical change, as against the re-run of Labour policies that the voters had heard before.

## Part II: The Alliance voter in 1983

By any standards, the success of the Alliance in the early 1980s was remarkable. When the Social Democratic Party came into being in March 1981 it immediately obtained the potential vote of a quarter of the electorate. Though these figures are impressive by themselves, they could represent no more than the passing attraction of a novelty, were it not for the fact that the same percentage figures were obtained in successive polls over eight months, followed by an increase to a 40% share during the last three months of 1981. This increase followed the announcement of the formation of the Alliance by the Social Democrats and Liberals to fight the next general election. In 1982, the percentage of potential Alliance voters remained at 30% or above until the Falklands crisis. Success in the polls was reinforced by the Alliance's concrete successes in three by-elections. For the remainder of 1982, vote intentions for the Alliance averaged around 23% and in 1983 around 21% until the beginning of the election campaign in May that year.

To attract voters, a new party needs to rely upon the mass media reporting its distinctiveness and successes even more than do long established ones. The novelty of the formation of the SDP and the even greater novelty of its joining with the Liberals to form the Alliance, together with favourable poll results and by-election successes ensured that the Social Democrats and the Liberals received considerable, and largely, favourable media coverage. Their experienced politicians were skilled at putting over in a very positive, combative style their conciliatory, centrist message. There seemed sufficient grounds for an Alliance optimist to believe, and party politicians have to be optimists or pretend to be so, that the Alliance was able, not just to get members of Parliament into the House of Commons as the Liberals had done before, but that the Alliance of the two parties was within reach of forming a government.

The 1982 Falklands crisis and its aftermath transformed the situation. It not only increased the standing of the Conservatives; it robbed the Alliance of opportunities to gain the electorate's attention. During the Falklands crisis the Alliance MPs, like the rest of the House of Commons, supported the government's action. Such criticism, where it occurred, and only as the war progressed, was voiced in a low key. The role of the Alliance MPs had become that of supporting bit players. For almost a year the Alliance had far fewer occasions than in the earlier period to make an impression on the public. Being so little reported by the press and broadcasters was perhaps more damaging than adverse criticism might have been.

The 1983 election campaign provided a much-needed opportunity for the Alliance politicians to make the electorate once more take notice of the Alliance as a viable choice. The agreement worked out between the parties and the broadcasters about the relative number of party election broadcasts was important not only because of the number of opportunities these provided to talk directly to the viewers, but also because by tradition the broadcasting companies apply the same ratio of air time given to the parties for party election broadcasts to the presentation of parties, candidates and leaders in News, current affairs and special election programmes. The ratio agreed for the 1983 election was five (party election broadcasts) for Labour, five for the Conservatives and four for the

Alliance.[8] The Alliance did well in the campaign. At the beginning of the campaign, the Alliance had a 21% share of the intended vote, at the end a 26% share, which was translated into actual voting by 25% of those who went to the polls. In the case of the major parties, the campaign served to reduce, not to increase, their potential vote (Worcester, 1983).

Did this record of success in the early 1980s imply that the Alliance, unlike the Liberal party in past elections, might turn out to be a party of *arrival* and not just a haven for the disaffected? The survey evidence available in 1983 suggests this was not so. Table 11.4 summarizes the evidence, showing that the Alliance voters, like the Liberal voters in previous elections, made up their minds later than voters for the major parties (as many as 44% during the campaign and 17% in the last few days) and more of them chose the party out of dislike for the other parties rather than because something attracted them to the Alliance. Only half the Alliance voters identified themselves with the Alliance (compared with about 85% of Labour voters and Conservative voters who identified with their parties) and as many as 33%, while voting for the Alliance, still saw themselves as either Labour or as Conservatives.

The Conservative voters almost without exception were the most positive about the policies, the team of leaders and the usefulness of their party "for people like

TABLE 11.4                                                                          *BBC/Crewe, 1983*

Distribution of party vote in the 1983 election by (A) time of decision making; (B) reason for voting for the party; (C) concordance between party identification and vote choice

|  | | Party voted for | |
| --- | --- | --- | --- |
|  | Con | Lab | Alliance |
| (A)  *Time of decision* | | | |
| 1.   Long time ago | 86% | 84% | 56% |
| 2.   Two or three weeks ago | 10% | 10% | 27% |
| 3.   Last few days | 4% | 6% | 17% |
|  | 100% | 100% | 100% |
| (B)  *Reason for party choice* | | | |
| 1.   Negative (dislike of other parties) | 48% | 33% | 57% |
| 2.   Positive (party attracts) | 40% | 54% | 33% |
| 3.   Both negative and positive reasons | 12% | 13% | 10% |
|  | 100% | 100% | 100% |
| (C)  *Voted for party and identified with it* | 85% | 90% | 53%* |

[8]The introduction of a new party which commanded a substantial number of potential voters but had not yet been tested in a general election posed problems for the joint committee of representatives of the political parties and the broadcasting authorities, which decides on the airtime to be allotted to the parties for their party political broadcasts. By tradition, this had been based on the parties' relative share of the votes in the previous general election.

me''; and the Alliance voters the least positive about their own party. They had a slight edge over Labour only in the proportion who saw their party as having the best team of leaders, no doubt due to the disastrous ratings by the electorate as a whole of the leader of the Labour party, Michael Foot.[9]

None of these findings is in any way surprising. Two parties, of which one is quite new, forming an alliance cannot engender the loyalty or the trust that the well established parties have built up over time.

## DIFFERENCES IN OUTLOOK BETWEEN ALLIANCE, LABOUR AND CONSERVATIVE VOTERS

The discriminant analyses reported in Tables 5.4 and 5.5 indicate that the Alliance voters, like the Liberals before them, were less accurately classified on the basis of their views on either issues or party leaders than were Labour and Conservative voters.

The discriminant analyses summarized in Table 11.2, comparing Alliance voters with the voters for each of the major parties in turn, also indicated that the issues that separated the Alliance voters from the voters for each of the major parties were the same as had separated the Liberals from them in earlier elections. In the 1983 election, in addition, what particularly differentiated Alliance voters from the Labour voters were their more positive views on Britain's relations with the EEC and from their Conservative counterparts, their views on the role that government as opposed to private companies could play in creating jobs, as well as their dislike of the siting of Cruise missiles in Britain and their lesser agreement about Polaris.

The 1983 British election BBC/Crewe survey offered an opportunity to gain a better understanding of the Alliance voters than had been possible when we tried with previous surveys to isolate the distinctive character of the Liberal voters. The very large size of the sample (over 4000) enabled us to differentiate between Alliance voters who had voted Labour in 1979 and those who had come from the Conservatives. If the place of *departure* matters more than the place of *arrival*, then a discriminant analysis should differentiate well between these two types of Alliance voters. Also, comparing the extent to which consistent Conservative voters can be distinguished from Conservative defectors to the Alliance compared with their Labour counterparts, should tell us something about the relative distances of these two types of Alliance voters from their respective home bases. The larger the distance, the less likely a return to that home base next time round.

The 1983 survey, in addition to the 12 questions on policy issues we described in Chapter 5, contained five questions designed by Crewe (1984) to represent different aspects of the Thatcherite style of government.

[9]Similar findings were obtained when assessing the percentage of voters in each party who saw their party as best in dealing with ten specific important issues, ranging from unemployment to the Health service.

These five questions asked for relative preferences for (a) sticking to one's beliefs in dealing with political opponents or trying to meet them halfway; (b) at difficult times, for the government to be caring or tough; (c) in making decisions about the economy, is it better to involve major interests like the trades unions and business or to keep them at arm's length?; (d) agreement or disagreement with the view that no party can do much about creating economic prosperity, but that it is up to the people; and (e) with regard to the rest of the world, is it better for Britain to stick resolutely to its own position or to meet countries halfway?

Here was an excellent opportunity to investigate how far the defectors from Labour and Conservatives to the Alliance differed from each other as well as from consistent Labour and Conservative voters in their views on policies *and* on this style of government.[10] Table 11.5 gives the results. It tells an interesting story: on policy issues defectors differed significantly from the party from which they came but so did the two types of Alliance voters from each other. Indeed the accuracy of their classification was almost as good as that between the defectors and the consistent voters for each of the two parties.

The issues on which the Conservative defectors differed from the consistent Conservative voter concerned the role of government in creating jobs, not wishing to de-nationalize, not approving the siting of Cruise nuclear missiles in Britain, and the desire for proportional representation. Labour defectors differed from the Labour voters with regard to their views of how Britain should handle its relations with the Common Market, on proportional representation, on nationalization, and on approving more of the Polaris

TABLE 11.5                                                                    *BBC/Crewe, 1983*

Results of six discriminant analyses grouping voters on the basis of 1979 recalled and 1983 actual vote. *Percentage accuracy of classification between:* (I) Conservative defectors to the Alliance with consistent Conservatives; (II) Labour defectors to the Alliance with consistent Labour voters; (III) Alliance voters with one another grouped by their 1979 recalled vote. *Using as independent variables:* (A) their views on 12 issues; (B) their views on five aspects of a "Thatcherite style of government"

| (A) Issues | | | (B) Thatcherite style of government | | |
|---|---|---|---|---|---|
| (I) Consistent Conservatives | Conservative Defectors | Overall | Consistent Conservatives | Conservative Defectors | Overall |
| 72% | 67% | 72% | 66% | 63% | 65% |
| (II) Consistent Labour | Labour Defectors | Overall | Consistent Labour | Labour Defectors | Overall |
| 72% | 71% | 71% | 62% | 51% | 53% |
| (III) Conservative Defectors | Labour Defectors | Overall | Conservative Defectors | Labour Defectors | Overall |
| 68% | 62% | 64% | 60% | 51% | 55% |

[10]We followed Crewe's procedure of developing a Thatcherism index for each voter, ranging from + 5 if the voter subscribes to the "tough" approach on all five questions, to – 5 if the voter chooses on each of these questions the alternative.

nuclear submarine programme. The two types of Alliance voters differed from each other in their views on the regulation of trades unions, withdrawing of tax privileges from private schools, and on the two nuclear issues — Cruise missiles and Polaris.

*While differing on policies, the three groups of Alliance voters were united in their dislike for the Thatcherite style of government.* The Alliance voters, like the Liberals, in earlier elections, react to the style of government as much if not more than to specific policy issues, and in particular to a strident doctrinaire approach.

## THE HIDDEN ALLIANCE VOTERS: OUTLOOK AND INCIDENCE OF TACTICAL VOTING AMONG THEM

In the 1983 election a third of Conservative and a third of Labour voters said that they had seriously considered voting for the Alliance. These are the potential defectors to the Alliance. In Table 11.6 we compare them (1) with those of their own party who had not considered voting for the Alliance and (2) with the group of actual defectors, with regard to their views about the Thatcherite style of government and whether they report that extremism and/or disunity in either party were factors influencing their vote choice. Finally, we show that the incidence of tactical voting among those who had seriously considered the Alliance was very high.

Table 11.6 shows a remarkably regular pattern of reactions to the Thatcherite style of government. Reactions were positive among the Conservatives who had not thought of voting for the Alliance, less so among those who had, and turned into dislike among those who defected. Alliance voters were nearly as extreme in their dislike as Labour voters irrespective of whether or not they had considered voting for the Alliance.

Dislike of extremism and/or disunity influenced the Alliance's voters' decisions regardless of their party of origin. About one fifth of Alliance voters reported that the extremism of the Conservative party and about a third that the extremism and/or disunity in the Labour party influenced their decision.

A sizeable proportion of voters who had seriously considered voting for the Alliance but did not, were as worried about disunity or extremism as were those who actually defected from the Conservatives or Labour. However, while defectors were equally worried about disunity or extremism in both the Labour and the Conservative party — regardless of their own previous affiliation — this was not so for those who stayed. Only 2% of voters having seriously considered the Alliance yet voted for the Conservatives cited *extremism in the party for which they voted* as a factor influencing their decision. The pattern is exactly the same for those who, having considered the Alliance, voted Labour. It is interesting to speculate whether this differential perception genuinely represents the individual's views *at the time* of making the decision or is the reaction to having made an unpalatable decision — a way of reducing *cognitive dissonance*, an uncomfortable state which arises where

TABLE 11.6

BBC/Crewe, 1983

Distinguishing three groups of Alliance voters (by 1979 recalled vote) from Conservative and Labour voters who had, or had not, considered voting for the Alliance on: (A) attitudes to Thatcherite style of government; (B) vote decision influenced by extremism and/or disunity in the (1) Conservative, (2) Labour party; (C) percentage not voting for the Alliance for tactical reasons

|  | Vote in 1983 | | | | | | |
|  | Conservative voters | | Alliance voters | | | Labour voters | |
|  | Did not consider Alliance ($n = 1014$) | Considered Alliance ($n = 358$) | Voted Conservative in 1979 ($n = 208$) | Voted Liberal in 1979 ($n = 277$) | Voted Labour in 1979 ($n = 272$) | Considered Alliance ($n = 216$) | Did not consider Alliance ($n = 682$) |
|---|---|---|---|---|---|---|---|
| (A) Mean attitude to Thatcherite style of government[a] | + 1·01 | + 0·58 | − 0·79 | − 1·27 | − 1·38 | − 1·51 | − 1·45 |
| (B) Percentage reporting being influenced by extremism and/or disunity in | | | | | | | |
| (1) The Conservative party | 1% | 2% | 22% | 24% | 19% | 19% | 13% |
| (2) The Labour party | 29% | 44% | 38% | 34% | 37% | 2% | 1% |
| (C) Percentage not voting for the Alliance for tactical reasons | 27% | 52% | — | — | — | 46% | 23% |

[a]The score is based on the answers to five questions: + 5 indicates that all answers favour the Thatcherite style of government, − 5 that all answers indicate dislike of it.

a decision made is at variance with the individuals' preferences. There is no way of disentangling these two possibilities.

Although the difference between the actual defectors to the Alliance and those who had never considered voting for the party was more pronounced than for the potential defectors, the latter was sufficient marked to make it likely that their vote decision was influenced by tactical considerations.

In the 1983 election all voters other than Alliance voters were asked whether they had decided not to vote for the Alliance for any of the following three reasons: (1) because it was obvious that the Alliance could not win the election; (2) because doing so might let the Conservatives in; (3) because doing so might let Labour in. If a voter agreed with any of these reasons, we classified him or her as not voting for the Alliance for *tactical reasons*. Approximately half the Conservative voters (52%) and half the Labour voters (46%) who had seriously considered voting for the Alliance came into the category of tactical voter. The picture is similar to that reported about the tactical voting of potential Liberals in the 1979 and earlier elections (Cain, 1978; Särlvik and Crewe, 1983).

Here we see the real importance of the policy to reform the electoral system within the Alliance's platform. If a change to a system of proportional representation could be secured, a party which is not "first past the post" in an election, but still obtains a substantial share of the vote is much more likely to have a say in government. The political implications of the findings reported here are discussed in the final chapter.

# 12

# Implications for social psychology

There are several reasons why the longitudinal study was particularly suitable for examining various psychological issues. First, the length and the period of the study are important. The fifteen years covered the 1960s to the mid-1970s, a time of much social and political change and a stage in the individuals' lives (from the early twenties until the mid-thirties) which for many was one of considerable development, both occupationally as well as personally. Secondly, through the larger study, we had detailed and repeated information about each individual, including his perspective on society, making it possible to set reactions to political issues in a broader context than is customary in voting studies. And finally, by concentrating on *one* decision which had to be made repeatedly, yet always in a different political and economic climate, we could develop and test the robustness of our model on more than one occasion. We could also examine the influence of the individual's own past decisions and those of his parents. Because everyone makes the decision on the same day using the same options, we could compare the reactions of different people at one point in time and of the same people across time. In most other real-life decisions, people's options and the timing of the decision tend not to be the same. And even in the present changeable matrimonial and economic climate, few people change jobs, spouses or homes sufficiently often that the influence of past successive decisions can be studied.

The core of the work concentrates on the process of decision making and on the role of the individual's cognitions within the process, issues which are central to the debate in social psychology about the relationship of attitudes to behaviour. It also throws light on the process of socialization in one particular domain and on adaptation to societal and personal change. We shall look at these aspects first and then at the methodological and theoretical implications of the study for our understanding of the relation of cognitions to behaviour.

## Socialization

Using our knowledge of adolescents' hypothetical vote choice and their parents' party preferences, we were able to trace the effect of parental example, beginning when that influence was strongest. We were surprised by the high degree of imitation or modelling[1] in view of the fact that politics are little discussed in most homes, except at election time every four or more years. Parents' party preferences, as opposed to their political views, were more readily echoed by their children (Jennings and Niemi, 1974). This suggests that imitation varies not only with the domain or with parental involvement but with the clarity of signals. To hear and recall the name of a party is far easier than to understand and piece together a person's political views, particularly where the views are infrequently expressed and moderate. Extreme views, especially extreme negative ones, tend to be more forcibly voiced.

Parental interest in politics increased the likelihood of modelling but *only* where the adolescents' relations to his parents were good. There is a subtle process of interaction at work in which parental involvement, parent–child relations and the ease of the task all play a part. In the socialization literature relatively little attention is paid to this interaction and to the clarity of signals. Also important here is the role of *cross pressures*. We found that far fewer adolescents who experienced cross pressures imitated their parents' vote choice than those who received consistent cues (Chapter 4). There were different types of cross pressures: the obvious one where parents made different choices and the more subtle ones where the father's vote differed from that of the majority of his social class, neighbourhood or parents of other pupils at school. Cross pressures proved equally important in the individual's subsequent political socialization as an adult. Despite the fact that as adults many of the adolescents voted differently from their parents, their early modelling continued to exert a surprisingly strong influence, particularly where the adult's reference groups provided conflicting cues — a repetition of the finding that in adolescence the school's influence mattered where the parents' vote choice differed.

Finally, despite the fact that politics are generally considered the man's domain, where parents made different choices the mother's vote was more influential. As the pressure for wives to echo their husbands' views loses its force and as parents feel less of a need to present a concerted front (genuine or stage-managed) to their children, so one would expect parental influence on children's views to become more diffuse. Similarity between generations may therefore depend less than now on direct parental influence and more on similarity in the political and economic climates in which the two generations live their lives.

Our results support Bandura's (1971) model of social learning, but we would urge that more attention be paid to the social context in which the behaviour or attitudes arise and the social conditions that cause them to change. Since we had repeated information about the individual's feelings about self, work, his goals and values as well as measures of his authoritarianism, eight and twelve years apart, we could look at the interaction between changes due to age and changes

---

[1] Half the adolescents chose their parents' party preferences and, if we omit the Liberals, as many as two out of three.

related to the individual's circumstances. There were definite changes; for example, the optimism of the men in their twenties had become markedly more muted in their thirties. Some goals became less important (for example, the wish for a quiet life without responsibilities), others more important: to feel needed, to be with people one can trust and to feel free to express oneself.

While a great deal has been written about the way in which individuals adapt to circumstances, it is rare to have clear evidence of the process. We found that the men adapted to their condition in part by changing the priorities they attached to certain goals. Working class men with little prospect of advancement who, in their twenties, had attached a great deal of importance to being successful and having an interesting, well paid job, made this a less important goal, and instead increased the importance they attached to the understanding and betterment of society. For them improvement in their situation was more likely to occur as a result of collective rather than individual effort. By contrast, for the middle class and the socially mobile for whom there were no clear barriers to further advancement, success became a more important goal in their thirties than it was in their twenties. Thus each group adapted to their condition by adjusting their goals. To adapt by redefining the perspective from which the situation is viewed takes time. That is why Campbell and Converse (1980) found that in the United States the older people tended to be more content than the younger ones. Inglehart (1971), in a cross-cultural study of values, showed that where there are particular economic conditions a society reacts — given time — by increasing the importance of those values which do not depend on the state of the economy.

In the short term, however, mismatch between goals and reality has different consequences (Tajfel, 1978). In a recent comparative study of employed and unemployed black and white youths in Britain, Gaskell and Smith (1981) showed that while black youths had internalized the society's values to the same extent as white youths, their chances of realizing them differed greatly. Here mismatch led not to a readjustment of goals but to despondency and anger. See also Jahoda's (1979) discussion of the effects of unemployment.

We need to pay more attention to the period needed for adaptation and to the conditions that make it more, rather than less, likely.[2] Is it the uniformity of a society's values, the rigidity with which society imposes them or the length of time needed for reality testing? The adaptation we are discussing is one in which a person's objective condition is redefined so as to make it more acceptable to the individual and less damaging to his or her self respect. This type of adaptation, while perhaps beneficial to the individual at least at first, may be disadvantageous for the group of which he is a member and for society at large because it may reduce pressures to improve objective conditions.

---

[2] We have just completed a four stage cross-sectional study in which the same questions were asked of comparable samples of men and women of different background and ages in 1971, 1975, 1980 and 1982 to see how people adapt to Britain's changing economic and political situation. The questions concern people's images of Britain and other countries, the priorities they attach to different goals and values and their views on selected political issues.

We confirm Rokeach's (1968) view that goals and values, and indeed measures of authoritarianism, are more stable over time than attitudes towards specific issues providing a general perspective on society which influences reactions to particular issues. It is this broader orientation which makes an individual select the more restrictive or the more liberal course when new issues arise and which affects his reactions to minorities or outgroups even though the particular groups in question may change.[3] Authoritarianism proved much less responsive to the social and political scene than political attitudes.

## Issues in social context

The nature of the relationship between attitudes and behaviour has preoccupied social psychologists for more than three decades. Four main views have been put forward. The traditional view, first expressed by Allport (1935) and further developed by writers like McGuire (1976), sees attitudes and cognitions as important predictors of choice behaviour. Bem (1972) turned that proposition upside down, suggesting that we know what we think and feel by observing what we do rather than having such feelings and acting on them. The third theory, expressed by Wicker (1969), claims that there is little or no relationship between attitudes and subsequent behaviour, so that attitudes do little to explain why a given behaviour occurs. And finally there are Kelman's (1974) and Jaspars' (1978) views which see attitudes and behaviour as mutually interacting in that an individual's attitudes may influence what he or she does, and the behaviour thus induced in turn modifies the attitudes.

The debate among psychologists' alternative explanations (which are, of course, all correct, depending on the situation, the behaviour or choice and the people concerned), has proved fruitful. It has led to better measurement of attitudes, has highlighted the need to distinguish between attitudes and beliefs, and has generated greater awareness of intervening factors, Ajzen and Fishbein's work being an outstanding example. But now, many hundreds of studies later, the debate has become sterile. This is not only because many of the studies were carried out in the laboratory, relying on skilful stage-management and using students taking an introductory course in psychology as subjects. It is also because the studies aimed at a rarified level of abstraction, where all kinds of behaviours were viewed as interchangeable, as were attitudes.[4]

[3] A similar relationship was found by Mussen and Haan (1981) in a longitudinal study of a Californian sample, where measures of authoritarianism obtained many years earlier correlated very significantly with their political attitudes in middle life.

[4] To cite just one example, Bentler and Spekart (1981) tested the proposition that attitudes cause behaviour and for purposes of replication examined three different behaviours: studying; doing exercises; and dating. When the researchers did not find the same relationship across domains — and there is no reason whatever why they should — they concluded, "the various domains *seem to require* more detailed understanding so that the crucial ways in which they differ could be tested by future work" (p.237, our italics). Yet in the same article and in many like it, there is little speculation about the behaviours that might account for differences in the relationship.

To treat attitudes or behaviours as interchangeable does not get one very far. *The individual's cognitions and the decision or behaviour itself are developed within the social context of a society at a particular moment of its history and are subject to change in meaning and usage by that society and the individuals in it.* When, over time, a behaviour becomes generally accepted as part of the customs of the society or a group within it, then attitudes towards that behaviour will no longer predict its occurrence. Equally, where an attitude becomes part of the consensus of the society, its predictive power decreases.[5] Alternatively, the relationship between attitude and behaviour might change because society, for historical reasons, no longer finds overt expressions of given attitudes acceptable, e.g. expression of anti-semitism soon after the Second World War.

There is therefore *a societal and a personal life history attached to the expression and significance of each attitude as there is to the meaning and the ease with which a particular behaviour is engaged in or a choice made.* The contribution that the type of societal social psychology we favour can make is not to show that attitudes matter—no psychologist is needed to tell people that—but to unravel the conditions in which cognitions play a greater or lesser part and to seek to account for the differences by considering the meaning, and changes in that meaning, of the attitude for the individual and for society. This includes investigating when *"cognitive thaw"* sets in (Lewin, 1951), that is, the point at which attitudes become more differentiated or change, and also where there is *"behavioural thaw"*, i.e. where behaviour previously governed by habit or tradition becomes more a matter of individual choice. This approach forces one to consider not only the individual's present behaviour and outlook but also to take into account the past as well as information extraneous to the study. As we could examine both the attitudes and the behaviour on more than one occasion we could begin to develop certain general principles about the way various factors played their part in the decision.

The study provided an opportunity for two novel ways of examining the relation of attitudes to behaviour. First, its longitudinal character permitted testing not only how well attitudes predicted voting but also how far attitude mismatch and attitude change led to changes in behaviour on a subsequent occasion (Chapter 7). Secondly, because there was already in existence a well documented but different model of electoral choice, the validity of our model had to be established by contrasting it with the Michigan model (Chapter 1). This meant that the debate shifted from whether attitudes predict behaviour to the more meaningful question of whether they do so better and consistently better than other sources of influence.[6]

We were therefore able to specify the conditions needed to show that it was indeed attitudes which were the primary source of influence. We list these

---

[5] This is not simply due to a reduction of the variance, but rather to a change in the place within society of the attitude or the behaviour.

[6] Our model gives pride of place to the individual's cognitions, the Michigan model to party identification and past vote, relegating attitudes to a subsidiary position.

conditions below, not to reiterate the findings reported in Chapter 5 to 9 but to indicate the variety of perspectives from which we have approached the problem. There were four conditions:

1. There had to be sufficient variation in the voting of the same individual across time for factors other than past vote to affect the decision. Had the correlations between vote choice and past vote been consistently very high, there would have been nothing left to explain. But this was not so; instead, we found considerable volatility (Chapter 3).

2. There had to be sufficient variance in the voters' reactions on those issues on which the parties took clear and dissimilar stands. We found this to be the case (Chapter 8).

3. Attitudes had to predict vote choice better and consistently better than party identification and past vote. Here we required confirmation across elections fought in different political and economic circumstances, which we obtained (Chapter 5).

4. To establish unequivocally a causal link from attitudes to behaviour, we also needed to show that a poor match between an individual's attitude and those of the majority of voters for the party would increase the likelihood of him defecting on a subsequent occasion. We did indeed find that more of the voters who were not in tune with the views of the majority of voters for their party made a different choice next time round. Also, where an individual changed his views, he was more likely to change his vote, moving to a party more in tune with his changed outlook (Chapter 7).[7] Whether attitude change leads to behavioural change depends therefore on a voter's initial attitudes, on the degree of shift and on the range of his or her views, on the overlap between these views and those expressed by the parties and on their beliefs about the competence of the different parties.

## Attitudes and beliefs

Our study confirms the importance of the distinction Fishbein (1967) made between attitudes and beliefs about issues and draws attention to the need for two further distinctions — this time between the issues themselves. The first differentiates between *consensus* and *non-consensus issues*. For example, controlling inflation is generally evaluated as desirable (consensus), whereas selling council houses to tenants is generally evaluated as contentious (non-consensus). The second differentiates the issues on the basis of the perceived beliefs about the likelihood of different parties implementing different policies. The difference here is between accuracy, where the ordering is the same for the sample as a whole, irrespective

---

[7] Provided, of course, that the shift is such as to bring his views closer to the range of views held by a party other than his own. Where the individual has moderate views which he modifies even further, this is likely to be the case. However, where the voter's initial views represented the extreme views of his party then even a considerable change in outlook might not be sufficient to bring his views in line with those of a different party.

of the individuals' own preferences, and projection where the beliefs differ in line with the voters' party preferences.

Using these distinctions we found an interesting relationship between evaluation and beliefs: where there is consensus of evaluation there is no consensus among the beliefs, and where there is consensus of beliefs there is no consensus in evaluation (Chapter 8). Since we show in Chapter 9 how a voter's degree of preference for a party is based on his or her evaluation of issues and beliefs about the party's stand on them, it follows that — in theory at least — each issue makes a contribution to the decision regardless of the type of consensus involved, since *either* evaluations or beliefs will vary in a way that influences preferences.

However, in practice consensus issues contributed less to the prediction than did non-consensus issues. This is not surprising. Consensus issues, like keeping prices and unemployment down, comprise the major problems of our society that successive governments of both parties have been unable to solve. Consequently the voters shared a common belief in the parties' inability, but differed in the degree of inability which they assigned to each party. This led to a very restricted range of replies by contrast with non-consensus issues, like nationalization of building land, where voters typically used the full range of evaluation from very good to very bad.

These findings have implications for the discussion about the salience of issues. It has often been suggested that provided salient issues are tapped, only a few are needed to predict the voter's choice (Butler and Stokes, 1974; Crewe, 1977). But if the salient problems are the unsolved problems then they can affect the decision only so long as the voter believes that one or other of the parties can ameliorate the situation. If they do not, it is more likely that less salient but more manageable concerns, and in particular specific policy proposals, will prove the more influential.

In most studies of the predictive role of attitudes, there is very little discussion on whether failure to establish the relationship at the expected level is due to the content, the adequacy and range of the attitudes sampled, or to the way the questions are put and answers sought. It is as if the onus of proof that the individual's cognitions are important rests with the respondent. He or she has to make do with what is offered. This makes little sense. The majority of choices an individual makes, of which voting is just one instance, depend on a balancing of many preferences and dislikes. This is particularly so where none of the available options inspire much enthusiasm or loyalty. The more heterogeneous the population studied and the more difficult the choice (because none of the options satisfy or because the individuals do not feel strongly about any one issue), the greater the range of issues which needs to be tapped. We found that the voters cared more about concrete issues than abstract principles and about issues couched not in general terms but translated into specific policy proposals.

## Methods of analysis

Don Campbell (1968) and others urge that a variety of methods of analysis be used to examine the validity of a model, not only because each method has its own built-in bias that needs to be corrected, but because each approach provides different insights. We used various methods of analysis which collectively yielded results showing that voters' attitudes proved a stronger and less variable influence than their past votes. The three methods we used were discriminant analysis, multi-attribute utility theory and path analysis. The last two have received less attention in social psychology than they deserve.

*Discriminant analysis* proved very useful in showing that voters could be well differentiated on the basis of their attitudes. It also demonstrated that the Liberals and the Alliance voters in 1983 had no distinctive attitude profile but were to be found in the middle between two sharply differentiated groups of Labour and Conservative voters. The method therefore provided useful information about each of the options, drawing attention to the fact that one option, the Liberal or Alliance vote, was effectively a "non-option", selected not for its attraction but because it did not have the manifest disadvantages of the other two. The second advantage of the discriminant analysis lay in the measure of *goodness of fit* of each individual's cognitions relative to those of the other voters of the party for which he had voted. This measure provided a way of identifying potential defectors.

Discriminant analysis, however, has three limitations. It can make use only of those attitudes which differentiate *across the board* between different groups of voters, while attitudes which matter to a particular individual but not to others who voted for the same party merely reduce the accuracy of the overall classification. The method is therefore a wholesale rather than an individually tailored way of relating preferences to choices made. Also, it does not predict but classifies voters *after* the event and does so by optimizing the weights to be assigned to each attitude in order to achieve maximum differentiation. Such optimization of course relates to the particular election and has all the disadvantages of bias through hindsight. And finally it fails to take account of the individual's beliefs about the likelihood that the parties will in fact implement the policies he values.

*Multi-attribute utility theory* (MAUT), on the other hand, overcomes these three limitations. It predicts how the individual will behave, draws on beliefs as well as attitudes, and is custom-built to reflect each person's individual mix of preferences. Each individual's utility score for each party is based on *his* evaluation of the issue and his beliefs about the party's action with regard to the issues, the simple prediction being that the individual will vote for the party with the highest utility score for him. There is no optimization here based on hindsight; the weights given to an issue arise solely from the individual's cognitions (see Chapter 9). Accuracy of prediction was very high because the method draws on the individual's cognitions without reference to those of others in the sample. Thus for the first time in our gamut of analyses the Liberal voters were well predicted. As their vote was one of disaffection, they shared too few views in common with other Liberal voters for group-based statistical estimates to be of use.

MAUT has clear advantages over other techniques of prediction, not least because of the simplicity of its calculations. The method makes use of the components of each person's cognitive map and, through its flexible method of scaling, provides important information about the perspective the voter uses in making his choice. The scaling can be varied in accordance with different assumptions about the voter's view of the status quo. If he sees the status quo as very bad, any change would be for the better, while if he sees the status quo as partly good and partly bad, some changes would improve things, others would make things worse. We carried out two MAUT predictions setting the status quo at the two levels just discussed and found that one level predicted the Liberals very well, the other badly, and that the reverse was the case with the Conservatives (Chapter 9). This is a good example of the way in which methods of analysis can be used not only to predict but to understand the nature of the decision.

In the example just given, MAUT provides information about how the voter arrives at his decision. Repeated MAUT surveys could be used to monitor the public's reactions to given policies and events by indicating not only whether a change has occurred over time but whether such change was due to a change in the individual's evaluation of the policy or issue or to a change in their beliefs about the competence or willingness of the parties or institutions to carry out the policy. MAUT can therefore act as a *sensitive and informative barometer of public opinion*. Such surveys could with profit be carried out separately among those who decide on the policy, those who have to implement it and the public who has to live with it. Politicians and public servants react to their perceptions of what the public thinks. Here is one way of updating such knowledge.

The third method which requires longitudinal data is the *path analysis*. This provides a way of studying the interaction of a variety of influences on the decision making as well as the pathways through which the influence is exerted — for some people such influence is direct, for others indirect through affecting the attitudes which in turn influence the decision. This approach was of particular importance for us since we did not want to substitute for the tyranny of party identification that of the individual's cognitions, but take into account other factors such as the individual's political socialization through home, his social background, education and social status, his own past vote decisions as well as his values and general perspective on society. (The method and its findings are presented in Chapter 4). Such analysis is valuable provided it is based on information collected at the time at which the event occurred and not years later through recall. There is a considerable body of evidence that voters make errors in recalling their vote at previous elections and that such errors are biased in favour of making the past consistent with the present (Himmelweit *et al.* 1978). This has the effect of inflating the importance of past vote as a determinant of subsequent vote choice. Also if insights are to be gained it is important that the analysis is not restricted to the voters at either end of the continuum, that is to Conservative or Labour voters only. By omitting the middle ground, the degree of polarization that exists in the society is exaggerated and its consensus underestimated.

## Use of secondary data

Most countries have available a rich source of data about people's cognitions and behaviour that social psychologists rarely use. These are the surveys of people's attitudes, values and conduct, carried out periodically either by government agencies or research organizations increasingly lodged at data archives for secondary analysis.

For the initial development and testing of the model, as indicated in Chapter 2, there were many advantages in designing a special study. But it would have been irresponsible to claim that the model applied to the population at large without checking that this was indeed the case. The representative British election studies and the panel studies that were built on them proved of inestimable value. We were able to test the applicability of the model not just by using one representative survey conducted at the time of a particular general election, but to do so on five occasions, each of the elections taking place in a different economic and political climate. Sometimes Labour, sometimes Conservatives were in power. We were impressed by how much the results of the larger studies agreed with the findings derived from the special enquiry, but this need not always be so. Using large samples also makes it possible to see whether the prevalence and the meaning of the behaviour or cognitions in question are the same for different subgroups of the population.

Social psychologists tend to test the validity of a given hypothesis or theory designing studies using undergraduates as subjects. While many articles begin drawing attention to the a-typical characteristics of the sample, just as many conclude their article implying that a general phenomenon has been demonstrated without indicating that it might hold only for a young, educated and highly selected subgroup within the population.

## Societal social psychology

In this chapter we have brought together some of the social psychological insights gained from a study in depth of *one* social phenomenon. The approach we have adopted is a *systems approach* which examines the individuals' cognitions and behaviour, not in isolation, but within the context of the society from which both attitudes and behaviour derive their meaning. In the case of voting the need to examine the interaction between social and historical factors, the individuals' and the parties' reactions is obvious. Nor is this interaction the same at different periods; indeed the only constant in the system is change, requiring an explanatory model which is dynamic rather than static. The model of electoral choice we have developed allows for change, indicating both the sources of influence that bear on the decision and the conditions under which one or other source will carry more weight.

The study is an example of what we have called *societal social psychology:* a study not of individuals *in* society but of their *interdependence*. Social psychology, through its methodology and theories, has a substantial contribution to make to the explanation of social phenomena, provided that researchers develop a sensitivity for the problems they investigate at the societal as well as the psychological level, looking at the life history of issues as well as the socialization of the individuals (Deutsch and Hornstein, 1975). This involves more use of the insights of the other social sciences and of historical and comparative data than is currently the practice. Too often social psychologists have used a particular situation or issue merely as an opportunity for making or testing predictions about individual behaviour. The approach we advocate gives pride of place instead to the study of the issue or phenomenon itself, the actors involved being one, but only one, relevant factor. There is of course all round gain since such an approach will inevitably sharpen our insight into individuals' reactions including their reactions to change.

If social psychology is to make the contribution to the understanding of society and of social change of which it is capable, then social psychologists need to focus more on the study of social phenomena than they do at present and develop conceptual frameworks which are dynamic allowing for societal influences which, like the individuals' circumstances, change over time. It is worth recalling Kurt Lewin's statement that "Observation of social behaviour is usually of little value if it does not include an adequate description of the character of the social atmosphere or the large unit activity within which the specific social act occurs". (1951).

# 13

# Implications for political science

A distinction is conventionally made within the political science literature between *social psychological* and *economic or rational* models of vote behaviour, and political scientists reading this book may be wondering how to categorize our model — is it one or the other, or a hybrid? Our contention is that any attempt at such categorization is ill-advised as the distinction is bizarre, since all decision making involves the operation of cognitive psychological processes. The Michigan model is viewed as social psychological, not because the authors are social psychologists, but because of the key role in that model assigned to party identification. Attachment to a party is seen as primarily affective, and hence "psychological", with its roots in the individual's past. By contrast, arranging preferences in order of their utility and acting on them takes place in the here and now and, as Downs (1957) suggests, is rational and therefore apparently not "psychological" but a characteristic of economic man. Economic man, it would appear, has but one ability, that of ordering his or her preferences, and but one set of motivations, namely to obtain profit or reduce costs whether this be money, possessions, power or prestige. This oversimplified and truncated version of man does not even allow for past decisions to influence the present even though, as S. Himmelweit (1976) has shown, this matters considerably when examining the purchase of goods or the disposal of money. Nor does it allow for a wider range of motivations, often in conflict with one another, to affect the preferences. In modelling a decision process we cannot be content with just studying the individual at the point of making the decision without also taking account of the reasons why individuals hold particular views.

In this chapter we provide insights from the perspective of our model and its findings about four issues which currently receive much attention in the political science literature: (1) a re-evaluation of the role of party identification; (2) the relative role played by evaluation of issues and candidates; (3) the importance of voters' assessment of the parties' performance and style of leadership, and (4) the relevance for vote choice of the voters' general perspective and values.

## Re-evaluation of the role of party identification

Party identification has occupied the centre of the stage in political science studies of voting behaviour at least in the United States since the key role assigned to it by Campbell *et al.* (1960).

In Europe, party identification has not been given quite the same prominence although its role as a standing decision and its link with political involvement has been the subject of many cross-cultural studies (Barnes and Kaase, 1979; and Kaase and Klingemann, 1981). In Britain where the first election surveys were carried out with Stokes as co-author, who had previously worked with Campbell on the development of the Michigan model, the model made more of an impact (Butler and Stokes, 1974). Since the mid-1970s, however, its importance has receded (Särlvik and Crewe, 1983).

In the last 15 years, a number of factors have come together which have necessitated a re-evaluation of the role of party identification due to an increase in people's awareness of the parties' stands on issues, a greater link between the voters' own views and those of the party for which they have voted, as well as a decline in the number who identify with a party and a quite dramatic decline in the number who identify strongly. This decline is especially pronounced among, but not restricted to, the young. Because in the early studies those not identified with any party were found to be badly informed, little involved in politics and disinterested in the outcome of elections, for many years political scientists devoted hardly any attention to them. Instead research concentrated on those who identified with the major parties, thereby exaggerating the degree of polarization of attitudes among the electorate.

Originally, party identification was seen as an affective link to a party, and by some enthusiasts as akin to an extension of the individual's ego, with allowance being made for people to deviate occasionally in their vote choice in one or other election. The increasing frequency of that deviation in recent years, however, has cast doubt on the assumption of a continuing strong bond to a party from which the voters deviate so readily.[1]

In the United States, the re-evaluation of party identification has taken two forms. The first, represented by the work of Brody (1978), Katz (1979), Weissberg (1980) and Dennis (1982a), seeks to develop more differentiated measures of party identification, particularly between types of independent voters. Here the differentiation sought is between those who lean towards one or other party without identifying with it and those who neither lean nor identify. The second tradition, exemplified by Markus and Converse (1979), seeks to isolate what portion of the voters' evaluations of candidates and issues can be attributed to *persuasion*, i.e. to the candidates and policies themselves, and what portion to *projection*, a spill-over

---

[1]Miller and Shanks (1982) draw attention to the substantial increase between 1972 and 1980 in the percentage of voters deviating from their party identification when voting in Presidential elections. In 1980 40% of weak Democrats voted for Reagan.

effect of the individual's affective identification with a party. To differentiate between persuasion and projection, Markus and Converse used an elegant simultaneous equation model, concluding that party identification remains a powerful influence by entering the decision process at various stages.

The British election representative and panel surveys offered an excellent opportunity to examine the role of party identification. We carried out a series of analyses which convinced us that there was no way of isolating the influence of party identification or attachment from voters' cognitions. Discriminant and MAUT analyses showed that where individuals identified with the party for which they voted, attitudes differentiated much better between the voters for the three parties than when there was no such congruence.

The most telling evidence of the virtual impossibility of isolating that influence came from a LISREL analysis which we carried out using the BES 1974–1979 panel.[2] Here we subdivided the voters for each party in 1979 into four groups on the basis of the strength of their identification with that party for which they had voted in the previous election: strong identification, fairly strong, not very strong, and no identification. We then computed for each group the mean discrepancy scores for two measures: one on attitudes to welfare, the other concerning their views on trades unions and nationalization. The discrepancy score consisted of the difference between the voters' own views and their perception of the Conservative stand minus the difference between their own views and their perception of Labour's stand. A high score indicated a close fit to the Conservative platform, a low score to that of Labour. We found that *the ordering of the voters by degree of identification was identical to their ordering on the basis of their cognitions. There was no single deviation in that ranking on either measure.*

Strengths of party identification and partisan attitudes co-vary[3] and evidence of prior party identification is not sufficient to establish a causal direction from party identification to attitudes. It is as likely that stability of "party identification" across elections is a result of a good fit between individual's views and a particular party's platform as an indication that identification with a party has affected the voter's views. It is also worth noting that no adequate explanation has been given by the Michigan school to account for differences in strength of identification independent of voters' views. In our view, party identification is a generalized attitude to a party possessing, like all attitudes, an affective as well as a cognitive component. Such attachment is strengthened where the voter has over many elections supported the party at the polls and associates with others who do the same. Where these links are strong, it may be easier for people initially to amend their views rather than their party attachment. However, inconsistency is an uncomfortable state, and sooner or later a move away from the party's stand will

[2]This analysis was carried out in collaboration with David Kenny. The results will be reported more fully in a separate publication.
[3]Cross-lagged correlational analysis of vote and party identification using the 1974–1979 British election panel obtained correlations of 0·42 between vote 1974 and party identification 1979 and 0·44 between party identification 1974 and vote 1979.

be followed first by a reduction in the strength of the identification and later by a refusal to identify with the party altogether.

Our analyses indicate over the last two decades a progressive decline in the consistency of voting for the same party across elections, an increase in people's awareness of the parties' stand and a reduction in the pressure to label oneself in terms of any group membership. A consequence of these changes is that "party identification" may come to be little more than a summary expression of people's views and not, as has been suggested, a directing and initiating force to guide people's evaluations (Budge, 1982, 1976).

We concur with Dennis's (1982a) description of partisanship as an accounting exercise, a retrospective evaluation of party promises and performance. If this is so, knowing an individual's party identification at the time of a particular election, as well as his or her vote choice, is useful when predicting the likelihood of the individual voting the same way the next time around. For example, in 1983 as many as 30% of the Liberal and Social Democratic Alliance voters identified with a different party while voting for the Alliance (Chapter 11). Once sizeable numbers of voters identify with the Alliance this would indicate that they were beginning to share the views of the party rather than voting for the party merely to express their disaffection with the party they had previously supported. It would signal arrival.

To understand better the role of party identification today, in-depth interviewing of people with different degrees of attachment to a party, or who have recently changed their allegiance, could throw new light on the origins and significance of that attachment, provided that such interviews include an equally searching exploration of the individual's political views. Until a satisfactory explanation can be given, independent of the individual's cognitions, for differences in strength of party identification, it seems to us more appropriate to follow the dictum, "Action speaks louder than words", and to concentrate in voting studies on the forces within society and within the parties that influence vote choice. Such analyses would include party identification as a summary statement of the voters' general political preferences which, as suggested in the cognitive model of vote choice, would interact with their preferences on specific issues and candidates.

## Evaluation of parties and leaders; the role of salience

Political science literature tends to concentrate on the voters' ignorance and lack of involvement and on their being so unlike Schumpeter's (1950) idealized version of the democratic citizen. Evidence of people's ignorance is found in voters' lack of factual knowledge (e.g. which countries belong to the Eastern bloc or make up the EEC); their inability often to give "appropriate" explanations of what the political labels of left and right stand for; the lack of stability across time of their political attitudes, and the greater emphasis that they place on the evaluation of leaders or candidates in deciding how to vote rather than issues.

While there are many studies which come to the not totally unexpected conclusion that either education or, in the absence of education, strong political involvement leads to more informed understanding of political issues, there are relatively few studies which examine in detail why some issues are well understood and others are not, or which seek explanations in the environment for differences in the stability of attitudes across time.

In this book we have proposed and shown some advantages of a more finely-grained analysis of voters' reactions than is generally carried out, one which differentiates between consensual and non-consensual issues. By examining individual issues, Särlvik and Crewe (1983) and we ourselves have shown that correct identification of the parties' platforms is generally quite high among voters. Where it is not, it is often because the issue is a new one for which the individual does not yet have an appropriate frame of reference, because the parties shy away from a discussion of their respective positions (race and incomes policy being two such issues), or because conflicting cues are offered as a result of parties changing their minds between elections.

This is not to say that a cognitive model of vote choice should concentrate solely on attitudes towards *issues*. Indeed, there seems to be an implied pecking order in political science literature how good citizens should form their judgements, a list of democratic desiderata for making vote choices. Issues are best, followed by the assessment of the candidate's or the leader's competence and integrity, with an evaluation of liking for them coming bottom of the list. The approach we have taken does not try to establish any pecking order. Quite the contrary: the general cognitive model we outline in Chapter 1 explicitly provides for multiple influences on the voter's decision making, with the relative strengths of their influence varying with the circumstances of the voter (including his or her past history) and the climate in which the election is fought. Our major emphasis on attitudes towards issues in analysing electoral surveys was appropriate for the electoral climate of the 1960s and very early 1970s (see the rise of issues voting (Nie *et al.*, 1976). However, in the changed climate of the 1970s and early 1980s, given the growing distrust by the electorate in the ability of any party to mount an effective policy on such key issues as unemployment, adequate provision of social services and management–trade union relations, voters' attitudes towards the leaders have become increasingly important, even decisive (a realization that this was so was very effectively demonstrated in the general election campaign of 1983).

Voters have learned over the years to appreciate the importance of the personality of the President of the United States and of the Prime Minister in affecting the conduct of affairs (Kinder, 1981).[4] When people are asked whether they like a given leader or presidential candidate, we suggest that their answer

[4]Miller and Wattenberg (1982) found that more of the better educated than the less well educated volunteered the information that personal facts about the candidates had influenced their vote choice. This difference was found in every election since 1952.

is given as though the voter had been asked, "Do you like him as President (or Prime Minister)?" That is, the question is not responded to in terms of interpersonal attraction but in terms of the candidate's suitability for his or her future role. We have some evidence to support this view, in that in the earlier British election studies, the voters were asked simply to indicate their liking for the three leaders of the parties, while in 1983 they were asked instead for a comparative judgement as to who would make the best and the worst Prime Minister; yet the predictive value of either measure was equally high (Chapter 5). The former question would seem to have been answered as though the latter question had been put.

This is not to suggest that in a political climate where personalities count, issues should be ignored. Both matter (Chapter 5). There is, however, no point in establishing a pecking order since we cannot make any clear distinction between issue and candidate evaluation. Canonical correlations between issue and leader evaluations in 1979 showed the two sets of evaluations to be highly correlated. Nor is this surprising; most leaders or candidates in the course of their many appearances on radio and television touch on policy proposals and it makes good sense for the voter to treat the leader as embodying, or at least reflecting, the party's stand.

We showed earlier that if one is to understand the voters' political thinking one needs to take the *life history of issues* into account. Nor is there any reason why revision of one's views through experience is any less desirable for a good citizen or for democracy than sticking to one's views, i.e. why stability of attitudes across time is necessarily a measure of political sophistication. There are, after all, quite a number of issues where negative side effects come for the fore only after the policy has been in operation for some time, or where the situation that made the policy initially attractive was changed.

Issues are taken up or dropped by parties, a point well made by Campbell *et al.* (1960) who refer to issues as coming into the political orbit or moving out of it. As we have shown, the issue of homosexuality has moved out of the political orbit, that of race relations may move more closely into that orbit, however hard politicians try to keep it out. It is also important to examine why reactions to certain policies are so resistant to change, the clamour for the restoration of capital punishment being one example. In Chapter 10 we described techniques based on multidimensional scaling which allowed a much closer examination of the issues that are raised in a particular election than is usually attempted in the literature by locating their positions within the voter's cognitive map of social and political attitudes, and by charting how these positions move in relation to one another as the life history of issues unfolds.

## The importance of the voters' assessment of the parties' record and style of leadership

Fiorina (1981) emphasized the importance of retrospective evaluation of the incumbents in the voters' decision which party to support. Confirmation for this came from Lipset's (1984) macro-analysis of elections, showing that where in a country economic conditions deteriorate significantly, the party in office tends to lose the next election. The reason for this is generally not so much because voters have changed their opinions on policy issues and are therefore attracted to the opposition, but simply because they tend to blame the government for its failure to arrest the economic decline. Lipset shows that among 20 elections in Western democracies since 1979 in which economic conditions were bad, 17 governments were put out of office. This was irrespective of their ideological position: half were left, the other half right of centre. Had the general election in Britain taken place before the Falklands War, it is likely that Britain would have provided the eighteenth confirmation of Lipset's thesis. At that time, Mrs Thatcher's rating as effective Prime Minister was lower than that of any British Prime Minister since opinion polling began.

That Britain's recession did not have the expected effect on the 1983 election was due to the new appraisal voters made of Mrs Thatcher during and after the successful conclusion of the Falklands War and due to the failure of the Opposition to present themselves as a credible alternative. The relative evaluation of the leaders of the two main contenders by the voters indicates the importance of obtaining information from the respondent not only about the party he or she is likely to support but for each of the parties under consideration concerning their evaluation of the leader, of specific policy proposals and their assessment of the likelihood of implementation by the party. We would have wished the Liberal party to have been included in such assessments or in future elections the Alliance formed by the Liberals and the Social Democrats.

Care needs to be taken in the wording of the assessment questions. We found it better to ask, not about each party's stand, but about the party's willingness once in office to implement a policy. Asking merely about parties' past record means that for the party in office this question relates to the party's *actual* performance, while for the other parties to their hypothetical performance had they been in office. Not asking an *explicit* question about past record does not, however, mean that the voter does not take the party's past record into account. After all in arriving at evaluations about a party's future performance people will draw on their experiences of how the party had behaved in the past.

Election campaigns are aimed at impressing the electorate with the parties' statesmanship, ability and willingness. Repeated MAUT surveys carried out during the campaign would be helpful in revealing whether changes in vote intentions that were found were due to changes in the voters' attitudes towards issues as the campaign progressed or due to changes in their perceptions of each party's capabilities. Such changes could then be related to the conduct of the campaign and its presentation by the media.

## The role of the individual's general predisposition and value orientation

There are a considerable number of studies relating individuals' predispositions and value orientation to their political outlook, involvement and participation. Among general predispositions, sense of efficacy, inner and outer-directedness and authoritarianism have been studied (for example, McClosky (1964), Lane (1973)).

In recent years, the role an individual's value system plays in political behaviour has received much attention, stimulated by the work of Inglehart (1977) who finds that the level of economic development of a country as well as people's social and economic situation during their formative years affect the relative priority they attach to one of the two value-orientations: a *materialistic* one stressing personal success, financial rewards and matters of individual and national security, and a *post-materialistic* one concerned more with social equality, improvement in the quality of life and of the environment, and with self actualization. Inglehart suggests that the former arises in times of economic scarcity and the latter in times of economic abundance and general optimism. The *Zeitgeist* and the individual's own experiences and education, relate to the development of these values. The 1960s was a period of economic abundance in the United States and Western Europe and the generation brought up then indeed attaches greater importance to post-materialistic values than the earlier generation brought up in the Depression. Within the same generation a post-materialistic orientation tends to be more prevalent among the educated and the middle class.

Kaase and Klingemann (1981) confirm Inglehart's thesis in a cross-national study they carried out into the relation of social structure, value orientation and the party system. They found that social status and education indeed encouraged a post-materialistic value orientation and that such people tend to be more politically concerned and more ready to seek political change outside the framework of a conventional party system, taking more part in protest activities including demonstrations. They draw attention to the current difficulty facing the British Labour party, which contains the Old and the New Left, the latter consisting of the younger and more educated section with a post-materialistic orientation.[5] We concur with Kaase and Klingemann's (1981) view that:

> Value orientations are evaluative standards which serve to assess social and political situations and which constitute a set of intervening variables between social structure and political behaviour. For this reason, and because the major interest–conflicts in society are usually fought out with reference to such value orientations, this set of variables holds a central place in our theoretical approach. Only a cultural interpretation makes interest–conflicts behaviourally relevant. (p. 367)

The model of vote choice we outline traces the complex interrelation of factors to which Kaase and Klingemann refer. It was put to the test in the path analysis

---

[5]It is incidentally worth noting that the dominant values in the Western democracies were materialistic values and that what we are discussing is not a rejection of materialistic values but a reduction in the salience assigned to them (Inglehart, 1977).

which we carried out (Chapter 4, pp. 64–68) which showed the interrelation between social class, education, measures of authoritarianism, the relative priorities attached to the advancement of personal or of societal goals,[6] and how these in turn relate to the individuals' views about law and order and other liberal issues as well as to their preference for Conservative or Labour policies. The dependent variable in the path analysis was the individual's vote choice. What made the path analysis so useful was not only the inclusion of a wide range of information about each individual, but also that the measures of social status, goals and values, authoritarianism and policy preferences were repeated after an interval of eight years. This enabled us to show how a person's goals and values and authoritarianism, though they had no direct influence on vote choice, had an indirect one by affecting his subsequent preference for specific policies. Stress on personal success and an authoritarian outlook were correlated with reluctance to subscribe to liberal policies (e.g. the liberalization of the law with regard to capital punishment, abortion and immigration) and to preference for Conservative policies.

How far an attitude affects vote choice varies with the issues raised in the elections. For example in 1970, but in no other election, individuals' liberal attitudes related to vote choice. This was not because they were more strongly held on that than on other occasions, but because the issue of law and order featured prominently in that particular election. Change is the order of the day and more research is needed on why factors which played so great a part in one election were not relevant in another. When focussing on change rather than on stability, it is particularly valuable to have available longitudinal studies, however small scale, so that the effects of societal changes which are not always overt can be properly charted.

By not restricting the model of vote choice, as both the Michigan and Downsian versions do, to the final component in that choice, but by also considering what factors make for particular evaluations, we show that a change in any one of the components, e.g. a change away from post-materialistic to materialistic, and, in our case, away from personal success to societal aspirations, is as important in evaluating the tensions within the party system and within the electorate as changes in reactions to specific policy proposals at election time.

We hope to have shown that a model which mirrors both past and present influences and is therefore more complex than one concentrating only on the point of decision making can still be clearly defined and systematically examined. We argue for highly focussed special studies permitting a wider range of data to be collected and across a longer period of time alongside the expensive national election surveys; the former to explore in depth the various factors and their

[6]We developed these measures in the early 1960s. Though not identical to those used by Inglehart, they bear some relation to them.

change over time and the latter to examine their prevalence in the general population.

The approach used we call societal psychological approach, one which is essentially dynamic, and incorporates changes in society as well as in the individual's circumstances, thus elucidating the speed and extent to which such changes are reflected in people's cognitive maps of their society.

# 14

# Political implications, including the conduct of election campaigns, the role of the media and the prospects of the parties

The parties are not only what their leaders do or say. The parties are also what their followers believe they are, expect them to be, and therefore think they should be . . . What the parties do affects what the voters think they are and what the voters think they are affects what they subsequently do. Out of this interaction between subjective perception and objective reality mutually affecting one another over decades emerges not only our definition but the reality of a political party's role . . . Today's subjective unreality in the voters' minds affects tomorrow's objective reality in the political arena. (Berelson *et al.*, 1954, p. 216)

In what follows we shall distinguish between the period up to 1974 (the end of the longitudinal study) and the period from 1974 up to the 1983 election, only where differences in findings make this necessary. We have been struck by how many observations made in the earlier period applied equally to the late 1970s and early 1980s, suggesting that we have touched on a trend or a general phenomenon that is here to stay despite the many changes in the political and economic climate. The differences between the two periods were marked. After 1974, inflation increased substantially and was brought under control only in 1982; there was the Falklands War in the same year, the deepening of the recession and the monumental rise in unemployment between 1979 and today. The period also brought in two successive Conservative governments with Mrs Thatcher as Prime Minister, the first with a comfortable and the second with a massive majority in Parliament.

Reactions to the body politic, however, cannot be understood by reference to political or economic happenings alone. They are also a response to, and a reflection of, the *Zeitgeist*, including the social and cultural climate of a society. They reflect people's general orientation to that society and its institutions. The 1960s brought about a change in this orientation, the effects of which continue to reverberate. The period was not only one of considerable social and political change, nationally as well as internationally, but also — and it is this which is particularly relevant — a period of increased questioning of authority and of the status quo. There was growing demand for more openness, accountability and consultation and less willingness to be at the receiving end of paternalism, however well intended. This applied to all walks of life; parents wanted more say in the selection and conduct of schools, students in the running of universities and workers in their industry; consumer councils were formed, shareholders demanded information about the conduct of companies, patients about the decisions of doctors, and Members of Parliament about the workings of the Civil Service.[1] Once critical questioning became widespread, political slogans demanding *carte blanche* approval, such as "Trust us", "We have served you well", "We too come from a mining background", "We have the experience", which might have served well in the past, lost their appeal.

Labelling in terms of class or sex became less acceptable, and less indicative of outlook and reactions, not only because of the increased employment of women and the Women's Movement, but also because of the considerable and largely upward social mobility. While in the 1950s such mobility, according to sociological research, tended to be associated with strain (a sense of marginality, of not belonging), there was no evidence of this in Goldthorpe's studies (1980) of the socially mobile of the 1960s and 1970s. Goldthorpe points out that boundaries between the classes had become more permeable and less significant, and life styles both more individualized and more uniform across social classes, helped by mass production, an increase in the provision of further education, increased travel and the homogenizing influence of television. In schools and at work there was correspondingly more emphasis on individualism and less on group conformity. The emphasis was on expressing one's own views rather than taking over packaged views on social, religious or political questions from others, whether these came from parents, the church, one's workmates or from political parties.

There were other factors too. Despite the many severe national and international problems, the great majority of the working population experienced a steady improvement in their living standards in the 1960s, with real earnings more than keeping pace with inflation. People learned to expect that year by year their work would bring improved returns. Yesterday's success in raising living standards became today's baseline for setting expectations. This led to impatience with another rhetoric, that of using the past as a guide to the future, "Remember the thirties" and "You've never had it so good". What mattered was not yesterday, but tomorrow; modernity, not tradition. There were some profound changes in the voters' orientation towards the institutions of society and their role within that society.

The quotation from Berelson *et al.* at the beginning of the chapter suggests that

---

[1]The mood of the time was reflected in the decision of the BBC to put on, and the instant success of, the television programme *That Was The Week That Was* which satirized the most venerable institutions of The Establishment: the Church, the Monarchy, the Prime Minister, Parliament, the Civil Service, captains of industry and trade union officials.

politicians are responsive to changes in the public's mood. During the period in question the two main parties put less emphasis on sectional concerns and more on shared ones. There was a shift from an avuncular approach, "The party knows best", to more discussion of particular issues, the effect of which was multiplied by the increased coverage of political events by news and current affairs programmes.[2] All this helped to increase the electorate's awareness, if not understanding, of the policy proposals of the different parties.

Social scientists, like politicians, respond to societal changes. During these same years interest grew in the individual's internal representation of the social world. Goffman (1974) calls this the "frame", Schank and Abelson (1977) the "script". These terms refer to the intuitive theories individuals develop about the complex environment in which they live, theories which provide an ordered view of social relations and the social order, their antecedents and consequences. They are fashioned through the individual's past socializing experiences and present situation, and represent what Berelson (1954) called "the subjective interpretation of objective reality". Their importance lies in the role they play in affecting behaviour and reactions to events. Where the members of a society share a particular interpretation or develop a common script, such interpretation *de facto* becomes a social reality. It defines the possible: the public act on it as do the politicians. The names given to such shared scripts have varied over the years: Durkheim (1898) called them "collective representation"; Moscovici (1984) "social representation", and Barthes (1972) simply "myths". Such scripts both reflect social change and are important precursors of such change.

What this suggests is that cultural change, or change in the social representations which took place during this period, though related to structural change, was not identical with it. There was also the growing and, for Britain, novel feeling that her future depended increasingly on factors outside her control and that neither party could do much to improve the economic and industrial situation. When we asked the voters in 1974 which of the three parties, once in power, would be able to deal with two salient issues — to keep unemployment and prices down — the voters made it clear that they did not think any party could do so. Relative to the other parties they merely believed their own .to be *less unable*.

Almost ten years later, in the 1983 election, with 72% naming unemployment as the most important problem facing the country, the voters expressed even less confidence in the parties' ability to reduce its level. Asked whether, if either the Conservatives or Labour were to win the election, they would bring down the level of unemployment, 80% thought that the Conservatives and 60% that Labour would *fail* to do so. With regard to other problems too, the majority thought it unlikely that any party could effect substantial improvements. Not only has there been a considerable lessening in recent years in people's trust in politicians'

---

[2]While fewer people view such programmes compared with serials like *Dallas* or *Coronation Street*, their numbers are still vast; also more than 90% view or hear one news programme or news headlines each day.

ability to handle the country's problems, but also a growing cynicism about their readiness to keep election promises. In 1983, half the voters thought the parties would not keep their election promises once in power (Worcester, 1983).

Many assumptions about consistency of vote, the role of party identification and of social class membership and about political belief systems which might have been appropriate in the 1950s were inappropriate when describing the voter and his reactions in the 1970s and 1980s.

## Volatility of vote

Where the past becomes less of a guide to the future, where the influence of group membership becomes less pervasive and where trust in the parties' wisdom and competence is at a low ebb, it is not surprising that the commonly held assumption that voters stay loyal to a party turns out to be the exception rather than the rule. However, when we charted the vote history of individuals across four or more elections, the extent of volatility of voters in both the longitudinal and the BES 1963–1970 panel studies surprised us. The consistent voters for Labour and Conservative were far smaller than had been envisaged and consistent Liberals hardly existed at all. Even more striking was the lack of similarity in voting profiles. There were 80 different voting histories among the 178 men and a startling 188 among the BES panel of 750 men and women (Chapter 3).

Political scientists have tended to dismiss such volatility as short-term fluctuations around a stable party identification. But neither *short-term fluctuations* nor Butler and Stokes' (1969) concept of *homing* continue to have much meaning. Fluctuations from what stable pattern? Homing to what nest? Even Casanova returned to the same woman on more than one occasion, but no one would call him either a "homing" husband or a faithful lover. While the majority of voters still voted for one party more than any other, they varied as to the elections at which they deviated and whether they deviated by abstaining or voting for another party. *There is every sign that volatility is here to stay and will increase rather than diminish*, not least because the parents of the next generation will provide fewer consistent cues than the previous generation.

In recent years, not only has the frequency of volatility increased, but also the extent of movement across the political spectrum. Before 1979, the majority of voters who were dissatisfied with their party would vote for one of the smaller parties or abstain; crossing over to the opposition was very rare. In 1979 and again in 1983, this was no longer so: a sizeable number moved right over, including Labour supporters whose working class background and trade union membership might have been expected to act as barriers to such a move.

In our model, the habit of voting for a party has a direct influence on vote. Psychologists point to the force of habit in affecting future behaviour and rightly so, but this applies either where the behaviour is frequently performed or else satisfies each time, as in the case of smoking. Voting comes into neither category;

it is practised infrequently and the choice made rarely satisfies. Either the party chosen loses or, if it wins, fails to carry out its promises. It is therefore not surprising that the effect of habit on voting for a party should be relatively weak except where buttressed through the pressure of significant reference groups or the homogeneity of the environment. But willingness to conform to group pressure has decreased and there is now access to a greater diversity of views, not least through television, even in the most closely knit community. *In the future the influence of the individual's past habit of voting on his or her subsequent vote will, if anything, decrease further.*

## Decrease in the role of social determinants in vote choice

Commentators in this country and abroad describe Britain as a class-ridden society, seeing in this an important reason for low productivity and industrial unrest. While reference is made to historical factors, the Empire, the early industrialization of Britain, the structure of the trade union movement, and the lack of technological training of management, equal prominence is given to the pervasive and continuing effects of class division. Indeed, at the launching of their party in March 1981, the Social Democrats cited as one of their principal aims, the "healing of class divisions". The implication is that class divisions in the more industrially efficient European countries are less pronounced and that as a consequence there is a more effective partnership between management and the workforce. Our research shows such analysis to be over-simplistic, as it fails to take into account the importance of people's current attitudes. Moreover, we found that it was possible to predict attitudes to political issues little better than chance from knowing solely a person's social origin, education and social status. Only attitudes towards big business and Britain's membership of the EEC were linked to class (Chapter 4). In Chapter 6 we showed that the political views of people within a given social class varied a good deal, and that such social determinants as class, education, age, sex and even trade union membership discriminated between the voters less well than did attitudes. Adding the social determinants to the cognitions made no independent contribution to the accuracy of voter classification.[3]

People's political attitudes, although important, are not, of course, by themselves sufficient for an appraisal of the strength of class divisions in society.

Education and social status also have a direct influence on an individual's general perspective on society, including his or her goals and values. These in turn help shape reactions to specific issues. Thus the middle class and the socially mobile were more concerned with personal success and less with societal betterment — an echo of Runciman's (1966) distinction between egocentric and fraternalistic aspirations (Chapter 4).

---

[3]In the economic period of 1983, being self-employed and owning one's own home irrespective of class were the only social determinants that were closely linked to voting Conservative.

Goldthorpe's (1980) study of social class and social mobility found not only a good deal of upward social mobility, resulting from changes in the occupational structure in Britain, but also that many of those who remained in the working class described themselves, relative to their fathers, as having ''risen''. Perceived mobility, whether through change in status or living standards, increased personal as opposed to collectivist aspirations (Chapter 2).[4] This would account not only for the growing reluctance of people to label themselves in class terms,[5] but also for the marked decrease in class-linked voting compared with former times. Up to and including 1974 much of it was due to an increase of Labour voters among the middle class (from 17% in 1964 to 27% in 1974, in addition to the 19% Liberal voters drawn from all social classes). By contrast, in 1979 there was a marked swing to the Conservatives, particularly among the skilled and semi-skilled working class.

Our study provides some further clues about the development or absence of class-related attitudes and voting. Early political socialization through parental examples was strong only where there was a consistency among the cues generated by the adolescent's environment. Imitation was also less where the father's vote was atypical of his social class or where parents disagreed. Parents' vote continued to exert an influence in adult life on the adults' vote choice. Where parents, whatever their social class, had voted Conservative, movement away from Labour was strongest, and weakest where the parents had voted Labour.

Class-linked voting still exists, of course. More of the middle class vote Conservative even though less than in the 1960s; in the working class, however, the decline in Labour's share of the vote has become almost a rout. In 1959 62% of the working class voted Labour, by 1983 only 38% did so. The decline was so steep that among working class voters, Labour had only a 5% advantage over the Conservatives. Crewe (1983b) suggests that it would be more accurate in the 1980s to describe Labour as a party of *a segment of the working class*, the segment that is engaged in the declining heavy manufacturing industries in the North and in Scotland. Among more prosperous members of the working class, particularly those owning their homes, or working in industries that are holding their own, Labour was often the third rather than the first choice.

We make a distinction between class-*linked* voting and class-*determined* voting, whose decline is unlikely to be reversed. While the historically determined relations between labour and capital are of course structured along class lines, what emerges from our studies is that the political views of individuals, or indeed their political actions, are to a much smaller extent influenced by their social class position or

[4]We found that upward mobility led to a move towards the Conservatives, away from Labour. In line with Dahrendorf's predictions (1959), it was strongest where, through further education, the individual had achieved upward mobility by the time he entered the labour market and least where mobility came after some years of doing a manual or routine white collar job.
[5]Crewe (1981a) found only 39% of the manual workers spontaneously described themselves as working class.

their social mobility than a view of them as members of a class-ridden society would lead one to suspect. Such a view fails to differentiate between the effect of economic and social structures and their history on *society* as a whole and the effects on *individuals* for whom these structural categories represent one experience among several that form their view of society.

## THE FUTURE RELATION OF CLASS TO VOTE

The degree of class-linked voting is time bound and election specific except in socially homogeneous areas (the industrial North or the South) with a long and unbroken tradition of voting Labour or Conservative. In the absence of specific regional and traditional ties with one party, the greater the geographical mobility, the more socially varied the neighbourhood, the smaller the place of work, the looser the relation between class and vote (Rose, 1980). Increase in standard of living, home ownership, upward social mobility and a middle class occupation encourage individualistic rather than collective aspirations (Strumpel, 1976). In our study, where concern with personal success was high, this coloured the individual's reaction to political issues (Chapter 4). By contrast, reduction in living standards, fear of inflation, high levels of unemployment and a working class job with little security or prospect of advancement led to more collectivist aspirations and the support of policies which in the 1970s were closer to those of the Labour than the Conservative Party.

What matters are the priorities of the voters at the time of each election. Where economic conditions are bad and mobility at a standstill, where unemployment hits society differentially and hardships fall unevenly, and where the government, by word or deed, does little to correct the imbalance, class-linked voting could increase. These conditions prevailed in 1983. There was also an increase in the polarization of the views of the two parties which should have yielded, at least among manual workers, more class-linked voting rather than less. We had expected that former Labour supporters from the working class who had voted Conservative in 1979, largely we thought as a reaction against the "winter of discontent", would return to Labour in 1983. This did not happen. Disillusionment with a party's promises and performance would be a sufficient reason for change of vote *only* where there is trust in the leadership and the realism of the proposals of the opposition.[6] Both were absent.

It is the economic conditions of a society and the performance of the government in office which make the potential for voting along social class determinants more or less likely. But it is the beliefs that individuals develop about the available

[6]At the beginning of the 1983 election campaign, 67% were dissatisfied with Michael Foot's competence as leader of the Labour party; only 17% of the electorate voted him best potential Prime Minister, and a far higher percentage the worst. Nor did his standing improve in the course of the election campaign (Worcester, 1983).

alternatives which will largely determine how far disillusionment with the party for which they had voted is translated into a move away from that party the next time around.

In the last 15 years, voting has entered a new era in which once familiar landmarks no longer operate or have been reversed. For example, in the early 1970s, trade union membership proved a significant factor over and above other social determinants in favour of a Labour vote. Since 1979, this has not been the case; indeed, in 1983, more trade unionists than non-union members voted Conservative. This was only partly due to an increase in the membership of white-collar unions; above all, it is an indication that those joining a union do not necessarily share the same political views, nor that membership generates such similarity.

The relevance of age to vote choice has changed as well, at least among the young. In every election since World War II up to 1979 new voters favoured Labour over the Conservatives. In the 1964 and 1974 elections, which Labour won with a very small majority, it was in fact their votes which tipped the scale. In contrast by 1983, despite unprecedented levels of youth unemployment, no more than 18% of the new voters opted for Labour as their first choice.

In the period after World War II the Conservatives consistently attracted more women than men. By 1979, this difference too had disappeared, largely because of increased voting for the Conservatives by male manual workers. In 1983, the pattern was actually reversed, with more men than women voting Conservative.

Comfortable landmarks on which politicians and political scientists have relied are disappearing one by one. For how long no-one can tell. What is certain, however, is that such landmarks no longer indicate invariant or even a strong predisposition for one party rather than another, unless other favourable conditions are also present.

## The increased importance of voters' assessments of policies, parties and their leaders

In the past voters were thought to have made their task easier by voting in line with party loyalty and significant reference groups. These supports, as we have seen, no longer have much force. Since the task of deciding has become more difficult, it is not surprising that the number of people who make up their minds during the campaign has increased, with a considerable percentage deciding only in the last few days. There has also been an increase in the number who change their vote intention during the campaign.[7] In voting as in any other decision making where previous guidelines have lost their force, individuals need increasingly to draw on their own assessments.

[7] In 1983, 17% changed their voting intention and 11% changed the party they wanted to vote for between two weeks before the election was called and a few days before election day (Worcester, 1983).

In Chapter 1, we outlined our cognitive model of vote choice which indicates the factors influencing the decision. We compared the way the voter decides how to vote with how he decides what goods to buy. Instead of buying goods, the individual purchases a party, in the manner we described in Chapter 10. We drew this particular analogy to highlight the extent to which the individual searches for the best fit or least misfit between his or her views and preferences and the parties' platforms. In doing this, he or she may also be affected by two other more variable and weaker influences. The first of these is the habit of voting for a party, like the loyalty people develop for a particular brand, which predisposes them in its favour. Where preferences between competing goods are evenly matched, brand loyalty — or in the case of voting, party identification — may well tip the scale. The second influence is the example of others. Here we draw an analogy to the influence of spouses, friends and colleagues whose purchases at times influence our own.

In the case of most purchases, the final choice is a compromise. The same is true of voting. Some preferences are met, others are incompatible and others not reflected in the stance of any party. There are other similarities between voting and the purchase of goods: in both cases individual preferences matter as does the voter's attempt to examine the realism of the claims made by the parties in competing for votes.

While the analogy between purchasing a party and purchasing goods is a useful one, there are aspects which make choosing a party that much harder. In the case of voting, options are few and the policies on offer are those generated by the parties, not the voter. The timetable too is fixed by government. *De facto*, there are few opportunities for the ordinary voter, only moderately interested in politics, to hear the parties' claims seriously challenged, except by the other parties' counter claims. There is also no Trade Description Act to limit the claims of the parties, nor is there a consumer guide like *Which?* to assess their realism. Relative costs and incompatibility of policies are rarely mentioned; for example, that it would be difficult to reduce government expenditure while improving the lot of the needy, health and education services, as well as provide help for the developing countries. Yet all parties claim these as their objectives.

Is it any wonder that there are wide fluctuations in the opinion polls and that the voter is particularly critical of the party for which he had voted last time or the one he tried "for size" in the pre-election period? It is for this reason that a party which does very well early on in a campaign needs to be particularly on its guard. For some voters the final choice is as often as not dictated by a general wish for change or a growing *dislike* of some posture of one party about which the voter already felt ambivalent, rather than attraction for another party. With the loosening of party ties negative partisanship is becoming more prevalent (Crewe, 1984).

Even though we found certain of the attitudes to be remarkably stable over a 12-year period, the model itself does not require stability of attitudes since each election is like a new shopping expedition in which familiar and new goods are on offer—some perennials, others shop-soiled and others still pristine in their wrappings.

Finally, our model of the voter as consumer does not imply that a voter who is in favour of two apparently incompatible policies lacks political acumen. When we buy goods, for example furniture or clothes, we want cheapness, elegance and good workmanship, generally incompatible qualities, but then decide between the available options by giving more weight to one rather than to the other quality. On another occasion the priorities as to which qualities matter most might well be reversed. For example, in most Western developed societies, voters want a reduction in public expenditure but no reduction in welfare provisions for which government is generally responsible: two apparently incompatible requirements which stem from different considerations; the first is economic, while the second derives from a shared value orientation which accepts that society has some responsibility for its poor. In Victorian times, when the poor were deemed to be responsible for their own plight, such incompatibility of views would have been less frequent.

EVALUATION OF PARTIES' STANDS ON ISSUES

While practically all studies of voting use the individual's attitudes to issues as ingredients for their analyses, far fewer (Fiorina, 1981; Fishbein et al., 1976; Särlvik and Crewe, 1983) take into account the voters' beliefs about the parties' stands and about their ability or willingness to implement their policy proposals. Yet such assessments are an integral part of the decision process.

In our study, we paid special attention to this aspect of the voters' decision, which led us to make a differentiation between *consensual* and *non-consensual* issues; the former are issues about whose desirability everyone is agreed, e.g. the need to bring down inflation and unemployment. The latter are issues on which views diverge, e.g. on nationalization or comprehensive education. We showed in Chapter 8 that only on consensual issues was there evidence (supporting here Markus and Converse, 1979) that people's party preferences affected the relative ordering of their perceptions of the parties' ability or rather inability to do something about these issues. On most non-consensual issues voters agreed on the relative ordering of the parties' stands, irrespective of their own preferences.

By using MAUT, a method which takes account of the particular concerns of each voter (Chapter 9), we established not only the importance that beliefs about the parties' ability and competence play in the final decision, but also the need to re-evaluate in that decision the role that the salience of an issue plays. Much has been written elsewhere about the importance or *salience* of an issue in the prediction of vote. Of course salience matters, but not in isolation. We need no research to predict that if there were an election tomorrow, the recession, unemployment, prices and wages would be uppermost in people's minds and that the parties would canvas around their particular remedies. Whether these concerns would affect the vote, however, would depend on the voters' assessment of the validity of the parties' claims that they could improve the situation. If the voters saw only a marginal difference between the parties because they believed them all to have little to offer then other attitudes to specific policies even though less salient, would have the stronger influence.

## Life history of issues

In Chapter 10 we described why it is important to consider not just correlations between given attitudes and the behaviour in which one is interested, but to look at the *life history of the issues themselves.*

For example, the men in the longitudinal study were asked, in 1962, 1970 and 1974, about their attitudes to a number of issues whose life histories illustrate the link between attitudes and issues and the social context which gave rise to them. An issue can move from the periphery to the centre of political debate, as in the case of comprehensive schools during this period. In 1962 a third of the men had no views about comprehensive schools. As it was a relatively new issue in 1962, views about it correlated neither with other views about education nor with the politico-economic cluster of attitues. By 1970 many such schools had been introduced and almost everyone had views about their value. By that time too comprehensive schools were in the forefront of political debate and attitudes to comprehensive schools now correlated with attitudes to trade unions, to strikes and to big business, all issues which differentiated the parties. This was even more so by 1974. Then the question had changed from whether people were in favour of having comprehensive schools to one of whether all schools should be comprehensive. From an issue about inequality of opportunity it became one of parental freedom and of the abolition of grammar and public schools. This is an example of an issue moving into the political arena and in the course of time changing its character.

An example of an issue which ceased to be part of a liberal belief system and becomes part of the consensus of the society is the legalization of homosexuality among consenting adults. In 1962, prior to legalization, the men in our sample were opposed to this change, as was the electorate at large. Views about it correlated with not wanting capital punishment abolished and not respecting nuclear disarmers; that is, attitudes to this issue formed part of a liberal belief system. By 1970, a few years after the change in law, the men's opposition had died down and even more so four years later. Once legalization had become accepted, the correlation of attitudes to this issue with other liberal beliefs became much smaller.

Voters' attitudes to the Common Market not surprisingly underwent many changes over the period from 1970 to 1983. We were able to trace the life history of this issue through analysis of the longitudinal study 1979–1974, and the BES studies of 1979–1983. When first questioned in 1970, people reacted to a hypothetical situation; between 1972 and 1979, once Britain had become a member, the issue became one of leaving or remaining, and more recently, it changed to one of re-negotiating terms. The parties' attitudes too have changed: in 1970, Labour was in favour, by 1974 it was opposed to membership. Since 1980, Conservatives have become more critical of the EEC and Labour more accepting that Britain is likely to remain a member.

Despite the fact that many people had definite views about Britain's membership in the EEC, prior to 1983 these views did not affect their vote decision. In 1983, they proved to be among the few that best differentiated between the voters for the three parties. The issue by then had changed from one of Britain's membership to one of re-negotiation of the terms of that membership. Britain's contribution to the EEC budget received much attention just before the General Election and, of course, related very directly to Britain's precarious economic condition. Also the issue had moved from one of ideology (to be in or out of the Community) to one of the relative effectiveness of the parties in getting better terms. Here Mrs Thatcher's ability to do so was presented as a continuation in peace time of the value of her resolute approach to other nations that had proved so successful in the Falklands War.

Berelson *et al.* (1954) suggest that an issue goes through certain stages which have bearing on its relevance to vote, from initial rejection through resistance to hesitant acceptance and then acquiescence, at which stage the issue becomes part of the social representation of that society. It is important to know what issues are in the political arena during a campaign, but also which ones are just approaching or just passing "the critical gateway phase of precarious balance between acceptance and rejection", as these are likely to be the most critical. Our research provides much evidence of the importance of considering the life history of an issue in the way we described in Chapters 5, 6 and 10, when assessing its bearing on the vote choice and its relation to the individual's belief system.

It is unfortunate that pollsters who have so much information about voters' reactions to a number of issues report only changes in each attitude over time but do not consider how their interrelation changes.

## Portrait of the British voter in the 1970s and 1980s

Two commonly made claims about voters received no support from the studies described in this book. These are Bell's (1962) claim that because of consensus of social attitudes among voters within Western developed societies, coherent and distinctive belief systems and goals were held only by politically concerned minorities; and Converse's (1964) claim that only the élite and not the general public had a coherent set of views. The views of our sample in 1970 and 1974 and those of the 1974 and 1979 British election samples were well structured, forming two belief clusters which showed considerable stability across a four- and a 12-year period—one concerned with a liberal versus a restrictive outlook on the law, civil liberties and minorities, and the other encompassing those political and economic issues which have traditionally separated the Labour and Conservative parties (Chapter 10). Separate analysis of the structuring of views of two contrasting groups, those with a university education and those without any educational qualifications at all, showed both to have similarly organized and equally clearly structured sets of beliefs.

The presence of such clearly articulated sets of beliefs within all sections of the electorate makes rapid change in response to the parties' propaganda much less likely than in a society where the individual's attitudes represent a set of discrete and unrelated beliefs. The portrait that emerges from our study of the voter of today is of someone who is not simply conforming to his or her own past or follows other people's example, but makes up his own mind. While little interested in politics and fairly unsophisticated in his or her political thinking, the voter is nevertheless quite aware of the parties' major policy proposals and has views about the parties' ability concerning the parties' leaders and or willingness to implement them; he or she also has fairly definite views about a variety of political issues, particularly those which have a bearing on his or her own life.

We give below inevitably rather stylized portraits of the consistent Conservative, Labour, Liberal and now Alliance voters drawing on the information we have about their reactions to the parties, their political outlook and goals and values.

## THE CONSERVATIVE VOTER

The consistent Conservative, compared with the consistent Labour voter, tends to identify more strongly with the party, to follow more in the parents' footsteps in his or her voting, and if middle class, to be more likely to vote Conservative than a member of the working class to vote Labour. Conservative voters of all social classes attach greater priority than Labour voters to being successful and to having a job with good financial rewards. Their outlook is more authoritarian: they have a greater tendency to see issues in terms of "we and they" and to subscribe to restrictive rather than liberal policies, whether these concern law and order issues, demonstrations, student unrest, immigration or attitudes to "coloured people" born in this country. They disapprove of trade unions and strikes, are against nationalization and the abolition of selective secondary grammar and public schools. Change, though not generally opposed, is viewed more cautiously, and seen often more as a threat than an opportunity. The Conservative voters wish to maintain the *status quo*. That makes them more consistent in their voting than Labour voters, particularly since they dislike the Labour party more than Labour voters dislike the Conservative party. They are, therefore, more ready to vote Conservative to keep Labour out even when not in tune with many of the Conservative party's policies. That is why fewer Conservatives voted for the Liberals when a Labour government called the election. Voting Liberal is a luxury which the Conservative voters feel they cannot afford when their primary task is to oust the Labour party.

## THE LABOUR VOTER

The Labour voter, particularly the middle class Labour voter, is also concerned about personal success but attaches more importance to improving society than do the Conservatives, tends to be less hostile to immigrants and less opposed to the liberalization of the law. Note that we speak of *less* hostile; neither group is supportive of immigrants and both are opposed to the liberalization of the law, wanting capital punishment restored. Since Labour voters tend to be less in tune with their party's ideological stand and policies than are the Conservative voters with those of their party, their allegiance to the party requires more "rootedness". The work environment, the area in which they live and family tradition in voting Labour all play a more important part in retaining allegiance than in the case of the Conservative voter.

## THE CENTRIST VOTERS: THE LIBERAL OR ALLIANCE VOTER

Whereas relatively distinct portraits emerged from our data about the consistent Labour or Conservative voters, this was not so in the case of the Liberal voter of former elections nor of the Alliance voters of the 1983 election. There were hardly any Liberal faithfuls.[8] Deciding to vote Liberal or Alliance has a different meaning from deciding to vote Labour or Conservative. It is a one-off affair, a vote of departure rather than arrival, so much so that these voters have more in common with the voters of the party from which they have come than with other Liberal voters who may have come from the opposition.

Liberal or Alliance voters in any one election represent a pale, and also a more differentiated, version of the voter of the party from which they came and to which they are likely to return. A detailed description of their outlook was given in Chapter 11. In general, Liberal or Alliance voters hold similar views to the Conservative voters on economic issues but are more liberal on issues of law and order. They are similar to the Labour voters in some of their liberal ideas while opposing Labour's economic policies. Those who came from the Labour camp were alienated from their old party by its stridency on economic issues; and those from the Conservative camp by its stridency on the issue of law and order.

Liberal or Alliance voters have no social or regional base. They tend to come from all walks of life — a party of individuals whatever their background — drawn somewhat more from the educated middle class and from the Conservatives. In

[8]This is apart from the constituencies where, for historical reasons or because of the popularity of the Liberal candidate, there is a tradition of voting Liberal (see Chapter 11).

Chapter 11 we likened the Liberal voter to the comparative shopper *par excellence*, someone who decides late, is primarily influenced by current proposals, by the conduct of the election campaign and by the behaviour of the politicians who take part in it, particularly those of their own party. They are sensitive to a strident doctrinaire approach as in 1983, or begin to feel uneasy when, as in the 1974 election campaign, one issue is overstressed and one group (in this case the miners) held responsible for society's problems.

Since few voters read party manifestos, their impression of the Liberals or the Alliance comes mainly from the party's television performance. As shown in Chapter 11, the television appearances of the centrist party plays a particularly important role and has been conducted with consummate skill by successive leaders of the party. The Liberal, and now the Alliance, party provides a kind of screen on which the individuals' dissatisfaction with their own party can be projected without voters becoming too sharply aware that in doing so they might be purchasing policies with which they do not agree. Nor did many vote for the Liberals or the Alliance in the hope that they would be able to form a government. It is rather that the voters wanted to give expression to their dissatisfaction with the stand, whether on liberal or economic issues, of the party from which they defected to the Alliance.

## RECENT CHANGES IN THE PORTRAITS OF THE LABOUR AND CONSERVATIVE VOTERS

The portraits just drawn are stylized and exaggerate the differences that were found in the samples we studied. In fact, during the 1970s, consensus became more pronounced, with the Conservatives supporting aspects of the welfare state while Labour voters became less certain about increased expenditure on social services; Conservatives began to accept comprehensive schools more and Labour voters became less certain about abolishing grammar schools and about further nationalization. Both disapproved of what they saw as the excessive power of trade unions, both saw strikes as harmful, with over 90% wanting secret ballots on whether or not to strike. Both were against arming the police. There has been a general shift to the right, particularly marked among certain sections of working class Labour voters. Särlvik and Crewe (1983) found that the Conservative party's views in 1979 were more representative of the electorate as a whole on six out of eight issues. They drew attention to the spectacular decline in support for what they described as the Labour party's "collectivist trinity of public ownership, trade union power and social welfare". In 1979 only a third of manual workers supported them. By 1983 only a quarter did so.

Yet in 1983, while many of the Conservative policies continued to receive strong support from the electorate, there was, compared with 1979, a 10% drop in the size of the majority that endorsed the need for laws to regulate trade union activities, and that thought new jobs should be created by the private sector from profits rather than by government from taxes. At the same time there was an even stronger acceptance (increasing from 71 to 80%) that taxes should not be cut if this meant a reduction of government services in either education, health or welfare, leading Crewe (1984) to comment that "Keynes might be out of fashion, but Beveridge is not".

Aspects of these portraits are time-bound and depend on the brand of Conservative and Labour governments experienced by the voters. Up to 1979 this was neither the right-wing doctrinaire brand of Conservatism practised by Margaret Thatcher nor the more left-wing doctrinaire Labour policies advocated by Tony Benn and his followers. Then the voters had only experienced the muted versions of the respective philosophies of the two parties in the Conservative governments of Sir Alec Douglas Home and Edward Heath and in the Labour governments of Harold Wilson and James Callaghan.

A government is judged by the record of its administration, by its policy proposals but also by its style, especially that of the leader of the party in dealing with conflict, whether this relates to pressure groups within the country, to general dissent or to negotiations with other nations. We showed in Chapter 11 that where the style jars, it becomes a reason for voters to defect even where they are in agreement with the party's policies. Such a reaction will tend to be ephemeral however, since it is likely that governments change their style or their leader when there is evidence of continued and widespread disapproval of it, particularly among the party's own ranks.

## The conduct of election campaigns

To get the timing and the conduct right has become more difficult with each election. In the 1950s and early 1960s governments might call an election when things went well, claiming "You have never had it so good", hoping that the voter would associate the upturn in the country's economic affairs with the stewardship of the government. In the increasingly difficult times in which the last four elections were, and the next is likely to be, fought, there is little to which a government can point as an achievement that is not dwarfed by the increase in the scale of other problems. Since responsibility for problems tends to be laid at the foot of the government of the day, being an incumbent has become a liability where formerly it was an asset.

Two advertisements which the Conservatives used in the 1979 election campaign illustrate how the opposition builds on the voter's association of problems with the government of the day. The first reads "1984. What would Britain be like after another 5 years of Labour?" The caption of the second, placed above a long queue of people waiting outside an "unemployment office", reads "Labour isn't working." Given the unprecedented rise in unemployment since the Conservatives came to power, this advertisement has a macabre charm all of its own. What makes these advertisements unusual is that the message about the Conservatives themselves "Britain's better off with the Conservatives" is found in each advertisement only in very small print at the bottom right-hand corner rather like an artist's signature. It is smaller even than the health warning that cigarette advertisements have to carry. The purpose of the advertisement is clearly to loosen the voters' ties with Labour. If the aim had been primarily to attract the voter to the Conservatives, this would testify to a degree of modesty unprecedented in politics.

One reason for the difficulty in knowing when to call an election and how to conduct its campaign has therefore to do with the state of the economy and the demonstrated inability of governments of both parties to overcome the problems facing them. As one problem comes close to being solved, another arises; what differs is their mix.[9]

A second reason has to do with the volatility of the voters and their consequent unpredictability. More and more voters make up their minds only during the campaign; since 1974 that percentage has doubled. In 1983 8% claimed to have made up their minds in the last day or so. This explains why only polls conducted on the eve or better still on the day of the election accurately reflect the electorate's decisions. The increase in volatility stems not from a lessening of political involvement, which has always been low, but from increased disaffection with the parties' records and promises. In 1983, for the first time, more people said that they had voted for a party not because it appealed to them but because of their dislike of the alternatives — among the late deciders three out of four gave this answer.

A third reason has to do with what Dahrendorf (1979) described as the lessening of the linkages, with fewer shared perspectives among people of the same age, sex and even social class, making it more difficult for the parties to know how to target their message.

Regional variations have become more pronounced, compounding the difficulties of targeting a message which will be transmitted nationwide through the media. The safe Labour seats are in Scotland and the North where unemployment is exceptionally high. There no Conservative appeal could convince the voters that a Conservative government would have the will, or be able, to revitalize the region's dying industries or improve the people's living conditions. The safe Conservative seats are in the rural areas in the South, in the New Towns and the suburbs. The Conservatives advanced most where there was some indication of economic stability if not expansion or at least no clear sign of a rapid, unstoppable decline of the area's industrial base.

The fourth difficulty has to do with the role that the press and broadcasting play in the campaign which we come back to later in this chapter.

Finally, there is the enormity of the task facing any government in this country today. Not only the public, but also politicians seem to think that the most that

---

[9]The achievements Labour could point to in 1979 (the easing of inflation and of the balance of payments crisis) were dwarfed by the upturn in the number and severity of strikes.

can be achieved is a small upturn in the economy rather than a genuine turn-around of Britain's fortunes. To bring the latter about would require a transformation of existing institutions: the Civil Service, the trade unions, industry, banking and many of the professions which have worked well in the past but are ill equipped to meet present and future needs. The time scale required for such transformation, if it is to be more than cosmetic, is a long one. Parties, however have a short time scale; their primary consideration is, after all, how to remain in, or regain, power.

It is salutary to look again at Schumpeter's comments about party objectives, voters' decisions and the conduct of campaigns. They are as apposite today as when they were first published over 30 years ago.

> The first and foremost aim of each political party is to prevail over the others in order to get into power or to stay in it. Like the conquest of a stretch of country, or a hill, the decision of the political issues is, from the standpoint of the politician not the end but only the material of parliamentary activity.
>
> Since politicians fire off words instead of bullets and since those words are unavoidably supplied by the issues under debate, this may not always be as clear as it is in the military case. But victory over the opponent is nevertheless the essence of both games.
>
> Its choice — ideologically glorified into the Call from the People — does not flow from its initiative but is being shaped, and the shaping of it is an essential part of the democratic process . . . Voters do not decide issues . . . voters confine themselves to accepting this bid in preference to others or refusing to accept it.
>
> The psychotechnics of party management and party advertising, slogans and marching tunes, are not accessories. They are of the essence of politics. So is the political boss. (Schumpeter, 1950, p. 283)

Of the three statements, the only one in need of revision is the second, where Schumpeter sees the voters only as reacting to what is on offer. Today, the voters have more influence on the parties' message and style of presentation than was the case before the ready and frequent use by each party of opinion polls. During the 1983 election campaign the Conservatives conducted daily polls (*Operation "Fast Feedback"*), whose results were available within 24 hours to help shape the party's press conference next day (Cockerell *et al.*, 1984).

THE 1983 ELECTION CAMPAIGN

It is interesting to look in detail at the 1983 election campaign because the results contradicted the general observation so amply demonstrated by Lipset's (1984) analysis of recent election outcomes in Western democracies, namely that a party which presides over a recession and a steep rise in unemployment or inflation loses the next election. The 1983 campaign is also particularly interesting because it demonstrates the influence on the style of the election campaign of a specific event (in this case the Falklands War), unrelated to the country's main problems, highlighting also the role of the leader of a party in influencing people's preferences. Above all, it brings out clearly the interdependence of the major parties' fortunes, showing that winning depends as much on the availability of credible alternatives as on the particular party's record and promises.

It was also the first election in which the newly formed Social Democratic party took part, joining with the Liberals to contest seats as the Alliance. While Liberals had always been a feature of the election campaign and had improved their share of the vote over the years, their metamorphosis into the Alliance created a different and largely unknown contender as the third party. Not only the parties but also the media needed to adapt, as their rhetoric had been geared primarily to a two party contest.

First, the facts: the Conservative party's share of the vote (42·5%), by comparison with 1979, was reduced by 1·5%. (It was less than in 1964 when the Conservatives lost the election.) Labour's share was 26·7%, its lowest overall vote for almost half a century. The Alliance gained 25·4%, taking second place in 312 constituencies. The massive majority of the Conservatives in the House of Commons was based on less than 50% support by the electorate!

> Never in the field of electoral conflict was so much owed by so many Conservative MPs to so few Conservative voters. (Crewe, 1984)

The difference between the electoral share of the vote and the number of seats in Parliament has of course to do with the first-past-the-post British electoral system, which has never accurately reflected the electorate's preference. The degree of distortion in the 1983 election was, however, exceptional, the worst since the introduction of the general franchise in 1918.

Election analysts (Crewe, 1984; Worcester, 1983; Hall and Jacques, 1983; Cockerell, 1984) attribute the Conservatives' victory, or more accurately, Labour's defeat to four factors: the first was "The Falklands factor".[10] As Brody and Page (1975) and Brody and Sigelman (1983) found, a sudden international crisis rallies the country round its leader and increases the leader's popularity, provided the crisis does not last long and is resolved. The Falklands War was successful on all these counts: short, sharp and decisive, not too costly in human lives, and high in symbolic value showing that although Britain had lost her pre-eminent position in the world and was in a poor state economically she was a force to be reckoned with, standing for the rule of law and the protection of her people. The second and third factors had to do with the state of the Labour party and its leadership. The Labour leader, Michael Foot, was unpopular; two-thirds of the electorate thought he would make a bad Prime Minister. The Labour party's reputation as a divided party, unsuccessfully seeking to contain its extreme elements, was reinforced by its conduct during the election campaign. (Seventy-two per cent of voters saw the party as divided at the beginning, and 79% at

[10]In December 1981, less than one quarter of the electorate was satisfied with Mrs Thatcher; in April 1982, when the invasion took place, her popularity rose to between 45% and 50% and has remained at that level. The increase in Mrs Thatcher's standing reflected on the party. By the summer of 1982 the Conservatives had gained a 20% lead over Labour and the Alliance's potential share of the vote had dropped from around 30% to 20%.

the end of the campaign.) The fourth factor was that the electorate preferred on most of the ten major issues Conservative policies. On only three: import controls, unemployment and the workings of the Health Service, had Labour an edge over the Conservatives, but that advantage was less than the advantage that the Conservatives had over Labour on policies to do with defence (where the majority wanted Britain to retain her own nuclear weapons), the economy, trade unions, and council spending. It was an election in which voters' perceptions of the leaders and the issues favoured the Conservatives.

In the cognitive model of vote choice, we point to the different aspects of the individual's cognitions which enter the decision. Four are of particular relevance for the conduct of election campaigns: (1) the individual's value system, that is the relative priorities he or she assigns to given values which may be in conflict with one another. (Such values, while less easily changed than people's views on individual issues, are still amenable to shifts in emphasis due to events or to persuasion.); (2) the individual's evaluation or preference for existing or proposed policies; (3) the individual's beliefs concerning the competence and/or willingness of the parties to affect change and to implement desirable policies; (4) beliefs about the relative suitability of the leaders of the parties.

Given the need to make a strong impact on the electorate within a short time, a party tends to concentrate in a campaign on no more than two of the four aspects. The contrast between the Conservatives' 1979 and 1983 campaign strategy illustrates this well. In 1979 when the Conservatives were trying to regain power, they were faced with a Labour government whose record in office had been relatively good (reducing inflation and improving the balance of payment) marred only by the severity of the strikes in the "winter of discontent" prior to the elections, and whose leader, Jim Callaghan, was more popular than Mrs Thatcher. In that election, the Conservative campaign concentrated on the electorate's general value system; and on specific policy proposals.

In 1983, the situation was quite different. Over the years a subtle shift had taken place in the electorate's values in the direction of a Conservative rather than a Labour orientation towards the role of government. Although the government's record was dismal (the country was in a deep recession and unemployment had tripled), Mrs Thatcher's handling of the Falklands crisis had provided an opportunity for the government to show that it could take tough and effective decisions and for the Prime Minister to display the calibre of her leadership. Also people largely accepted the structural character of mass unemployment so that less blame attached to the government of the day than might otherwise have been the case. A party in government speaks in generalities rather than making specific policy proposals since it could be argued that such proposals should have been implemented during the party's term of office.[11] A party in opposition, on the other hand, has to back worthy intents with worthy and workable

[11]In 1979, when Labour was in power, Callaghan also spoke in very general terms about the achievements of the party rather than proposing specific new policies.

policy proposals. In 1979, the emphasis in the campaign was on the rekindling of the values of initiative and individual choice which, it was suggested, had been stifled by Labour's policy of state intervention and on selected policies like council tenants buying their own home. In 1983 the Conservative campaign concentrated on two other aspects, both to do with beliefs about the relative competence of the parties and their leaders. The Falklands factor provided the impetus to do so, as did Labour's disunity and poor leadership. The party also stressed beliefs in the electorate's capacity to surmount obstacles and to face unpalatable realities.

Much of the Conservative campaign was centred on persuading the electorate that the resolve, toughness and decisiveness that Mrs Thatcher displayed during the Falklands War was needed now and that the British people, having demonstrated their own resolve and toughness, were capable, under appropriate leadership, to deal with hard facts and the long struggle needed for economic recovery. While no direct reference was made in the manifesto and in speeches to the Falklands War, its metaphors were used to evoke its memories in the electorate's mind. In her introduction to the party's manifesto, Mrs Thatcher wrote:[12]

> In the last four years, Britain has *revived her confidence* and *self-respect*. We have *regained the regard and admiration of other nations*. We are seen today as a people with integrity, *resolve* and *the will to succeed* . . . our history is the story of a free people . . . linked by a common belief in freedom and in Britain's greatness. All are aware of their own responsibility to contribute to both. (Our italics)

The theme was "We can overcome", "Trust us". Everything in the campaign favoured this approach, not least the contrast between Mrs Thatcher's combative style, always taking the offensive, and Michael Foot's vacillating and wordy approach. Also, given the state of the Labour party, it was easy to draw a contrast between a united Conservative and a divided Labour party and, again using the rhetoric of war, to dismiss Labour's proposals about unemployment as unworkable, a gimmick, characteristic of that party's refusal to face hard facts.

Labour's campaign was doomed from the outset — the manifesto papered over profound disagreement on defence and other policies, which surfaced later in the campaign — it also promised an unrealistic reduction in the number of unemployed by means of familiar Labour remedies of further nationalization and public works. These remedies were out of step with the mood of the electorate and judged by them to be ineffective. All this, quite apart from the lack of unity in the conduct of the election campaign and the unsuitability of its leader.

The Alliance faced a difficult task — being new the party had to show that it was creditable as well as "nice", and the need to attract voters from both the main parties required it to operate on three fronts simultaneously: to change the electorate's view of the value of the existing electoral system (the need to break the mould); to attack both parties for their extremism; and to convey distinctive policy proposals on the main issues of the day. In spite of these difficulties, the

---

[12]Cockerell *et al.* (1984) write "She was the Falklands factor made flesh" (p. 203).

Alliance was the only party whose standing improved in the course of the campaign and where the opinion polls in the last week showed a steady rise, putting it within reach of becoming the main opposition party.

It is particularly interesting, in distinguishing the approaches of the three parties, to note that in each case their campaigns were based on the parties' stand on political issues, rather than on traditionalist appeals to the faithful. However, the way in which issues were presented by each party were quite different. Labour learned to its cost, and the Alliance to its advantage, that issues concerning party leadership were of importance to the electorate. But the Conservatives went even further, not only promoting the desirable characteristics of the leader, but also using the recency of the Falklands success as a metaphor suggesting that they were the only party who could offer the resolute leadership that was required. With this style of leadership went a new perspective about the issues that mattered. Hence much of the valid criticism levelled by the other parties at the Conservative's past record was successfully neutralized in Conservative propaganda (with the aid of operation "fast feedback") as "irrelevant" to voters' concerns in deciding how to vote.

## The role of the media and the polls

> The general election of 9th June was an election fought by the parties almost wholly through broadcasting, and principally through television. This characteristic has intensified in every general election since 1959, the first election campaign when broadcasting really came into its own. (Glencross, 1983)

Just as election campaigns become more important as more voters make up their mind late and fewer can be relied upon to act on former loyalties, so does the role of the media. Blumler *et al.* (1985) describe it as "the engine by which the campaign is predominantly driven".

Changes in the organization and conduct of campaigns are linked to the role that the press, and in particular radio and television play in the campaigning. For the vast majority of voters, television has become the main source of information about the election with over 70% having seen one or more party political broadcast and as many as nine out of ten see the News almost every day (half of its time being generally devoted to the campaign). This is quite apart from the other day-time and evening programmes covering the election which, together with radio, provide a wide range of contact between the public and the politicians. Such contact ranges from press conferences to open forum and from interviews with journalists to phone-ins, and other forms of questioning by the public.

In the parties' response to this increasing role and power of the media in the campaign, power has shifted decisively from the constituency to each party's headquarters, where staff, resources and role in masterminding and orchestrating the campaign have all substantially increased. Each party's central organization has also been strengthened to exploit or minimize the impact of unexpected favourable or damaging happenings, including leaks, gaffes, planned or inadvertent expressions of dissent.[13] There is greater reliance on experts (advertising agencies, producers, polling experts and scriptwriters), and less on the politician's intuitions or on the power of their oratory (Butler, 1985). What matters is the marketing of the party's politicians and promises (Cockerell et al., 1984).

In the 1950s, radio relayed the speeches of the politicians; there were no interviews, no press conferences, no confrontations. The two sides never seemed to meet, nor comment on the points made that day by the other side. "Each seemed to be manoeuvring on a separate battlefield against straw armies of its own devising" (Butler, 1985). Today, by contrast, there is constant challenge and rebuttal with the rhythm of the news programmes ensuring that most issues are exhausted within a few hours and with the press and broadcasters constantly on the lookout for new themes.

Leaders have always dominated election campaigns, but do so even more now that television and press journalists follow them throughout the day. In 1983, 48% of the news coverage of the Conservative party was devoted to Mrs Thatcher and 43% of Labour coverage to Michael Foot. Set speeches by leaders are fewer now: in 1974 Wilson gave 17 long addresses, in 1983 Mrs Thatcher made six set speeches, but she provided 40 "happenings" aimed at television. These were set up not to discuss issues, but to display her mastery of the important "three C's": confidence, competence and caring. Contact with voters in any real sense of a dialogue was avoided wherever possible.

> What American presidential candidates called photo opportunities abounded, particularly if they involved the Prime Minister wearing some kind of industrial hat. She drove a mechanical dumper truck; she sorted peanuts on a conveyor belt, she operated a micro computer and the cameras purred. All was stage managed. The secrecy surrounding the itinerary meant that few hostile demonstrations had the chance to organise in advance, but local Conservative agents were told to arrange for crowds of loyal supporters to turn up at the main stopping points. (Cockerell et al., 1984, p. 207)

A joint study by the BBC and IBA (Wober et al., 1985) of viewers' perceptions of the 1983 election campaign showed that while no more than a quarter said they made a special point of watching as much election coverage as they could, less than 10% said they switched off or turned the sound down, and a considerable number of viewers (43%) felt they had learnt a good deal or a fair amount from the television coverage and an almost equal number from the press (37%).

In Chapter 11, we showed that in 1970 those who were less happy with their own party sought more information about other parties and their leaders from

[13]Enoch Powell's speech during the 1970 election campaign on race and immigration, despite the party's wish not to have these issues raised, is an example of planned dissent, Mr Pym's comment during the 1983 election campaign that too large a majority would not be advisable is an example of an inadvertent expression of dissent. Denis Healey's dissociation from Labour's defence policy regarding Polaris, while not as premeditated as Enoch Powell's speech in 1970, was not of course just an off-the-cuff remark.

television. Another set of self reports indicates that among those who made up their minds in the last two days (4% of Conservatives, 6% of Labour and 15% of Alliance voters), as many as 40% said they had been influenced by television coverage — a striking figure when contrasted with the 10% among them who said they had been influenced by discussions with family, friends or colleagues. Crewe (1983b) adds to this picture by singling out those who were both late deciders and had said they had been influenced by one or other party political broadcast. He shows that such influence is not necessarily to the party's advantage: in the case of Labour broadcasts, more defected than were recruited; in the case of the Conservatives, the defectors and recruits were more evenly balanced, while out of the 184 who made reference to the Alliance broadcasts, as many as 128 became recruits. For the Alliance, television exposure was of particular importance, as were their party political broadcasts, providing one of the few occasions where their views and approach could be presented directly without journalistic intermediaries.

Not too much reliance should be placed on the actual percentage who report such influence, since it is very difficult to become conscious of the distinctive role any one factor plays in the process of decision making. What is more relevant is that for the public, television along with radio and the press provide the raw material that shapes their perception of the current state of the country, they interpret events, provide an agenda, and present and analyse the parties, their message and their leaders.

Before discussing the practices of press and television and their role in the campaign, we shall consider the growing passion, in the present volatile electoral climate, for taking the pulse of the nation.

## THE ROLE OF THE POLLS

There has been a remarkable increase in the number of polls between the two last elections: in 1979, 26 national polls were commissioned, by 1983 14 newspaper and television programmes commissioned almost double that number (46). In addition, there are the many private polls conducted by the parties, and those conducted in particular regions, in marginal constituencies and with special groups, e.g. young voters. The majority were quickies, asking for vote intentions, leader and policy preferences, with field work and reporting completed within 48 hours.

The role of the polls and their accuracy have been analysed in particular by Crewe (1983a) and Worcester (1983). Our concern is less with the adequacy of the samples or the appropriateness of the questions than with the use to which the polls have been put and the influence, if any, they have on the voters.

Polls are both seen and understood. Sixty per cent or more had seen some poll results and the majority of voters knew from poll results at the start of the campaign that the Conservatives would win. Among the Crewe/BBC sample 1983, 14% of the few very late deciders said they had been influenced by the polls compared with only 4% of the remainder: a small difference only and unlikely to be very reliable.

While the degree of influence is difficult to determine, inaccuracy of reporting of the results by press or television is not. And it is here that there is justified criticism and the need for more responsible reporting, treating poll results with the same care as the reporting of any other events. The main criticisms have been addressed to press headlines and to some television reporting where these speak of victory and defeat, even though the shifts in vote intentions were small and within sampling errors and where often insufficient reference was made to the large number of undecided voters (Crewe, 1981b; Worcester, 1983).

From time to time there is some discussion as to whether publication of polls close to the election day should be banned. There is no justification for this: the news media should be free to canvass and report the voters' views. Instead the discussion should focus on the responsibility of press and broadcasters to present such findings accurately and include the necessary caveats.

To this we would add that, given the barrenness of the information obtained from such quickies that there is need for subtler and more in depth questioning if one wants to understand why individuals make their decisions or later change their minds. Politicians and the media would gain more useful information if they were to commission rather fewer superficial polls and instead devote resources to the building up of small panels whose attitudes and beliefs could be sampled more searchingly, preferably several times during the campaign and once immediately after the election. In this way useful information about the voters' decision-making could be related to the campaign strategies of the parties, to an analysis of media coverage and to external events that occurred at the time. This would also provide the basis for more informed post-mortems after the election.

To understand the reporting of the election campaign and through it the information made available to the public, we need to look more closely at the organizational practices, values and norms of the two major communication industries that are involved: the press and the broadcasting industry. While television is certainly the medium with the largest reach, the press remains an important source of potential influence. Three out of four people read a daily paper and almost as many (37%), as in the case of television, felt they had learnt a good deal from the newspapers they read (Wober *et al.*, 1985).

THE PRESS

In Britain the press has always been largely Conservative. In recent years, this imbalance has increased. Up to 1970, one in five Labour voters read a Conservative daily paper. By 1979 three quarters of Labour voters and three quarters of the working class did so. There was not only an increase in the predominance of Conservative papers (largely because the *Sun* tabloid had successfully drawn readership away from the *Daily Mirror* that favoured Labour), but also in the degree and openness of their partisanship, particularly by tabloid and middle level papers.

How the papers handled the election depended on their customary style of reporting. The quality papers provided background information and analysis, while the tabloids concentrated on personalities and sensationalism. The *Sun* outshone all others in its vituperative comments on the Labour party and its leader, and in the hyperbole used to describe Mrs Thatcher. Nor is the style of the middle level papers necessarily more restrained. While the *Sun* described the Labour party as having "a parody of a programme . . . which is extreme, extravagant and nightmarish . . . and which would virtually wipe out freedom", the *Express* described Michael Foot as "half socialist . . . half politician, half journalist, half ranter, half raver, half baked and half gone", and in that same paper Mrs Thatcher inspecting a field in Cornwall is described as "vibrating with crusading passion . . . Superwoman who could take off from Gatwick without her BAC 1-11 wings . . . Mrs. Big, Britain's boss" (Harrop, 1985).

It is clear that those reading the tabloids and some of the middle level newspapers with their increasing emphasis on sensationalism, get little information about the policy proposals, their rationale and implications. It is no wonder that tabloid readers said they gained more from television than from the newspapers, while those readers of the quality papers cited newspapers rather than television (Wober *et al.*, 1985).

## TELEVISION AND RADIO

Television and radio, like the press, are powerful institutions with their own norms and values, sets of practices and rituals. Like the press they need to attract, or at least not to lose, audiences. They have the largest reach and the most heterogeneous audience but, unlike the press, also have the statutory requirement to be impartial and to inform and educate.[14]

Television and radio mediate between the parties and the electorate. In the pre-broadcasting period, communication between the parties and the public was generally without an intermediary. Now with television this is so only for party political broadcasts whose number is decided by a joint committee of the main parties and the broadcasters (see Chapter 11). All other appearances of the parties or their message are matters for the broadcasters. It is they who allot space and exercise editorial control. They do so within the conventions set by the reporting of previous elections, and in the knowledge that they need the good will of the parties just as much as the parties need the attention of the broadcasters.

While the requirement of balance applies to the reporting of all events, compliance with it is most closely watched by political parties, particularly at

[14]This is one of the reasons why the BBC and IBA routinely commission a study of viewers' opinions of the broadcasters' handling of the election campaign in terms of the amount of coverage (which is generally seen as being rather too much) and balance. The majority judge the BBC and ITV to have presented a balanced view, with the remainder disagreeing as to which party was given greater prominence (Wober *et al.*, 1984).

election times. There is balance by time and by treatment. The former is achieved by applying to the appearances of the three parties and discussion of them across all programmes the same ratio of air time as for party political broadcasts. Balance by treatment as distinct from time is, of course, far more difficult to document, hence the stopwatch syndrome with parties watching like hawks their relative exposure on News or discussion programmes. It is an interesting way of solving the problem of balance but one which inevitably mitigates against new parties and new or complex issues which, if they are to be meaningfully discussed, require more exposition than do old and familiar themes — proportional representation being one such issue which the Alliance alone features as a high priority in its programme.

The parties have become attuned to television's practices in the selection of items for News programmes, and to the medium's preference for the visual and the arresting or novel. This has affected how the party leaders use their time and the places they go to. Media events are created to increase the chances of transmission. Where set speeches are made, these take place with the television audience primarily in mind and are written for the easy lifting of excerpts. Atkinson's (1985) linguistic analysis of the speeches of Margaret Thatcher, David Steel, Roy Jenkins and Michael Foot showed that it is the three-part pithy statement and the two-part contrast much used by the first two which achieves ready applause. This in turn signals that the item may be newsworthy and therefore tends to be more readily repeated in a News programme than other parts of speech. It is the style and not the content that matters here. Most excerpts are less than a minute long. Oratory is not dead, but, if it is to be given the opportunity to make an impact, needs to be attuned to the varying "needs" of different radio and television programmes.

Blumler *et al.*'s (1985) analysis of the problem facing the BBC in its coverage of the election, based on interviews and participant observation, distinguishes four approaches to the coverage of the election which they termed respectively the prudential, the reactive, the journalistic, and the analytic approach. The first seeks primarily to avoid trouble and accusation of bias; the second to put "what is out there" on to the screen, that is to act as translator or transmitter rather than interpreter of events. The third, the journalistic approach, values accurate reporting but also the journalistic coup: the gaffe. And finally the analytic, more probing approach provides background information and comment characteristic more of current affairs programmes like Newsnight on BBC2, and those shown on Channel 4 rather than on BBC1 or ITV. Blumler found that the institutional separation in the BBC of news and current affairs, although modified during the election campaign, meant that the journalistic approach predominated on those channels which attract the largest audiences.

News journalists generally have less relevant political background information than their current affairs counterparts and are not as well equipped to ask searching questions about issues raised in the daily press conferences, as there is no advance notice of the issues to be raised. Inadvertently they act as reporters of the parties' statements rather than as questioners probing inconsistency of views or the cost of proposals. This was particularly so in the case of the Conservative press conferences masterminded by experts in marketing and broadcast presentation and helped by Mrs Thatcher's readiness to learn "the tools of the trade" (Cockerell et al., 1984).

The more combative and epigrammatic the style, the more clear cut the presentation of the issue, and the more skilled the parties are at operating within the broadcasters' constraints and preferences, the greater their chance of retaining the initiative in determining the agenda. Much has been written about the agenda-setting function of the media, far less about *agenda-generating by the parties themselves*. Here the Conservative party was highly effective in ensuring that the Labour party's policy with regard to Polaris remained in the forefront and in avoiding probing questions about the Conservative record and about its proposals concerning unemployment and the National Health Service. Labour's management of the media was much less effective.

The introduction of the Alliance into the election campaign created another problem for the broadcasters — over many elections, their style of presentation had been built on a two-party conflict, a horse race with two favourites and a third, the Liberals, trailing behind. This time one could not be sure. Blumler observed uncertainty in their handling of the Alliance, though they were generally treated like the Liberals before them — nice, but of little moment. Only when the polls showed a substantial gain in the Alliance's potential vote share during the last week of the campaign, suggesting that the Alliance might replace Labour as the main opposition party, were its policies given more attention. Glencross, Director of Television at the Independent Broadcasting Authority, comments on the election reporting as follows:

> Television is sometimes accused of setting the agenda: but in the 1983 General Election the party leaders set the agenda of television coverage to a far greater extent than any television producer would have dared to attempt. . . . Certainly issues did emerge — but they were filtered through the personalities of the leaders. Monetarism appeared not as an economic policy to be debated but as a seal of good housekeeping. The politics of deficit financing took on the aura of compassion as known only to the early socialist pioneers. Defence and foreign policy were tossed between jingoism and guilt. (Glencross, 1983, p. 8)

Analysts of television reporting of the 1983 election (Cockerell et al., 1984; Crewe, 1984) have considered that too much prominence was given to the gaffes and disunity of the Labour party while the Conservatives were let off lightly; that the broadcasters incorporated the Alliance inadequately into the party mix, and were too ready to present the election as a horse race rather than inform on policy choices; and that in the reporting of the polls they commissioned, too much was made of small, generally unstable differences in vote intentions which transformed a non-event into a happening.

There are three aspects to communication: (1) the raw material of events; (2) what is selected from such material and how it is presented; and (3) the reception of that presentation by the public. So far only the third aspect has been examined, and this in a rather superficial, stereotyped way. The public which lacks any information as to what is available is asked to judge the fairness, balance and amount of coverage of that reporting. An interesting but not very informative exercise (Wober *et al.*, 1985).

What is also needed is an assessment of the relation of what is presented to the raw material. It would be a great step forward if the editorial staff of each of the channels, if necessary with the help of experts, were to carry out their own *content analysis* examining the cumulative way in which the parties, the leaders, their policies and the poll results have been presented. Such analysis needs then to be related to the raw material available; the manifestos, the speeches, the press conferences, poll reports and to relevant factual data about the economy and other issues. Only then can one look for errors of *omission* as well as commission. In a recent study of the newspaper reporting of a congressional election in the United States (from candidates to copy) which included also interviews with journalists and a study of the electorate's reactions, Clarke and Evans (1984) found that the incumbents received twice as much coverage as the challengers and that issues were given far less attention than personal information about the candidates. The scene here may well be different.

If on the basis of such content analysis, the editors of British broadcasting are satisfied that the journalists have indeed performed their function of standing in for the viewer in examining and questioning; that the agenda has not been unduly constrained with equal justice done to the potential of new proposals as well as to familiar themes; and if the horse race analogy is found not to be justified, well and good. If not, one would expect these distinguished organizations to experiment with new approaches. Our own research and that by Worcester (1983) show that the electorate likes to hear politicians develop arguments and be challenged in discussion and would like to see in this country a debate between the leaders of the three parties along the lines of the debates between the presidential candidates in the United States, an innovation which the broadcasters too have urged.

The broadcasters are undoubtedly in a different position — their need to hold audiences conflicts with the task of presenting in some depth an election campaign extending over three to four weeks, in which much is repetitive and predictable. But there are by now also many repetitive, almost ritualistic features in their election reporting which may well add to, rather than detract from, the viewers' indifference. Experimentation becomes more urgent with the increase in local broadcasting outlets and with the advent in the not-too-distant future of cable and direct broadcast satellites.

When all is said and done, much of the responsibility for the level of debate during the campaign now rests with the broadcasters since the parties adapt and up-date their campaign strategy to what they detect to be the broadcasters' preferences. If, as in the last election, photo opportunities prove irresistible to the broadcasters, such opportunities will mushroom as they did this time compared to previous elections. If, however, the broadcasters become more selective, provide more opportunity for debate and analysis on the programmes the majority of voters watch, this too will affect the conduct of the campaign. As Glencross points out,

> the actual campaign period left the broadcasters with a good deal more freedom of manoeuvre than they might have supposed. The doubt which nags is whether, altogether, the broadcasters made best use of that freedom. (1983, p. 8)

It would be good if the Governors of the BBC and the Independent Broadcasting Authority were to look afresh at the conventions which have grown up in the interpretation of the statutory requirements laid down by Parliament about balance and impartiality. Balance by time may create an imbalance in presentation by mitigating against the exploration of common ground between the parties, of the aims and policies of new parties or of the changed perspective of well established ones. It may also mitigate against the presentation and analysis of more complex policy proposals. Such re-interpretation cannot be done by the broadcasters alone; the politicians too have to be convinced that it is in their, as well as in the public, interest to create a more effective dialogue between politicians and between the politicians and the public, and not just at election time.

## Future prospects of the parties

After the General Election in 1979 or even halfway through the Conservative period in office, few would have predicted their return in 1983 with only a marginally smaller share of the vote. Indeed a number of signs pointed to the likelihood of their defeat: (1) the first time vote for the Conservatives by previously loyal Labour supporters, many from the skilled working class; (2) the uneven distribution of Conservative gains across the country, testifying to the continued strength of Labour's support; (3) the fact that a substantial amount of Conservative support came from 1974 Liberal voters who, even if they had previously voted Conservative, were among the least committed and therefore the most likely to defect again; (4) the state of the country: economic recession, attendant bankruptcies and unemployment which should rebound against the party in office.

The forecast was wrong on four counts: (1) The move of former Labour supporters to the Conservatives was more than just pique with Labour's record in office, but disaffection with the party's ideology and preference for several Conservative policies without necessarily subscribing fully to the Conservative's view of society. (2) There was an overt split within the Labour party between its more extreme and centrist elements, each fighting for control and the inability of its leader to present a unified, convincing programme. (3) Senior members of the Labour party resigned and founded the Social Democratic party in March 1981. (4) The Falklands War in 1982.

We begin with this analysis of the past to show that to predict the outcome of an election some years before it occurs is likely to be little better than crystal gazing. However, what we can do, drawing on the model and the findings reported here is to indicate those factors which would enhance or detract from voting for each of the main contenders. This is quite different from an actual prediction which depends on the particular mix of these factors and their relative weight at the time of the election.

In discussing future prospects five factors need to be borne in mind:

1. The advent of the Alliance profoundly changed the party constellation. The Alliance's 25% share of the vote in the 1983 election and its by-election and local election record since, makes it a serious contender and not a minor also-ran like the Liberals in earlier elections. It is worth recalling that during the last week of the 1983 election, the Alliance came close to being the main opposition party, relegating Labour to third place. Although this did not happen, it was a close thing; in twice as many seats which returned a Conservative MP it was the Alliance and not Labour which came second.

A three-party constellation makes forecasting even more difficult than a two-party one. Even if we were able correctly to predict loss of support for the Conservatives, for example, the effect on the outcome of the election would depend not only on the size and distribution of the reduction of its vote share, but on how they were redistributed across the other two parties: if all former Labour supporters were to return to Labour, the Conservatives would lose; if, on the other hand, the majority voted instead for the Alliance or abstained, in places where the Alliance was in third place the Conservatives might still be returned to office.

2. The outcome of elections is decided not by the solid supporters of the main parties, but by the large numbers whose support for them is hesitant and variable, and whose final decision is based on an amalgam of factors which together tilt the individuals' choice, often only marginally in favour of one party. This means that recent events and the election campaign itself, particularly in its final week, will play a very important part as will the interpretation of that campaign by the media.

3. People's memory of a party's successes and failures whether in government or opposition is short. In government, the ease with which recent events can overshadow a party's record was shown particularly vividly in the case of Conservatives, with the Falklands War cancelling out the party's poor economic record and unpopularity, and equally, in 1979 when the "winter of discontent" cancelled out the effect of Labour's successes in controlling inflation and improving the balance of payments.

4. The particular constellation of internal and external factors within the parties and within the country which operate at the time of, or close to, the election.

5. There is every indication that partisan de-alignment to which reference has already been made will continue, making it more difficult to make any predictions about either the size of swings or about the extent of movement across the political spectrum. The Alliance is not necessarily the beneficiary of the increase in de-alignment, although a strong candidate for it. Given the increasing trend towards negative voting, the vote decisions of many will depend more on the juxtaposition of the programmes and conduct of the parties rather than on the attraction of a particular party's programme or leader.

The task for each party during the 1980s is, of course, different; in the case of the Conservatives it is to hold onto those voters who moved over from Labour; in the case of Labour it is to seek their return and to recruit the first time voters of whom the majority had voted Labour before 1979, and for the SDP/Liberal Alliance to draw in the same first-time voters and also the dissatisfied voters from the two main parties.

The fate of all the parties depends largely on the economic situation and on the degree of strife or harmony in the society, but none more so than the *Conservatives'*. As was discussed earlier, the Conservatives fought the 1979 election around values: a new radicalism which stressed the values of initiative, personal freedom and free enterprise. In 1983, the election was fought on beliefs, on the need to trust the government's direction and competence. That is why the Conservatives' record in office will be so important, given also that re-election for a third term is very rare. There needs to be solid evidence of an upturn in the economy and a reduction in the number of unemployed. A second Falklands factor overriding the effects of continued recession is unlikely to occur.

There are other aspects too which are important. When a particular policy or approach is continued for too long, or pursued too stridently, it may backfire even where initially welcomed. Two such policies intitiated by the Conservatives in 1979 fall into this category. The first was the call for reduction in expenditure on welfare services and the second control of the rate of expenditure by local authorities. The impression conveyed was that most of the reduction could be achieved by reducing waste. When real cuts in the services began to make themselves felt in the early 1980s, the public changed their concern about "welfare scroungers" and "spendthrift local authorities" to anxiety about the maintenance of the services themselves. This is why in 1983, 80% said they wanted to preserve the level of the services rather than cut taxes, and was also one of the reasons for the shift in people's views during 1982–1984 about the value of the large metropolitan authorities including the GLC.

Equally, Mrs Thatcher's strong leadership initially attracted voters including former Labour voters. But a very definite style of leadership is a double edged sword. While attractive to some, it alienates the moderates in the party, already vulnerable to defection because they are less in tune with the party's policies than the consistent voters. In Chapter 11 we showed that those who had seriously considered voting for another party and those who had actually moved over to the Alliance in 1983 disliked the style of Thatcherite conservatism.

These three examples indicate the difficulty a party faces during its period of office, requiring not only adjustment of its programme to events, but also an adjustment of its rhetoric and style. Particularly where a government takes a strong stand, it needs to remain in tune with the public's changing perceptions as they experience the real consequences of a policy that had previously been judged on a theoretical basis alone.

The erosion of support for *Labour* during the late 1970s and early 1980s extended beyond lack of approval of its leadership to lack of approval of its programme, ideology and rhetoric. Values and beliefs are involved. This makes the task of revival of such support so difficult. At the level of beliefs, it requires evidence of strong and consistent leadership as well as evidence of the party's ability to work together and agree on a programme of action. Any disagreements will undoubtedly be highlighted and exaggerated by the largely Conservative press and will also be amplified by television.

At the level of values, the Labour party faces two major problems during the 1980s. Unlike the Conservatives whose supporters tend to share a common outlook differing on matters of degree or emphasis, the Labour party contains members who disagree quite fundamentally in their views, not only about the role of the party and that of trade unions in relation to the party, but in their ideology. This disagreement is well illustrated by members' attitudes to the Common Market and the party's attempt in its 1983 election manifesto to arrive at a policy which would encompass these divergent views. To satisfy those who wish to remain in the EEC, the proposal in the manifesto stresses tough negotiation which puts Britain's interests first, and to satisfy those who are opposed to membership it includes the option of withdrawal should the negotiations prove unsatisfactory. "If" statements are neither good for negotiations with the EEC nor for electioneering. Nor are they convincing. On other issues, like defence, the divide is equally wide.

Quite apart from the difficulty of reconciling within the party genuine divergence of views, the party has also to take on board the increased consensus among the electorate for the "middle ground" which in 1984 appears to fall to the right rather than to the left of centre.

Labour fought the 1983 election proposing old remedies and using the old rhetoric associated with these remedies. Regaining support requires working out new specific proposals for particular issues rather than an overarching ideology, and for Labour to convince the public that its objectives are realistic. The claim to be able to effect a large reduction in unemployment which Labour put forward in 1983 did little for the party simply because it was deemed improbable. The party needs to be in closer touch with its potential supporters, especially young voters, to understand better how they see society's problems, how they interpret events, and what they think about possible solutions.

The Labour party might, of course, decide on an alternate strategy and go for an updated, radical approach even if it alienates its supporters, in the hope of attracting young, particularly first-time voters: a risky but perhaps necessary strategy to arrive at a convincing programme of action. Much will depend on whether in the intervening years consensus within society will become less and whether there will be a move away from the right. There are some indications that this is currently beginning to happen (Ashford, 1981; Crewe, 1984).

Of the three parties, the *Alliance's* task is particularly formidable. A new party, it fought its first general election in 1983 with remarkable success. It has inadequate financial backing since it depends primarily on donations from individuals and on the subscriptions of a small number of members. While the Liberals have well established local organizations, the SDP has still to develop theirs. There is also the disadvantage that it is a coalition of two parties with the attendant lack of clarity about how its overall future leadership will be determined. The Alliance's initial campaign built on people's disaffection, on the consensus in the electorate and on the preference for the middle ground to which reference has already been made. It appealed to two sets of values important within British society: a sense of compassion and responsibility for others, wanting liberal rather than repressive solutions, and a preference for pragmatism, as opposed to the rigid, doctrinaire economic ideology of either left or right. But this may also be the Alliance's electoral weakness — it can too easily look as if it wants to be all things to all men, borrowing the policies from left and right, scaling them down and calling them Alliance policies. In the 1960s and 1970s the Liberals had no pretensions about forming a government and so could speak in general terms, offering a convenient resting ground for those disillusioned with the major parties. But the Alliance's hopes are set higher, asking the electorate to consider the party as a potential government. To succeed, their policies (or the packaging of their policies) has to be seen as both distinct from, and more attractive than those offered by either of the other two parties.

The Alliance's campaign, like Labour's, has to be directed at both values and beliefs but with the added task of convincing those inclined to vote for the Alliance that their vote will not be a wasted vote. This is why the emphasis on a change to proportional representation is central to any Alliance campaign. But a massive and extended educational campaign would be needed to bring home to the electorate how inadequately the views of Alliance voters are represented in Parliament given the existing first-past-the-post electoral system. After the 1983 election campaign, 51% of the voters still did not know that the Alliance was in favour of proportional representation (Worcester, 1983); probably few know what proportional representation is. Nor does the electorate fully appreciate that it is not in the interest of the major parties to change the system from which they benefit so much and that therefore the only way to achieve electoral reform is to succeed in strengthening the Alliance share of the vote in such a way that a hung Parliament results with the Alliance holding the balance of power. Under those conditions the Alliance could make electoral reform a precondition of giving its support to one or other of the parties which need it to form a government.

This is, of course, easier said than done given that the Alliance, unlike the major parties, has no regional or social base. On the other hand, the opportunity to create a climate of opinion favourable to change in the electoral system has been strengthened by the results of the 1983 general and the 1984 European elections, each of which highlighted to an unusual degree how little the actual pattern of the public's choices was reflected in the composition of the parliament that was elected.

## Returning the voter to the centre of the stage

We have presented a model of the influences and the way they operate in affecting the individual's vote decision and a method for learning more about how the voter arrives at that decision.

While the model has been developed and tested within the British electoral system, we believe it to have applicability also in countries that have a larger number of parties. In such countries, the voter does not of course consider all parties but only those which fall into what psychologists call the individual's "latitude of acceptance". After all, few voters in Britain, when trying to choose between one of the major parties and the Liberals, set about the task by first comparing each with the National Front. By asking a voter to list the parties that he or she would be considering, and by restricting the enquiry to those, the methods used here could readily be applied.

In Chapter 12 we stressed the importance for social psychologists, when studying attitudes and behaviour, to take more account of the social context in which these arise. Here we should like to urge the obverse, namely that political scientists, politicians and the media look more closely at the psychology of the voter of today — not at his or her personality make-up or early childhood experiences — but at the psychological processes involved in arriving at the decision.

While a great deal of resources and skill go into the planning of the campaign and its presentation and coverage by press, radio and television, there is very little study of the impact that these make on the public's thinking and what there is tends to be superficial. It tells of reactions but not why these reactions have occurred. Yet the cognitive maps that different sections of the community build up about the society and its institutions are important. They affect their reactions to events. It matters therefore, particularly in times of rapid social change, that politicians, policy makers and the media update their image of the public they serve. Elections provide a useful opportunity to do so as for once the public occupies the centre of the stage.

Appendices 1 to 3

# Appendix 1

Measures obtained at different stages of the longitudinal study[a]

| 1962 | 1970 | 1974 |
|---|---|---|
| *Liberal outlook*[b]<br>1. Capital punishment should be abolished.<br>2. The law on homosexuality should be made less severe.<br>3. I respect the nuclear disarmers. | *Liberal outlook*<br>1. Capital punishment should be restored.<br>2. It was right to make the law on homosexuality less severe.<br>3. I respect those who oppose the Vietnam war. | *Liberal outlook*<br>1. Capital punishment should be restored.<br>2. It was right to make the law on homosexuality less severe. |
| *Immigration*<br>1. The government must restrict immigration from the colonies and the Commonwealth.<br>2. If you give them an inch they take a mile might well apply to immigrants in this country. | *Immigration*<br>1. The government must further restrict immigration from the colonies and the Commonwealth.<br>2. If you give them an inch they take a mile might well apply to immigrants in this country.<br>3. It is wrong that coloured people born in this country are so often treated as outsiders (R).<br>4. The problem of immigrants has been greatly exaggerated (R).<br>5. It is wrong to control immigration to this country on the basis of a person's colour (R). | *Immigration*<br>1. The government must further restrict immigration from the colonies and the Commonwealth.<br>2. If you give them an inch they take a mile might well apply to immigrants in this country.<br>3. It is wrong that coloured people born in this country should be treated as outsiders (R).<br>4. The problem of immigrants has been greatly exaggerated (R).<br>5. It is wrong to control immigration to this country on the basis of a person's colour (R).<br>6. Encourage immigrants to return to their home country. |
| *Attitude to trade unions*<br>1. The way they are run now, trade unions do this country more harm than good. | *Attitude to trade unions*<br>1. The way they are run now, trade unions do this country more harm than good.<br>2. Power without responsibility is a good description of trade unions today. | *Attitude to trade unions*<br>1. The way they are run now, trade unions do this country more harm than good.<br>2. Power without responsibility is a good description of trade unions today. |

*Welfare*
1. The poor should be taken care of by the government.

*Common Market*
1. Britain should enter the Common Market.

*Management/employee relations*
1. Multiple choice answers: open warfare; full of conflict; ups and downs, generally amicable; full of trust

*Law*
There is one law for the rich and one for the poor.

*Welfare*
1. The government should spend more on pensions and social services.
2. A large number of people abuse the Welfare State (R).

*Common Market*
1. Britain should enter the Common Market.

*Management/employee relations*
1. Multiple choice answers: open warfare; full of conflict; ups and downs, generally amicable, full of trust

*Strikes*
1. Legal sanctions should be imposed to control strikes.
2. The government should not impose any restrictions on the right to strike (R).

*Strikes and secret ballot*
1. Voting to strike should be by secret ballot.

*Mergers*
1. Takeover bids and mergers are matters for management alone, employees need not be consulted.

*Welfare*
1. The government should spend more on pensions and social services.
2. A large number of people abuse the Welfare State (R).

*Common Market*
1. Britain should remain in the Common Market.

*Management/employee relations*
1. Multiple choice answers: open warfare; full of conflict; ups and downs, generally amicable, full of trust

*Strikes*
1. Legal sanctions should be imposed to control strikes.
2. The government should not impose any restrictions on the right to strike (R).
3. Cut social benefits to strikers.

*Strikes and secret ballot*
1. Voting to strike should be by secret ballot.

*Mergers*
1. Takeover bids and mergers are matters for management alone, employees need not be consulted.

*(cont'd)*

# Appendix 1 (continued)

| 1962 | 1970 | 1974 |
|------|------|------|
| | *Big business*<br>1. Until big business is subject to more control, prices will go on rising. | *Big business*<br>1. Big business should be subject to more control. |
| | *Law and order*<br>1. Stricter laws make for a healthier society.<br>2. The power of the police should be increased.<br>3. The so-called breakdown in law and order has been greatly exaggerated (R). | *Law and order*<br>1. Stricter laws make for a healthier society.<br>2. The power of the police should be increased.<br>3. The so-called breakdown in law and order has been greatly exaggerated (R). |
| | *Student unrest*<br>1. Students should get on with their studies.<br>2. Student violence, however mild, is never justified.<br>3. Students have the right the express their views on political and social questions (R).<br>4. Students are right to want more say in the running of their college (R).<br>5. Students who take part in sit-ins should have their grants suspended.<br>6. The real cause of student unrest is genuine grievance, not the work of a few agitators (R). | |
| | *Demonstrations*<br>1. The right to demonstrate is more important than its possible threat to law and order (R).<br>2. I have no patience with demonstrators, peaceful or otherwise. | |

*Secondary schooling*
1. More comprehensive schools.
2. Abolish public schools.

*Secondary schooling*
1. More comprehensive schools.
2. Abolish public schools.
3. Abolish grammar schools.

*Secondary schooling*
1. All should be comprehensive.
2. Abolish public schools.
3. Abolish grammar schools.

*Responsibility for unemployment*
1. Inefficient management and planning have led to the present high level of unemployment.
2. The high level of unemployment is due to the workers' excessive demands.

*Taxation of wealth*
1. Reduce company taxes.
2. Heavier taxing of the wealthy.

*Nationalization*
1. Keep private health service.
2. Nationalize building land.
3. Bring more companies into public ownership.

*Other individual policies*
Sell council houses to tenants.
Introduce statutory control of wage increases.
Subsidize the cost of essential foods.
Reform our electoral system.
Hold mortgage rates down.
Create more worker participation in industry.

[a] The replies for the majority of items were on a five-point scale ranging from 1 (agree very much) to 5 (disagree very much). (R) indicates that the item has been reversed when making the composite score.
[b] Items under each italicized heading were added to create a composite score.
[c] The replies ranged from 1 (very good) to 5 (very bad).

# Appendix 2

# Characteristics of the longitudinal sample

**Characteristics of the longitudinal sample
and the effects of sample loss**

TABLE 1                                                          *Longit. study*

Response rate at each wave of interviewing the subjects from age 25 to 38
(1962–1974)

| Year | Age of respondent | A Sample size | B Sample successfully contacted | C Response rate |
|------|-------------------|---------------|---------------------------------|-----------------|
| 1962 | about 25 | 450 | | |
| 1964 | ,,   27 | 450 | 371 | 82% |
| 1966 | ,,   29 | 371 | 325 | 88% |
| 1970 | ,,   33 | 325 | 246 | 76% |
| 1971 Oct. | ,,   37 | 246 | 178 | 72% |

Column A indicates the size of the sample, Column B the number of that sample successfully contacted,
and Column C the response rate.
Response rate over 12 years (1962–1974) = 40%.

Apart from biases (with regard to age, sex, schooling and residence) inherent
in the selection of the initial sample due to the aims of the original study,
there was differential loss at each round of questioning. The extent of the
loss is shown in Table 2 separately for both manual and non-manual
workers.

The requirements of the study were stringent: to be included in the
analysis a respondent had to have replied at *every* preceding round of
questioning. After 12 years (1962–1974) and five rounds of questioning,
the sample was reduced to 178 (40% of the 1962 sample of 25-year-olds).

In longitudinal studies there is always sample loss. To examine whether the effect of this loss would colour the relationships studied three comparisons were carried out: the 1970 sample with the 1962 sample who had dropped out, the 1974 sample with the 1962 sample who had dropped out; and the 1974 sample with those of the 1970 sample who had not replied in 1974. Comparisons were made on a wide variety of measures. The crucial comparisons relate to the distribution of votes, to demographic factors, and to the responses to those attitude questions which were found to be predictive of vote.

Up to 1970, sample loss was greater from those who, in 1962, were in manual jobs.[1] However, by 1974 the trend had reversed: a greater proportion of those who held manual jobs in 1962 and had remained in the study until 1970 replied in 1974 compared with men in white collar jobs. As a result the distributions of the 1962 social class of those who remained the entire course did not differ significantly from those in 1962 who had dropped out. Nor were there any differences in terms of inter-generational mobility or in the percentage who had voted along class lines.

To compare the dropouts at different stages of the study with who remained, we carried out 73 analyses of variance (the social class of the respondent in 1962 constituted one factor and the time of the final response the other). Only seven were statistically significant (hardly better than chance). There were no differences on the crucial attitudinal measures nor in their voting patterns (Himmelweit and Bond, 1974).

TABLE 2                                                          *Longit. study*

Response rates of manual and non-manual workers[a] at each wave of interviews of those who had been successfully contacted on the previous occasion. The sample is divided on the basis of their 1962 job level into manual and non-manual workers

| Year of survey | Total sample | Response rate | Non-manual workers | Response rate | Manual workers | Response rate |
|---|---|---|---|---|---|---|
| 1962 | 450 | | 289 | | 161 | |
| 1964 | 371 | 82% | 244 | 84% | 127 | 79% |
| 1966 | 325 | 88% | 219 | 90% | 106 | 83% |
| 1970 | 246 | 76% | 172 | 79% | 74 | 70% |
| 1974 | 178 | 72% | 121 | 70% | 57 | 77% |

[a] The division was based on the 1962 job level.

[1] Similar differential loss was found when the sample was divided into those with few or no qualifications, versus those with a fair number of qualifications. This is not surprising, given the dependence of job level on educational qualifications.

## Comparison of longitudinal sample with those from the British election surveys

SOCIAL MOBILITY

Table 3 cross-tabulates the social status level of jobs held by our respondents in 1962 and 1974.

The inter- and intra-generational mobility among our respondents was far greater than that of a representative sample. In 1970, 70% of the national sample came from a working class background compared with 61% in our sample, not a very great difference compared with the marked difference in upward *inter-generational* mobility; while 19% of the national sample were upwardly mobile, this was so for as many as 46% of our sample.

The considerable *intra-generational* mobility combined with differential sample loss yielded by 1974 only 48 manual workers.

VOTING TURNOUT

Table 4 indicates the percentage who voted in each election. Apart from 1959, the first election when our subjects were old enough to vote (abstentions of first time voters are generally very high), our sample had a higher turnout compared with the national sample. While our sample voted more regularly than the general population, its interest in politics was equally low: 10% were not at all interested, 75% moderately so and only 15% expressed a strong interest. These proportions did not vary across time despite the fact that the turnout in the 1974 election was one of the highest and that in 1970 one of the lowest.

DISTRIBUTION OF VOTING CHOICES AT EACH OF THE SIX ELECTIONS

Table 5 provides a comparison between the voting pattern of our sample and of the national samples. It will be seen that in 1964 our sample differed very little from the national sample. From that period onwards, while the proportion of Conservatives in the electorate remained remarkably constant (around 32%), our sample became increasingly Conservative and this at the expense of Labour. In 1964 35% voted Conservative; by October 1974 40%. In the same election 21% voted Labour compared with 36% of the electorate.

TABLE 3                                                          *Longit. study*

Cross-tabulation of job level of occupations in 1974 by the men's 1962 occupations.

| Job level 1974 | Job level 1962 | | | | | n | % |
|---|---|---|---|---|---|---|---|
| | Middle class | | | Working class | | | |
| Middle class: | 1. | 2. | 3. | 4. | 5. | | |
| 1. Upper middle | 46 | 37 | 11 | 10 | — | 104 | 58 |
| 2. Middle middle | 1 | 6 | 13 | 12 | 3 | 35 | 20 |
| 3. Routine non-manual | | | 4 | 3 | 1 | 8 | 4 |
| Working class: | | | | | | | |
| 4. Skilled manual | | 1 | 2 | 20 | 3 | 26 | 15 |
| 5. Semi- and unskilled | | | | | | | |
| manual | | | | 2 | 3 | 5 | 3 |
| n | 47 | 44 | 30 | 47 | 10 | 178 | |
| % | 26 | 25 | 17 | 26 | 6 | | 100% |

TABLE 4

Comparison of national turnout at British general elections 1959–
October, 1974: with that of the longitudinal sample

| | National turnout % of the electorate | Longitudinal sample % (n) |
|---|---|---|
| 1959 | 79 | 66 (246) |
| 1964 | 77 | 77 (246) |
| 1966 | 76 | 86 (246) |
| 1970 | 72 | 74 (246) |
| 1974 (Feb.) | 78 | 90 (178) |
| 1974 (Oct.) | 73 | 85 (178) |

TABLE 5

Distribution of votes of the longitudinal and of the national samples in the elections 1959–
October, 1974

*Longitudinal sample*

|  | Election year | | | | | |
|---|---|---|---|---|---|---|
| Vote | 1959 (%) | 1964 (%) | 1966 (%) | 1970 (%) | Feb.1974 (%) | Oct.1974 (%) |
| Conservative | 41 | 35 | 43 | 43 | 39 | 40 |
| Labour | 19·5 | 31 | 35 | 24 | 24 | 21 |
| Liberal | 4·5 | 10 | 7 | 7 | 27 | 23 |
| Abstention | 34 | 23 | 14 | 26 | 10 | 15 |
| Other |  |  | n (2) |  |  | 1 |
| n | 246 | 246 | 246 | 246 | 178 | 178 |

*National samples[a]*

| Vote | 1959 (%) | 1964 (%) | 1966 (%) | 1970 (%) | Feb.1974 (%) | Oct.1974 (%) |
|---|---|---|---|---|---|---|
| Conservative | 39 | 33 | 32 | 33 | 32 | 31 |
| Labour | 35 | 35 | 37 | 32 | 36 | 36 |
| Liberal | 5 | 9 | 7 | 5 | 17 | 15 |
| Abstention | 21 | 23 | 24 | 30 | 13 | 15 |
| Other |  |  |  |  | 2 | 3 |
|  | 100 | 100 | 100 | 100 | 100 | 100 |

[a]Data on national samples presented for the elections 1959 to 1970 were obtained from Butler and
Stokes (1974). Date for elections February and October, 1974 were from Särlvik and Crewe (1983).

# Appendix 3

# Tables and figures relating to Chapters 2 to 11

The tables and figures in this appendix supplement materials discussed in the text of the book. They are listed under the chapter headings where they are discussed.

# Chapter 2

TABLE 1                                                        *Longit. study*

Distribution of votes and party preferences for
elections 1959–1974[a]

| Election | | Vote (%) | Party preference (%) |
|---|---|---|---|
| 1959 | Conservative | 41 | (Not available) |
| | Labour | 20 | |
| | Liberal | 5 | |
| | Abstention | 34 | |
| 1964 | Conservative | 35 | 44 |
| | Labour | 31 | 36 |
| | Liberal | 10 | 16 |
| | Abstention | 23 | 4 |
| 1966 | Conservative | 43 | 48 |
| | Labour | 35 | 40 |
| | Liberal | 7 | 10 |
| | Abstention | 14 | 2 |
| 1970 | Conservative | 43 | 53 |
| | Labour | 24 | 32 |
| | Liberal | 7 | 9 |
| | Abstention | 26 | 6 |
| February 1974 | Conservative | 39 | 43 |
| | Labour | 24 | 25 |
| | Liberal | 27 | 29 |
| | Abstention | 10 | 3 |
| | Other | | |
| October 1974 | Conservative | 40 | 47 |
| | Labour | 21 | 23 |
| | Liberal | 23 | 26 |
| | Abstention | 15 | 2 |
| | Other | 1 | 2 |

[a]The distribution of votes 1959 to 1970 is based on the 1970 sample ($n = 246$) those of the two 1974 elections on the 1974 sample ($n = 178$).

# Chapter 3

TABLE 2A *Longit. study*

Voting profiles based on five elections from 1964 to October, 1974

| Type of voter | | $n$ |
|---|---|---|
| I. | *Consistent voter[a]* | |
| | Conservative | 44 |
| | Labour | 31 |
| | Liberal | 6 |
| II. | *Preferred Conservative deviated:* | |
| | to Liberal[b] | 22 |
| | to Labour[c] | 7 |
| | to Abstention | 6 |
| III. | *Preferred Labour deviated:* | |
| | to Liberal[d] | 10 |
| | to Conservative[e] | 3 |
| | to Abstention | 1 |
| IV. | *Preferred Liberal deviated:* | |
| | to Conservative[f] | 10 |
| | to Labour[g] | 6 |
| | to Abstention | 1 |
| V. | *Abstainers* | |
| | Consistent Abstainers[h] | 5 |
| | Preferred Abstentions[i] | 13 |
| VI. | *Voted for all 3 Parties* | 5 |
| VII. | *Equal preference in voting with 1 Abstention* | 4 |
| VIII. | *Other Party voters* | 2 |

[a]Includes 1 abstention. [b]Includes 3 individuals who abstained twice. [c]Includes 2 individuals who abstained twice. [d]Includes 1 individual who abstained twice. [e]Includes 1 individual who abstained twice. [f]Includes 7 individual who abstained twice. [g]Includes 2 individuals who abstained twice. [h]Includes 1 vote. [i]Those who abstained 3 times and voted twice.

TABLE 2B                                         *BES panel 1963–'70*

Voting profiles based on four elections from 1959 to 1970

| Type of voter | | $n$ |
|---|---|---|
| I. | *Consistent voters*[a] | |
| | Conservative | 228 |
| | Labour | 230 |
| | Liberal | 11 |
| II. | *Preferred Conservative, deviated:* | |
| | to Liberal | 29 |
| | to Labour | 17 |
| III. | *Preferred Labour, deviated:* | |
| | to Liberal | 18 |
| | to Conservative | 36 |
| IV. | *Preferred Liberal, deviated:* | |
| | to Conservative | 18 |
| | to Labour | 11 |
| V. | *Equal frequency of vote for:* | |
| | Conservative/Abstention | 15 |
| | Conservative/Liberal | 7 |
| | Conservative/Labour | 18 |
| | Labour/Abstention | 19 |
| | Labour/Liberal | 13 |
| | Liberal/Abstention | 5 |
| VI. | *Abstainers* | |
| | Consistent Abstainers[b] | 35 |
| | Preferred Abstainers[c] | 8 |
| VII. | *Voted for all 3 parties* | 19 |
| VIII. | *Other Party voters*[d] | 13 |

[a]Includes 1 abstention. [b]Includes 1 vote. [c]Excluding those who had equal preferences for abstention and Conservative, Labour or Liberal. [d]Those who voted for other parties at any time during the period examined.

TABLE 3 *Longit. study*

Interest in politics of consistent and floating major party voters

| | Type of voter | | | |
|---|---|---|---|---|
| Interest in politics | Conservative consistent (%) | Conservative floater (%) | Labour consistent (%) | Labour floater (%) |
| 1962 Great deal | 25 | 20 | 31 | 30 |
| Moderate | 54 | 70 | 62 | 47 |
| Not at all | 11 | 10 | 7 | 23 |
| 1970 Great deal | 22 | 6 | 22 | 15 |
| Moderate | 78 | 91 | 75 | 77 |
| Not at all | 0 | 3 | 3 | 8 |
| 1974 Great deal | 19 | 9 | 29 | 16 |
| Moderate | 79 | 85 | 68 | 84 |
| Not at all | 2 | 6 | 3 | 0 |
| (n) | (36) | (30) | (29) | (13) |

TABLE 4 *Longit. study*

Reasons for vote choice of consistent Conservative and Labour voters

| | Conservative | | Labour | |
|---|---|---|---|---|
| Reasons for vote choice | Consistent (%) | Floating (%) | Consistent (%) | Floating (%) |
| 1964 Party appealed | 41 | 33 | 58 | 46 |
| Best of bad bunch | 18 | 17 | 0 | 9 |
| 1966 Party appealed | 65 | 39 | 86 | 75 |
| Best of bad bunch | 18 | 25 | 3 | 8 |
| 1970 Party appealed | 78 | 61 | 84 | 87 |
| Best of bad bunch | 15 | 7 | 8 | 0 |

TABLE 5                                                                      *Longit. study*

Proportion of consistent and floating major party voters who made up their mind before
announcement of the election or in the last few days

| Time at which decision was made | | Consistent Conservative (%) | Floating Conservative (%) | Consistent Labour (%) | Floating Labour (%) |
|---|---|---|---|---|---|
| 1964 | before announcement | 81 | 69 | 75 | 77 |
|  | last few days | 3 | 12 | 12 | 7 |
| 1966 | before announcement | 84 | 50 | 87 | 92 |
|  | last few days | 11 | 28 | 0 | 8 |
| 1970 | before announcement | 90 | 82 | 84 | 75 |
|  | last few days | 5 | 14 | 4 | 0 |
| 1974 | before announcement | 77 | 30 | 90 | 61 |
| Oct. | last few days | 7 | 33 | 10 | 23 |

# Chapter 4

TABLE 6                                                    *Longit. study*

Percentage distribution of vote choice of adolescents by social class of father, type of school
attended and social class composition of the school

| Sample characteristics | | Con (%) | Lab (%) | Lib (%) | Abst (%) | (%) |
|---|---|---|---|---|---|---|
| *Social class of father* | Middle class | 52 | 24 | 8 | 16 | 100 |
| | Working class | 26 | 44 | 7 | 23 | 100 |
| *Type of school* | Grammar | 40 | 34 | 9 | 17 | 100 |
| | Secondary modern | 27 | 24 | 4 | 27 | 100 |
| *Social class* | Mainly middle class | 44 | 28 | 10 | 18 | 100 |
| *composition of school* | Mixed | 35 | 36 | 2 | 27 | 100 |
| | Mainly working class | 25 | 49 | 9 | 17 | 100 |

TABLE 7A                                                   *Longit. study*

Congruence of parental and subjects' vote for consistent and floating Conservative and
Labour voters

| | Father's vote | | Mother's vote | |
|---|---|---|---|---|
| Subject's voting history | Congruent (%) | Different (%) | Congruent (%) | Different (%) |
| Consistent Conservative | 45 | 55 | 57 | 43 |
| Floating Conservative | 48 | 52 | 55 | 45 |
| Consistent Labour | 65 | 35 | 71 | 29 |
| Floating Labour | 38 | 62 | 23 | 77 |

TABLE 7B                                                              *BES panel 1963–'70*

Congruence of parental and subjects' vote for consistent and floating Conservative and Labour voters

| | Percentage of | | | |
| --- | --- | --- | --- | --- |
| | Father's vote | | Mother's vote | |
| Subject's voting history | Congruent (%) | Different (%) | Congruent (%) | Different (%) |
| Consistent Conservative | 66 | 34 | 66 | 34 |
| Floating Conservative | 60 | 40 | 51 | 49 |
| Consistent Labour | 70 | 30 | 55 | 45 |
| Floating Labour | 39 | 61 | 22 | 78 |

TABLE 8                                                                   *Longit. study*

Prediction of political attitudes in 1970 from a knowledge of structural factors, and of goals and values (blockwise multiple regression)

| | Blocks of predictors | | |
| --- | --- | --- | --- |
| Attitude predicted[a] | I | II | III |
| 1. Liberal outlook | 0·24 | 0·41 | 0·46 |
| 2. Immigration | 0·17 | 0·56 | 0·59 |
| 3. Students | 0·17 | 0·60 | 0·62 |
| 4. Demonstrators | 0·14 | 0·42 | 0·44 |
| 5. Management–employee relations | 0·04 | 0·30 | 0·35 |
| 6. Common Market | 0·33 | 0·36 | 0·46 |
| 7. Secret ballot to strike | 0·14 | 0·28 | 0·32 |
| 8. Take over bids concern for managers only | 0·24 | 0·35 | 0·41 |
| 9. Big business control | 0·44 | 0·44 | 0·57 |
| 10. Trade unions | 0·22 | 0·57 | 0·60 |
| 11. Strikes | 0·24 | 0·52 | 0·55 |
| 12. Welfare | 0·14 | 0·51 | 0·52 |
| 13. Law and order | 0·14 | 0·50 | 0·51 |

[a]These 13 attitudes were those used to predict vote (Chapters 5 and 6).
The blocks of predictors are: Block I, Structural Factors (educational, social background, social class and social mobility); Block II, Authoritarianism and measures of relative importance attached to four sets of goals and values; Block III, Blocks I and II combined.
Each entry in the table is the multiple correlation coefficient for a regression of a block of predictors on a single attitude.

# Chapter 5

TABLE 9                                                                                    *Longit. study*

Mean replies by Labour, Conservative and Liberal voters to statements which were significant predictors of vote in mid-election, 1962 and in the 1970 and 1974 elections

| | Conservative | Labour | Liberal | Range | High score |
|---|---|---|---|---|---|
| | Groups of voters | | | | |
| **1962 Statements** | | | | | |
| 1. The way they are run now, trade unions do this country more harm than good. | 2·21 | 3·45 | 2·33 | 1–5 | Disagree strongly |
| 2. Public schools should be abolished. | 3·82 | 2·71 | 3·57 | 1–5 | Disagree strongly |
| 3. The poor should be taken care of by the government | 3·00 | 2·29 | 2·70 | 1–5 | Disagree strongly |
| 4. Britain should enter the Common Market. | 2·75 | 2·96 | 2·34 | 1–5 | Disagree strongly |
| 5. There is one law for the rich and one for the poor. | 2·95 | 2·27 | 2·53 | 1–5 | Disagree strongly |
| **1970 Measures** | | | | | |
| 1. Attitude toward schools.[a] | 6·32 | 2·71 | 4·00 | 1–9 | Pro-selective education |
| 2. Attitude toward trade unions.[b] | 3·15 | 6·03 | 3·94 | 1–9 | Pro-unions |
| 3. Until big business is subject to more control, prices will go on rising. | 3·65 | 2·41 | 3·29 | 1–5 | Disagree strongly |
| 4. View of management–employee relations. | 3·06 | 2·80 | 3·41 | 1–4 | Working as a team with trust |
| **1974 Measures** | | | | | |
| 1. Attitude toward nationalization.[c] | 3·29 | 9·84 | 4·92 | 1–13 | Pro-nationalization |
| 2. Attitude toward electoral reform. | 2·56 | 2·57 | 1·82 | 1–5 | Pro-reform |
| 3. Attitude toward schools.[a] | 10·45 | 4·43 | 8·22 | 1–13 | Pro-selective education |
| 4. Sell council houses to tenants. | 1·81 | 3·30 | 2·32 | 1–5 | Desirable |
| 5. Attitude toward trade unions.[b] | 2·74 | 6·30 | 3·55 | 1–9 | Pro-trade unions |
| 6. Attitude toward immigration.[d] | 9·80 | 11·38 | 10·10 | 1–21 | Pro-immigrants |

[a]Composite item dealing with attitudes to grammar, comprehensive and public schools.
[b]Composite item: "The way they are run now, trade unions do this country more harm than good" and "Power without responsibility is a good description of trade unions".
[c]Composite item: "Keep private health service", "Nationalize building land" and "Bring more companies into public ownership". (Last two items reversed.)
[d]Composite item: "Encourage immigrants to return home", "Government must further restrict immigration from the colonies and the Commonwealth". "If you give them an inch they take a mile might well apply to immigrants to this country". "The problem of immigrants in Britain has been greatly exaggerated", and "It is wrong to control immigration to this country on the basis of colour".

TABLE 10                                                                *BES 1974*

Accuracy of classification of vote from attitudes by class of voters; discriminant analyses

| | Percentage of voters correctly classified | | | | |
|---|---|---|---|---|---|
| Nature of sample | Con (%) | Lab (%) | Lib (%) | Total (%) | (n) |
| Non-manual, middle class | 67 | 74 | 48 | 65 | 841 |
| Manual, working class | 63 | 72 | 40 | 65 | 708 |

TABLE 11                                                   *BES 1970, Oct. 1974*

Percentage correct classification based on discriminant analysis of men and women voters: A. 1970 and B. Oct. 1974

| | | *Percentage of voters correctly classified* | | | | | | | |
|---|---|---|---|---|---|---|---|---|---|
| | | Men | | | | Women | | | |
| | | Con | Lab | Lib | n | Con | Lab | Lib | n |
| A. *Actual vote cast 1970* | Con | 70 | 15 | 15 | 195 | 73 | 18 | 8 | 250 |
| | Lab | 18 | 64 | 18 | 202 | 23 | 58 | 19 | 207 |
| | Lib | 37 | 26 | 37 | 27 | 25 | 36 | 37 | 44 |
| | | 65% correctly classified | | | | 64% correctly classified | | | |
| | | Men | | | | Women | | | |
| | | Con | Lab | Lib | n | Con | Lab | Lib | n |
| B. *Actual vote cast Oct. 1974* | Con | 66 | 5 | 29 | 337 | 71 | 6 | 23 | 367 |
| | Lab | 4 | 77 | 19 | 437 | 7 | 75 | 19 | 393 |
| | Lib | 31 | 17 | 52 | 152 | 27 | 24 | 49 | 200 |
| | | 69% correctly identified | | | | 68% correctly identified | | | |

# Chapter 6

TABLE 12

BES Oct. 1974, 1979; BBC/Crewe 1983

Percentage of voters correctly classified using discriminant analysis. The independent variables were: (A) structural data only; (B) structural data and attitudes to issues; (C) attitudes to issues only

Percentage Accuracy of Classification

| Set of independent variables | 1974 Election | | | | 1979 Election | | | | 1983 Election | | | |
|---|---|---|---|---|---|---|---|---|---|---|---|---|
| | Con | Lab | Lib | All | Con | Lab | Lib | All | Con | Lab | Alli | All |
| (A) Structural data only | 62 | 63 | 32 | 57 | 55 | 55 | 38 | 52 | 59 | 61 | 26 | 51 |
| (B) Structural data and attitudes to issues | 69 | 77 | 52 | 69 | 69 | 72 | 44 | 66 | 77 | 76 | 56 | 71 |
| (C) Attitudes to issues only | 69 | 76 | 49 | 68 | 69 | 71 | 46 | 67 | 76 | 73 | 54 | 69 |

# Chapter 7

TABLE 13A                                                          *Longit. study*

Discriminant analysis classification of vote 1974 from attitudinal fit 1970, attitudinal shift 1970–1974 and cumulative vote until 1970

|            |          | Predicted vote | | | |
|------------|----------|-----|-----|-----|-----|
|            |          | Con | Lab | Lib | *n* |
| Actual vote | Con (%) | 81  | 1   | 18  | 69  |
|            | Lab (%)  | 0   | 93  | 7   | 41  |
|            | Lib (%)  | 22  | 9   | 69  | 45  |

81% correctly classified overall

TABLE 13B                                                          *Longit. study*

Discriminant analysis classification of vote 1974 from attitudinal fit 1970 and attitudinal shift 1970–1974

|            |          | Predicted vote | | | |
|------------|----------|-----|-----|-----|-----|
|            |          | Con | Lab | Lib | *n* |
| Actual vote | Con (%) | 77  | 1   | 22  | 69  |
|            | Lab (%)  | 2   | 93  | 5   | 41  |
|            | Lib (%)  | 27  | 11  | 62  | 45  |

77% correctly classified overall

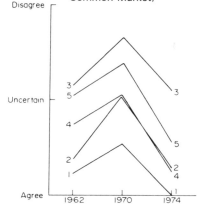

(a) Britain should join the Common Market
(1974 Britain should remain in the
Common Market)

GROUPS
1. Upper middle stable
2. Mid middle stable
3. Working stable
4. Mid upper mid mobile
5. Working to middle mobile

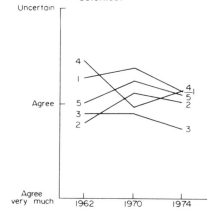

(b) Restrict (further) immigration
from Commonwealth and
colonies.

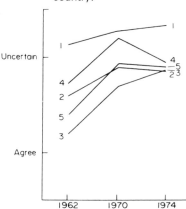

(c) "If you give them an inch,
they take a mile" might well
apply to immigrants in this
country.

Fig. 1. Changes in attitude over time by intra-generational mobility (1962–1974).
*Significance of results:*
(a) Groups: $p < 0.001$; Time: $p < 0.001$; Interaction: N/S.
(b) No significant differences.
(c) Groups: N/S; Time: $p < 0.001$; Interaction: N/S.

(d)  See the relation of management
     to employees

(e)  The way they are run now,
     trade unions in this country
     do the country more harm
     than good

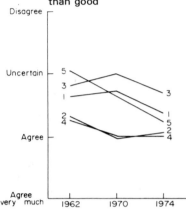

(f)  Capital punishment should be
     restored (1962 those who agreed
     that capital punishment should not
     be abolished)

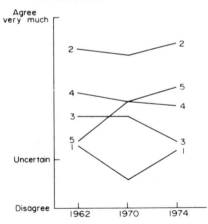

(g)  It was right to make the law on
     homosexuals less severe (1962 those
     who agreed that the law should be
     made less severe)

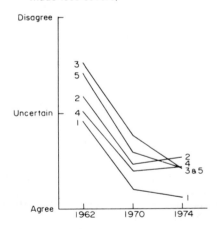

Fig. 1 (*continued*)
(d) Groups: N/S; Time: $p<0.005$; Interaction: N/S.
(e) Groups: $p<0.001$; Time: $p<0.02$; Interaction N/S.
(f) Groups: $p<0.01$; Time: N/S; Interaction: N/S.
(g) Groups: N/S; Time: $p<0.001$; Interaction: N/S.

(h)  Public schools should be abolished

(i)  In favour of comprehensive schools, (1974 "More comprehensive schools should be established")

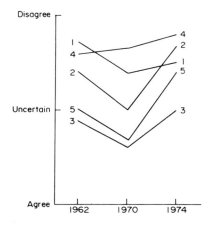

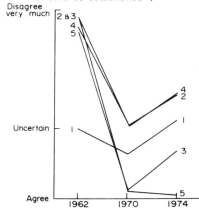

Fig. 1 (*continued*)
(h)  Groups: $p < 0.008$; Time: $p < 0.004$; Interaction: N/S.
(i)  Groups: $p < 0.03$; Time: $p < 0.02$; Interaction: N/S.

# Chapter 10

TABLE 14                                                        *Longit. study*

Five-factor solution of oblique factor analysis of replies in Oct. 1974 to 37 attitude statements

|  | F1 | F2 | F3 | F4 | F5 |
|---|---|---|---|---|---|
| 1. The law on capital punishment should be restored. | 0·38 | 0·61 | −0·12 | −0·34 | −0·05 |
| 2. It was right to make the law on homosexuality less severe. | −0·03 | −0·25 | −0·01 | 0·00 | 0·05 |
| 3. Encourage immigrants to return to their home country. | 0·24 | 0·79 | −0·16 | −0·11 | −0·10 |
| 4. The government must further restrict immigration from the colonies and the Commonwealth | 0·29 | 0·79 | −0·19 | −0·16 | 0·02 |
| 5. "If you give them an inch, they take a mile" might well apply to immigrants to this country. | 0·24 | 0·76 | −0·10 | −0·14 | −0·21 |
| 6. The problem of immigration in Britain has been greatly exaggerated. | −0·29 | −0·73 | 0·21 | 0·19 | 0·10 |
| 7. It is wrong to control immigration to this country on the basis of colour. | −0·28 | −0·42 | −0·01 | 0·21 | 0·35 |
| 8. Stricter laws make for a healthier society. | 0·30 | 0·49 | 0·03 | −0·13 | −0·03 |
| 9. The power of the police should be increased. | 0·31 | 0·39 | 0·02 | −0·24 |  |
| 10. The so-called breakdown in law and order has been greatly exaggerated. | −0·31 | −0·37 | 0·35 | 0·32 | −0·22 |
| 11. Britain should remain in the Common Market. | 0·16 | −0·33 | −0·00 | −0·22 | 0·41 |
| 12. The government should spend more money on pensions and social services. | −0·23 | −0·15 | 0·67 | 0·28 | −0·06 |
| 13. Spend more on our social services. | −0·24 | −0·22 | 0·81 | 0·21 | −0·04 |
| 14. Subsidise the cost of essential foods. | −0·31 | −0·02 | 0·50 | 0·46 | −0·26 |
| 15. A large number of people abuse the Welfare State. | 0·32 | 0·57 | −0·17 | −0·24 | 0·06 |
| 16. The way they are run now, trade unions do more harm than good | 0·76 | 0·40 | −0·31 | −0·50 | 0·09 |
| 17. "Power without responsibility" is a good description of trade unions today. | 0·76 | 0·40 | −0·31 | −0·50 | 0·09 |
| 18. Trust trade unions to honour the "Social Contract". | −0·40 | 0·40 | −0·31 | −0·50 | 0·09 |
| 19. Big business should be subject to more control. | −0·32 | 0·03 | 0·32 | 0·53 | 0·17 |
| 20. Reduce company taxes. | −0·51 | −0·07 | 0·53 | 0·62 | 0·01 |
| 21. Heavier taxing of the wealthy. | −0·51 | −0·07 | 0·53 | 0·62 | 0·01 |
| 22. Management–employee relations conflictful. | −0·09 | −0·18 | −0·07 | 0·09 | 0·35 |
| 23. Inefficient management and planning have led to the present level of unemployment. | −0·24 | −0·05 | 0·16 | 0·32 | 0·00 |
| 24. The high level of unemployment is the result of workers' excessive demands. | 0·64 | 0·41 | −0·29 | −0·38 | 0·02 |

| | F1 | F2 | F3 | F4 | F5 |
|---|---|---|---|---|---|
| 25. Introduce statutory control of wage increases. | 0·37 | 0·05 | −0·10 | −0·23 | 0·18 |
| 26. Cut social security benefits to strikers. | 0·71 | 0·48 | −0·36 | −0·56 | −0·04 |
| 27. Legal sanctions should be introduced to control strikes. | 0·86 | 0·38 | −0·09 | −0·41 | 0·07 |
| 28. The government should not impose any restrictions on the right to strike. | −0·60 | −0·12 | 0·24 | 0·30 | −0·05 |
| 29. Voting to strike should be by secret ballot, not just a show of hands. | 0·42 | 0·17 | −0·15 | −0·34 | 0·32 |
| 30. Sell council houses to tenants | 0·55 | 0·27 | −0·05 | −0·45 | 0·14 |
| 31. Keep a private health service. | 0·54 | 0·16 | −0·30 | −0·76 | −0·19 |
| 32. Nationalize building land. | −0·68 | −0·11 | 0·33 | 0·65 | −0·12 |
| 33. Bring more companies into public ownership. | −0·64 | −0·18 | 0·37 | 0·75 | −0·14 |
| 34. Abolish grammar schools. | −0·40 | −0·22 | 0·19 | 0·83 | −0·08 |
| 35. Public schools should be abolished. | −0·44 | −0·11 | 0·26 | 0·79 | 0·16 |
| 36. All schools should be comprehensive. | −0·37 | −0·26 | 0·28 | 0·71 | −0·10 |
| 37. Reform our electoral system. | 0·09 | 0·12 | −0·01 | −0·01 | 0·12 |
| Percentage variance accounted for: | 28% | 10% | 5% | 4% | 4% |

*Factor pattern correlations*

| Factor | 1 | 2 | 3 | 4 | 5 |
|---|---|---|---|---|---|
| 1 | | 0·32 | −0·25 | −0·55 | 0·12 |
| 2 | | | −0·09 | −0·15 | −0·09 |
| 3 | | | | 0·32 | 0·09 |
| 4 | | | | | −0·02 |

# References

Aaron, R. On the proper use of ideologies. In Ben-David, J. and Clark, T. N. (eds), *Culture and its creators: Essays in honour of Edward Shils*. Univ. Chicago Press, 1977.

Abelson, R. P. Script processing in attitude formation and decision making. In Carroll, J. S. and Payne, J. W. (eds), *Cognition and social behaviour*. Hillsdale, New Jersey: Erlbaum, 1976.

Abelson, R. P., Kinder, D. R., Peters, M. D. and Fiske, S. T. Affective and semantic components in political person perception. *J. Pers. Soc. Psychol.*, 1982, **42**, 619–630.

Abramson, P. R. Intergenerational social mobility and partisan preference in Britain and Italy: A cross-national comparison. *Comp. Polit. Studies*, 1973, **6**, 221–233.

Achen, C. H. Mass political attitudes and the survey response. *Am. Pol. Sci. Rev.*, 1975, **69**, 1218–1231.

Adelson, J. and O'Neill, R. P. The growth of political ideas in adolescence. The sense of community. *J. Pers. Soc. Psych.*, 1966, **4**, 295–306.

Adorno, T. W., Frenkel-Brunswik, E., Levinson, D. J. and Sanford, R. N. *The authoritarian personality*. New York: Harper, 1950.

Ajzen, I. and Fishbein, M. *Understanding and predicting social behavior*. New Jersey: Prentice Hall, 1980.

Allport, G. W. Attitudes. In C. Murchison (ed.), *Handbook of social psychology*. Worcester, Mass.: Clark University Press, 1935.

Almond, G. and Verba, S. *The civic culture*. Princeton: Princeton University Press, 1963.

Alt, J. E., Särlvik, B. and Crewe I. Individual differences scaling and group attitude structures. Paper given at conference on Surveys in Social Research. Southampton: 14 April, 1975.

Alt, J. E., Särlvik, B. and Crewe I. Partisanship and policy choice: Issue preference in the British electorate. *Br. J. Pol. Sci.*, 1976, **6**, 273–290.

Andrews, F. M. and Messenger, R. C. Multivariate nominal scale analysis: A report on a new technique and a computer program. Ann Arbor, Michigan: Survey Research Center, Institute for Social Research, 1973.

Ashford, D. E. *Policy and politics in Britain: The limits of consensus*. Philadelphia: Temple University Press, 1981.

Atkinson, J. M. The 1983 Election and the Demise of Live Oratory. In Crewe, I. and Harrop, M. (eds), *Political communication: The General Election campaign of 1983*. Cambridge University Press, 1985.

Bandura, A. *Social learning theory*. Morristown, New Jersey: General Learning Press, 1971.

Barnes, S. H. and Kaase, M. *Political action: Mass participation in five western democracies*. Beverly Hills: Sage Publications, 1979.

Barthes, R. *Mythologies*. London: Paladin, 1972.

Bell, D. *The end of ideology*. New York: Collier, 1962.

Bem, D. Self-perception theory. In Berkowitz, L. (ed.), *Advances in experimental social psychology*, Vol. 6. New York and London: Academic Press, 1972.

Benewick, R. J., Birch, A. H., Blumler, H. and Ewbank, A. The floating voter and the Liberal view of representation. *Political Studies*, 1969, No. 2, 177–195.

Bentler, P. M. and Spekart, G. Attitudes "cause" behaviours: a structural equation analysis. *J. Pers. Soc. Psychol.*, 1981, **40**, 226–238.

Berelson, B., Lazarsfeld, P. F. and McPhee, W. P. *Voting: A study of opinion formation in a Presidential campaign.* Univ. Chicago Press, 1954.

Berkeley, D. and Humphreys, P. Structuring decision problems and the "bias heuristic". *Acta Psychol.*, 1982, **50**, 201–252.

Bishop, G. F., Tuchfarber, A. J. and Oldendick, R. W. Change in the structure of American political attitudes: The nagging question of question wording. *Am. J. Pol. Sci.*, 1978, **22**, 250–269.

Block, J. H., Haan, N. and Smith, M. B. Socialisation correlates of student activism. *J. Soc. Issues*, 1969, **25**, 143–177.

Blondel, J. *Voters, parties and leaders.* Harmondsworth: Penguin, 1969.

Blumler, J., Gurevitch, M. and Ives, J. *The challenge of election broadcasting.* Leeds University Press, 1978.

Blumler, J., Gurevitch, M., Nossiter, T. Television news responses to the 1983 campaign: A view from the BBC bunker. In Crewe, I. and Harrop, M. (eds), *Political communication: The General Election campaign of 1983.* Cambridge University Press, 1985.

Brody, R. A. The puzzle of political participation in America. In King, A. (ed.), *The new American political system.* Washington, D.C.: American Enterprise Institute for Public Policy Research, 1978.

Brody, R. A. and Page, B. Indifference, alienation and rational decisions. *Public Choice*, 1973, **15**, 1–17.

Brody, R. A. and Page, B. I. The impact of events on Presidential popularity: The Johnson and Nixon administrations. In Wildavsky, A. (ed.), *Perspectives on the Presidency.* Boston: Little-Brown, 1975.

Brody, R. and Sigelman, L. Presidential popularity and Presidential elections: An update and extension. *Public Opinion Q.*, 1983, **47**, 325–333.

Budge, I. Electoral volatility: issue effects and basic change in 23 post-war democracies. *Elect. Stud.*, 1982, **7**, 147–168.

Budge, I., Crewe, I. and Fairlie, D. (eds), *Party identification and beyond.* London: Wiley, 1976.

Butler, D. The changing nature of elections. In Crewe, I. and Harrop, M. (eds), *Political communication: the General Election campaign of 1983.* Cambridge University Press, 1985.

Butler, D. and Kavanagh, D. *The British General Election of 1979.* London: Macmillan, 1980.

Butler, D. and Stokes, D. *Political change in Britain.* London: Macmillan, 1969.

Butler, D. and Stokes, D. *Political change in Britain*, 2nd ed. London: Macmillan, 1974.

Cain, B. Strategic voting in Britain. *Am. J. Pol. Sci.*, 1978, **22**, 639–655.

Cain, B., Ferejohn, J. and Fiorina, M. The House is not a home: British MPs in their constituencies. *Legisl. Stud. Quart.*, 1979, **4**, 501–523.

Cain, B. and Ferejohn, J. Party identification in the United States and Great Britain. *Comp. Polit. Studies*, 1981, **14**, 31–47.

Campbell, D. and Converse, P. E. *The human meaning of social change.* New York: Russell Sage Foundation, 1980.

Campbell, D., Converse, P. E., Miller, W. E. and Stokes, D. E. *The American voter.* New York: Wiley, 1960.

Campbell, D. T. Quasi-experimental design. In Stills, D. L. (ed.), *International encyclopaedia of the social sciences.* London: Macmillan and Free Press, 1968.

Clarke, P. and Evans, S. H. *Covering campaigns: Journalism in Congressional elections.* Stanford: Stanford University Press, 1983.

Clements, J. The volatility of voting behaviour. *J. Market Res. Soc.*, 1975, **16**, 291–301.

Cockerell, M., Hennessey, P. and Walker, D. *Sources close to the Prime Minister: Inside the hidden world of the news manipulators.* London: Macmillan, 1984.

Converse, P. E. The nature of belief systems in mass publics. In Apter, D. E. (ed.), *Ideology and discontent*. New York: Free Press, 1964, 206–261.

Converse, P. E. The concept of the normal vote. In Campbell, A., Converse, P. E., Miller, W. A. and Stokes, D. E. (eds), *Elections and the public order*. New York: Wiley, 1966.

Converse, P. E. *The dynamics of party support*. Beverley Hills: Sage Publications, 1976.

Cooley, W. W. and Lohnes, P. R. *Multivariate data analysis*. New York: Wiley, 1971.

Coombs, C. H. *A theory of data*. New York: Wiley, 1964.

Crewe, I. Do Butler and Stokes really explain political change in Britain. *Eur. J. Pol. Res.*, 1974, **2**, 83–87.

Crewe, I. Why the Conservatives won. In Penniman, H. (ed.), *Britain at the polls*. American Enterprise Institute for Public Policy Research, Washington, D.C., 1981a, pp.263–301.

Crewe, I. Improving but could do better: a report on the media and the polls in the 1979 General Election. In Worcester, R. and Harrop, M. (eds), *Media politics*. London: Allen and Unwin, 1981b.

Crewe, I. Surveys of British elections: Problems of design, response and bias. *Round Table Conference on Political Campaigns and Electoral Surveys*, Cento de Investigaciones Sociologicas, Madrid, October 1983a.

Crewe, I. The electorate: Partisan dealignment: Ten years on. *West. Eur. Pol.*, October, 1983b.

Crewe, I. How to win a landslide without really trying: Why the Conservatives won in 1983. In Penniman, H. and Ranney, A. (eds), *Britain at the polls, 1983*. University of North Carolina Press for American Enterprise Institute for Public Policy, 1984.

Crewe, I., Särlvik, B. and Alt, J. E. Partisan realignment in Britain, 1964–1974. *Br. J. Pol. Sci.*, 1977, **7**, 129–190.

Dahrendorf, R. *Class and class conflict in industrial society*. Stanford: Stanford University Press, 1959.

Dahrendorf, R. *Life chances: Approaches to social and political theory*. London: Weidenfeld and Nicolson, 1979.

Davis, O. A., Hinch, M. J. and Ordeshook, P. C. An expository development of a mathematical model of the electoral process. *Am. Pol. Sci. Rev.*, 1970, **64**, 426–448.

Dawes, R. M. *Foundations of attitude measurement*. New York: Wiley, 1972.

Dennis, J. New measures of partisanship in models of voting. Paper given at Midwest Political Science Association, April 1982a.

Dennis, J. The child's acquisition of partisanship and independence. Paper delivered at the Western Political Science Association meeting in San Diego, 1982b.

Dennis, J. and McCrone, D. J. Pre-adult development of political party identification in Western democracies. *Comp. Polit. Studies*, July, 1970, **3**, 243–263.

Deutsch, M. and Hornstein, H. *Applying social psychology*. Hillsdale, New Jersey: Lawrence Erlbaum, 1975.

Downs, A. *An economic theory of democracy*. New York: Harper and Row, 1957.

Dowse, R. E. and Hughes, J. A. Girls, boys and politics. *Br. J. Sociol.*, 1971, **22**, p.53.

Durkheim, E. Représentations individuelles et représentations collectives. *Revue Métaphysique*, 1898, **6**, 274–302.

Easton, D. and Dennis, J. *Children in the political system*. New York: McGraw Hill, 1969.

Edwards, W., Lindman, H. and Phillips, L. D. Emerging technologies for making decisions. In Newcomb, T. M. (ed.), *New directions in psychology II*. New York: Holt, Rinehart and Winston, 1965.

Ferejohn, J. A. and Fiorina, M. P. The paradox of not voting. *Am. Pol. Sci. Rev.*, 1974, **68**, 525–536.

Festinger, L. *Conflict, decision and dissonance*. London: Tavistock, 1964.

Fiorina, M. P. Formal models in political science. *Am. J. Pol. Sci.*, 1975, **19**, 133–159.

Fiorina, M. P. An outline for a model of party choice. *Am. J. Pol. Sci.*, 1977, **21**, 601–623.

Fiorina, M. P. *Retrospective voting in American national elections.* New Haven: Yale University Press, 1981.

Fishbein, M. Attitude and the prediction of behavior. In Fishbein, M. (ed.), *Readings in attitude theory and measurement.* New York: Wiley, 1967.

Fishbein, M. and Coombs, F. S. Basis for decision: An attitudinal analysis of voting behaviour. *J. Appl. Soc. Psychol.*, 1974, **4**, 95–124.

Fishbein, M., Thomas, K. and Jaccard, J. *Voting behaviour in Britain. An attitudinal analysis.* London: Social Science Research Council, 1976.

Franklin, M. N. and Mugham, A. The decline of class voting in Britain: Problems of analysis and interpretation. *Am. Pol. Sci. Rev.*, 1978, **72**, 523–534.

Gallup Poll Bulletins, 1974.

Gamble, A. The impact of the SDP. In Hall, S. and Jacques, M. (eds), *The politics of Thatcherism.* London: Lawrence and Wishart, 1983.

Gaskell, G. and Smith, P. Are young Blacks really alienated? *New Society*, 1981, **56**, 260–261.

Geertz, C. Ideology as a cultural system. In Apter, D. E. (ed.), *Ideology and discontent.* New York: Free Press, 1964.

Glencross, D. The General Election of 1983: Could we have used more freedom? *Independent Broadcasting*, Dec. 1983, **37**, 6–8.

Goffman, E. *Frame analysis: An essay on the organization of experience.* Cambridge, Mass.: Harvard University Press, 1974.

Goldberg, A. Social determinants and rationality as basis of party identification. *Am. Pol. Sci. Rev.*, 1969, **63**, 5–23.

Goldthorpe, J. H. *Social mobility and class structure in modern Britain.* Oxford: Clarendon Press, 1980.

Goodman, L. A. and Kruskal, W. H. Measures of association for cross classifications. *J. Am. Stat. Ass.*, 1954, **49**, 749.

Green, P. E. and Rao, V. R. *Applied multidimensional scaling: A comparison of approaches and algorithms.* New York: Holt, Rinehart and Winston, 1972.

Greenstein, F. L. *Children and politics.* New Haven: Yale University Press, 1965.

Hall, S. The "Little Caesars" of social democracy. In Hall, S. and Jacques, M. (eds), *The politics of Thatcherism.* London: Lawrence and Wishart, 1983.

Hall, S. and Jacques, M. *The politics of Thatcherism.* London: Lawrence and Wishart, 1983.

Harrop, M. Press coverage of postwar British elections: changes and consequences. In Crewe, I. and Harrop, M. (eds), *Political communication: the general Election campaign of 1983.* Cambridge University Press, 1985.

Hess, R. and Torney, J. *The development of political attitudes in children.* Chicago: Aldine, 1967.

Himmelweit, H. T. Political socialization. *Int. Soc. Sci. J. (UNESCO)*, 1983, **35**, No. 2, 237–256.

Himmelweit, H. T. and Bond, R. *Social and political attitudes: Voting stability and change.* Report to the Social Science Research Council. London: 1974.

Himmelweit, H. T. and Humphreys, P. C. The Liberal floater. *New Society*, 28 February, 1974, **27**, No. 595.

Himmelweit, H. T. and Swift, B. A model for the understanding of school as a socialising agent. In Mussen, P., Langer, J. and Covington, M. (eds). *Trends and issues in developmental psychology.* New York: Holt, Rinehart and Winston, 1969.

Himmelweit, H. T. and Swift, B. *Social and personality factors in the development of adult attitudes toward self and society.* Report to the Social Science Research Council. London: 1971.

Himmelweit, H. and Swift, B. Adolescent and adult authoritarianism re-examined: Its organisation and stability over time. *Eur. J. Soc. Psychol.*, 1978, **1**, 357–384.

Himmelweit, H. T., Jaeger, M. and Stockdale, J. Memory for past vote: Implications of a study of bias in recall. *Br. J. Pol. Sci.*, 1978, **8**, 365–376.

Himmelweit, H. T., Humphreys, P., Jaeger, M. and Katz, M. *How Voters Decide* (1st edition). London: Academic Press, 1981.

Himmelweit, S. A behavioural model of learning in production. *Rev. Econ. Studies*, 1976, **43**, 329–346.

Humphreys, P. C. Applications of multiattribute utility theory. In Jungermann, H. and de Zeeuw, G. (eds), *Decision making and change in human affairs*. Amsterdam: Reidel, 1977, pp.165–208.

Humphreys, P. C. and Berkeley, D. Handling uncertainty: Levels of representation of decision problems. In Wright, G. N. (ed.), *Behavioral decision making*. New York: Plenum, 1984.

Humphreys, P. C. and McFadden, W. Experiences with MAUD: Aiding decision structuring versus bootstrapping the decision-maker. *Acta psychologica*, 1980, **45**, 51–69.

Hyman, H. *Political socialisation*. New York: Free Press, 1959.

Inglehart, R. *The silent revolution; changing values and political styles among Western publics*. Princeton, N.J.: Princeton University Press, 1977.

Jahoda, G. Children's concepts of nationality: A critical study of Piaget's stages. *Child Development*, 1964, **35**, 1081–1092.

Jahoda, M. The impact of unemployment in the 1930's and the 1970's. *Bull. Brit. Psych. Soc.*, 1979, **32**, 309–314.

Jaspars, J. M. The nature and measurement of attitudes. In Tajfel, H. and Fraser, C. (eds), *Introducing social psychology*. London: Penguin, 1978.

Jennings, M. K. and Niemi, R. G. *The political character of adolescence*. Princeton: Princeton University Press, 1974.

Jennings, M. K. and Niemi, R. G. *Generations and politics*. Princeton, N.J.: Princeton University Press, 1981.

Kaase, M. and Klingemann, H. Social structure, value orientations and the party systems: the problems of interest accommodation in Western democracies. *Eur. J. Pol. Res.*, 1981.

Katz, R. S. The dimensionality of party identification: cross-national perspectives. *Comp. Pol.*, 1979, **11**, 147–165.

Keeney, R. L. and Raiffa, H. *Decisions with multiple objectives: preferences and value tradeoffs*. New York, Wiley, 1976.

Kelley, S. and Mirer, T. M. The simple act of voting. *Am. Pol. Sci. Rev.*, 1974, **68**, 572–591.

Kelman, H. Attitudes are alive and well and gainfully employed in the sphere of action. *Am. Psych.*, 1974, **29**, 310–324.

Kerlinger, F. N. and Pedhazur, E. *Multiple regression in behavioral research*. New York: Holt, Rinehart and Winston, 1973.

Key, V. O. *The responsible electorate*. Cambridge, Mass.: Harvard University Press, 1966.

Kinder, D. R. Presidents, prosperity, and public opinion. *Public Opinion Q.*, 1981, **45**, 1–23.

Kinder, D. R. and Sears, D. O. Public opinion and political action. In Lindzey, G. and Aronson, E. (eds), *Handbook of social psychology*, Third Edn. Mass.: Addison-Wesley, 1985.

Kneppreth, N. P., Gustafson, D. H., Leifer, R. P. and Johnson, E. M. *Techniques for the assessment of worth*. Technical Paper 254 (AD78462a) Arlington, Va.: Army Research Institute for the Behavioral and Social Sciences, 1974.

Kruskal, J. B., Young, F. W. and Seery, J. B. *How to use KYST, a very flexible program to do multidimensional scaling and unfolding*. Murray Hill, N.J.: Bell Laboratories, 1973.

Kubota, A. and Ward, R. E. Family influence and political socialisation in Japan. *Comp. Polit. Studies*, 1970, **3**, 140–175.

Lane, R. E. Patterns of political belief. In Knutson, J. (ed.), *Handbook of political psychology*. San Francisco: Jossey-Bass, 1973.

Lazarsfeld, P. F., Berelson, B. R. and Gaudet, H. *The People's Choice*. New York: Duell, Sloan and Pierce, 1944.

Lemieux, P. H. Political issues and Liberal support in the February 1974 British General Election. *Pol. Studies*, 25, 323–342.

Levin, M. L. Social climate and political socialisation. *Public Opinion Q.*, 1961, **23**, 596–606.

Lewin, K. *Field theory in social science*. New York: Harper, 1951.

Lingoes, J. C. *The Guttman-Lingoes non-metric program series*. Ann Arbor, Michigan: Methesis Press, 1973.

Lipset, S. M. The end of ideology and the ideology of the intellectuals. In Ben-David, J. and Clark, T. N. (eds). *Culture and its creators*. Chicago: Univ. of Chicago Press, 1977.

Lipset, S. M. The economy, elections and public opinion *The Tocqueville Review*, 1983, **5**, 431–470.

Luce, R. D. *Individual choice behavior*. New York: Wiley, 1959.

Maccoby, E. E., Matthews, R. E. and Morton, A. Youth and political change. *Public Opinion Q.*, 1954, **18**, 23–29.

Markus, E. G. and Converse, P. E. A dynamic simultaneous equation model of electoral choice. *Am. Pol. Sci. Rev.*, 1979, **73**, 1055–1069.

McCloskey, H. Conservatism and personality. *Am. Pol. Sci. Rev.*, 1964, **52**, 27–45.

McGinnes, J. *The selling of the President 1968*. New York: Trident Press, 1969.

McGuire, W. The concept of attitudes and their relations to behaviors. In Sinaiko, H. W. and Broedling, L. A. (eds), *Perspectives on attitude assessment: surveys and their alternatives*. Champaign, Ill.: Pendleton, 1976.

Merrin, M. B. and Le Blank, H. L. Parties and candidates in 1972: Objects of issue voting. *Western Pol. Q.*, 1979, **32**, 59–69.

Miller, W. and Shanks, M. Policy directions and Presidential leadership: Alternative interpretation of the 1980 Presidential Election. *Br. J. Pol. Sci.*, 1982, **12**, 299–356.

Miller, A. and Wattenberg, P. Cognitive representation of candidates' assessments. Paper given at the American Science Association, Denver, September 1982.

Morgan, J. N. and Messenger, R. C. *THAID: A sequential analysis program for the analysis of nominal scale dependent variables*. Ann Arbor, Michigan: Survey Research Center, Institute of Social Research, 1973.

Moscovici, S. The phenomenon of social representations. In Farr, R. and Moscovici, S. (eds), *Social Representations*. Cambridge University Press, 1984.

Mussen, P. and Haan, N. In Eichhorn, D. (ed.), *Past and present in middle age*. New York: Academic Press, 1981.

Nie, N. H. and Anderson, K. Mass belief systems revisited: A research role. *J. Politics*, 1974, **36**, 540–590.

Nie, N. and Anderson, K. Mass belief systems revisited. In Niemi, R. G. and Weissberg, H. F. (eds), *Controversies in American voting behavior*. San Francisco: W. H. Freeman & Co., 1976.

Nie, N. H. and Rabjohn, J. N. Revisiting mass belief systems revisited: Or, doing research is like watching a tennis match. *Am. J. Pol. Sci.*, 1979, **23**, 139–175.

Nie, N. H., Verba, S. and Petrocik, J. R. *The changing American voter*. Cambridge, Massachusetts: Harvard Univ. Press, 1976.

Niemi, R. G. and Weissberg, H. F. (eds), *Controversies in American voting behavior*. San Francisco: W. H. Freeman and Co., 1976.

Orum, A. M. *The seeds of politics: Youth and politics in America*. New Jersey: Prentice Hall, 1972.

Page, B. and Brody, R. Policy voting and the electoral process: The Vietnam war issue. *Am. Pol. Sci. Rev.*, 1972, **66**, 979–995.

Pedersen, M. The dynamics of European party systems: Changing patterns of electoral volatility. *Eur. J. Pol. Res.*, 1979, **7**, 1–26.

Pederson, J. T. Political involvement and partisan change in Presidential elections. *Am. J. Pol. Sci.*, 1978, **22**, 18–30.

Pitz, G. Decision making and cognition. In Jungermann, H. and de Zeeuw, G. (eds), *Decision making and change in human affairs*. Amsterdam: Reidel, 1977.

Pomper, G. M. *Voters' choice*. New York: Dodd, Mead and Co., 1975.

Popkin, S., Gorman, J. W., Phillips, C. and Smith, J. A. Comment: What have you done for me lately? Toward an investment theory of voting. *Am. Pol. Sci. Rev.*, 1976, **70**, 779–805.

Renshon, S. A. (Ed.) *Handbook of political socialization: Theory and research.* New York: Free Press. 1977.

RePass, D. E. Comment: Political methodologies in disarray: Some alternative interpretations of the 1972 election. *Am. Pol. Sci. Rev.*, 1976, **70**, 814–831.

Riker, W. and Ordeshook, P. A. A theory of the caculus of voting. *Am. Pol. Sci. Rev.*, 1968, **62**, 25–42.

Rokeach, M. *The open and closed mind.* New York: Basic Books, 1960.

Rokeach, M. *Beliefs, attitudes and values.* San Francisco: Jossey-Bass, 1968.

Rose, R. *Politics in England: An interpretation for the 1980s,* 3rd ed. London: Faber and Faber, 1980.

Runciman, W. G. *Relative deprivation and social justice.* London: Routledge and Kegan Paul, 1966.

Savage, L. J. *The foundations of statistics,* 2nd rev. edn. New York: Dover, 1972.

Särlvik, B. and Crewe, I. *Decade of dealignment: The Conservative victory of 1979 and electoral trends in the 1970s.* Cambridge University Press, 1983.

Schank, R. C. and Abelson, R. P. *Scripts, plans, goals and understanding.* Hillsdale, New Jersey: Erlbaum, 1977.

Schiffman, S. S., Reynolds, M. L. and Young, F. W. *Introduction to multidimensional scaling: theory, methods and applications.* New York: Academic Press, 1981.

Schumpeter, J. A. *Capitalism, socialism and democracy.* New York: Harper and Row, 1950.

Sears, D. O. Political socialization. In Greenstein, F. L. and Polsby, N. W. (eds), *Handbook of political science,* Vol. 2. Reading, Massachusetts: Addison-Wesley, 1974.

Sidanius, J. and Ekehammar, B. Political socialisation: A multivariate analysis of Swedish political attitude and preference data. *Eur. J. Soc. Psych.*, 1979, **9**, 265–279.

Smith, J. A. *American Presidential Elections: Trust and the rational voter.* New York: Praeger Special Studies, 1980.

Stimson, J. A. Belief systems: Constraint, complexity and the 1972 election. *Am. J. Pol. Sci.*, 1975, **19**, 393–417.

Stokes, D. E. Voting. In Sills, D. L. (ed.), *International encyclopaedia of the social sciences,* Vol. 16, p.394. Macmillan and Free Press, 1968.

Strumpel, B. (ed.), *Economic means for human needs: social indicators of well-being and discontent.* Ann Arbor, Michigan: University of Michigan Press, 1976.

Tajfel, H. *Differentiation between social groups.* London and New York: Academic Press, 1978.

Toda, M. The decision process: A perspective. *Int. J. General Systems,* 1976, **3**, 79–88.

Tullock, M. *Toward a mathematics of politics.* Ann Arbor: University of Michigan Press, 1967.

Turkle, S. *Psychoanalytic politics.* London: Andre Deutsch, 1979.

Wattenberg, M. P. The decline of political partisanship in the United States: Negativity or neutrality? *Am. Pol. Sci. Rev.*, 1981, **75**, 941–950.

Weissberg, H. F. A multi-dimensional conceptualization of party identification. *Pol. Behav.*, 1980, **2**, 33–60.

Wicker, A. Attitude versus action: The relationship of verbal and overt behavioral responses to attitude objects. *J. Soc. Issues,* 1969, **25**, 41–78.

Wober, M., Svennevig, M., Gunter, B. The television audience and the 1983 General Election. In Crewe, I. and Harrop, M. (eds), *Political communication: the General Election campaign of 1983.* Cambridge University Press, 1985.

Worcester, R. M. *British public opinion General Election 1983.* London: Market and Opinion Research International (MORI), 1983.

Von Winterfeldt, D. and Fischer, G. W. Multi-attribute utility theory: Models and assessment procedures. In Wendt, D. and Vlek, C. (eds), *Utility, probability and human decision making.* Amsterdam: Reidel, 1975.

# Author index

# Subject Index